Janice Campbell Paul was born in Provo, Utah, and raised in Southern California. She lived in Prescott Valley, Arizona, for fifteen years, before moving to India and later Nepal.

She has spent eleven years in India and Nepal, telling the story of her miraculous healing to the world. Her passion to serve the suffering, especially those affected by leprosy, led her to work with Nepal Leprosy Fellowship set up in the 90s by the legendary British missionary, Eileen Lodge.

She has owned two businesses in Southern California, and worked as an insurance agent and a bank consultant. She currently lives in Mexico, and is working on a novel as well as a sequel to *The Secret Wife*.

THE SECRET WIFE
Memoirs of An American Missionary in India and Nepal

Janice Campbell Paul

SPEAKING TIGER PUBLISHING PVT. LTD
4381/4, Ansari Road, Daryaganj
New Delhi 110002

Published in India by Speaking Tiger in paperback 2017

Copyright © Janice Campbell Paul 2017

ISBN: 978-93-86582-41-6
e-ISBN: 978-93-86582-39-3

10 9 8 7 6 5 4 3 2 1

Typeset in Sabon Roman by SŪRYA, New Delhi
Printed at Sanat Printers, Kundli

All rights reserved.
No part of this publication may be reproduced,
transmitted, or stored in a retrieval system,
in any form or by any means, electronic,
mechanical, photocopying, recording
or otherwise, without the prior
permission of the publisher.

This book is sold subject to the condition that it shall not,
by way of trade or otherwise, be lent, resold,
hired out, or otherwise circulated, without the
publisher's prior consent, in any form of
binding or cover other than that in
which it is published.

To my father, Ivan Campbell, who read to me as a child, encouraged me to 'write about it' and always believed that one day I would be an author. Thanks Pops. I miss you.

CONTENTS

1. In the Beginning — 1
2. Visions and Healing — 20
3. India, Finally — 41
4. Discovery of India—My Way — 49
5. Discovering Varun — 59
6. Dress Like An Indian — 66
7. A Big, Fat Indian Wedding — 72
8. Lessons in Leprosy — 78
9. The First Bible Study — 84
10. Unexpected Danger — 93
11. A Home of Our Own — 98
12. Prayers and Battles — 104
13. Spreading the Word — 116
14. A Surprise Homecoming — 121
15. Letting Go — 128
16. Back to India — 135
17. Sin or No Sin? — 143
18. Alien—or Indian? — 149
19. Living in a Man's World — 155
20. The 'Other' Wife — 163

21.	Blood Sacrifices	180
22.	Leaving Again	201
23.	Back in the USA	208
24.	After the Doors Were Closed	230
25.	Picking Up the Threads	234
26.	Deshbundho Road—Where Heaven and Hell Met	246
27.	An Unexpected Visitor—and a Prophesy	260
28.	Great Expectations	269
29.	The Next Chosen Wife	286
30.	Trials and Tribulations	293
31.	Then It All Fell Down	310
32.	The Betrayal	323
	Epilogue	340

1. In the Beginning

Our lives are like a tapestry with all the events interwoven in fine detail. It is not until we look back that we can see the beauty of the cloth that God has created. Such is my story. It began without me.

In the district of Purulia in West Bengal there was a young man. His left arm had been damaged in an accident when he was younger so he learned to survive with just one strong arm. He was full of anger, rebellion and mischief. He wandered the streets drinking, fighting and using his wits to trick people out of money.

He knew how to use deception well, having first learned how to close his heart to almost everyone. His life was spiraling downward into the darkest of worlds. A few years later he moved to a bigger city where he learned the ways of an even darker group of people, criminals, thieves and crooked politicians. His path seemed to have been set. To most people he was on the road of no return.

Then there was me…a pleasantly plump, middle-class 47-year-old American woman, mother of two grown children, grandmother of five. I had married young, just three months short of my sixteenth birthday. It was 1966, and the Vietnam war was on. My husband was in the US Navy, and left for Vietnam shortly after we married. When he returned, he proved himself to be abusive, a philanderer and an alcoholic. By the age of twenty-two, I was a divorcee with two small children, my daughter, Tracy, and son, Kevin.

In 1990, I married Rod Paul. Thirteen years older than me, Rod, had his own bank consulting firm. But the financial crisis of 1991 closed down his business, and a housing market crash followed. We sold everything we owned and moved to California, where we bought a 35-foot 'fifth wheel'—a caravan that hooks into the back of a pick-up truck—and moved into a trailer park for seniors (Rod was sixty by then, so he qualified as a 'senior').

Rod and I were escapees from the rat race. We settled down in the beautiful mountain area of Prescott Valley, Arizona. Our caravan was equipped with water and electricity for a long-term stay, and all the comforts of a regular home, only packed into a tiny space.

We became one of the 'year rounders', but the majority of the park was for the 'snow birds', those who escaped the rough winters in the east coast and camped temporarily in the warm climate of Arizona.

Soon after we moved there, I became the recreational director of the park. It was a demanding job that required me to organize all the events of the park to keep the seniors busy and happy. I was healthy, walking five miles a day and swimming laps in the pool. Though we were not rich, by any means, we were reasonably happy. We enjoyed the vacation and party atmosphere at the park. I spent my off-days fishing in the lakes in the area. Fishing was my passion, my 'alone time' and the only time I talked to God.

A few years later, we moved from the recreational park to a mobile home park, where we bought a 'fixer-upper', as the older mobile homes are known. Ours was built in the early '70s, and needed quite a bit of 'fixing' before we could live in it, but we got it cheap, and we loved the location. It sat on a large lot that had open land around it and a large hill behind. A mobile home is much more permanent than a 'fifth wheel'—much like a regular home in size and appearance, except that it is pre-made in a factory, and has wheels! Usually, though, once it is set up on one's plot, it is not moved again. We were no longer in a 'park' environment, but in a regular street in Prescott Valley. All the homes in this area, for several blocks, were mobile homes. At last, Rod and I felt we had a permanent home again.

On the day we closed the deal, Rod had a heart attack. The doctor called it a 'heart incident'. A week later he had another, this time sending him to a Phoenix hospital for two stents to be inserted in his arteries. This left him unable to do any heavy-lifting or strenuous activity. I became the caregiver and he became grumpy and demanding, supervising all the remodeling and redecorating work I was doing in our new home.

I also got a new job at Home Depot, part of a large chain of home improvement stores in the country, that provided everything from lumber to windows, plaster and roofing material.

The store was about 5 km from our home and my job was in the flooring department. I was the only woman in the department and the work required me to lift boxes of tiles and bags of mortar as well as drive the heavy equipment in the store. At home I shoveled tons of gravel, fixed tiles, and repaired the roof. As the mobile home was built of wood, I also put up 'dry walls'—pre-made plaster walls held together with strong paper, that had to be nailed or screwed onto the wood frames. I was, by any standards, doing the work of any able-bodied man in America and feeling kind of proud of it. But inevitably, all this physical activity began to take its toll on me.

∼

I started to notice changes in my body. Subtle changes like getting tired more quickly and aches that wouldn't go away. I began to drop things and stumble often. There was a pain that began at the base of my back and traveled down my legs.

As time passed, the pain increased and was with me night and day. Then I began twitching now and then and I noticed a slight shaking in my hands. I went to my doctor and he began a series of tests.

My feet felt heavy and my legs began to wobble and grow weak. I could no longer do the heavy-lifting my job required and had to quit, but took on assignments to install tiles in homes and businesses whenever I could, to bring in some money. I constantly pushed myself to move, to keep going in spite of the pain, but eventually I had to stop working altogether.

After three months off, Rod returned to his job at a popular food warehouse store, Costco, where he worked as a 'greeter', welcoming people as they walked into the store. He worked part-time, and began to do light work around the house.

In spite of my own physical ailments, he kept pushing me to do more, or he would tear out the work I had done, declaring it unsuitable for one reason or another. One day I came home from work to discover he had torn out a wall I had spent three days dry-walling and plastering. Needless to say, I was both livid and depressed. My physical pain just seemed to make Rod angry.

More tests were done and I saw more specialists as the symptoms worsened. Each doctor prescribed a new medication. Eventually I was on anti-depressants, pain suppressants, anti-seizure medicine to control the shaking, and sleeping pills. The doses were increased as the months went by without much relief. Finally the doctors gave it a name. Fibromyalgia.

I knew it was a little-known or accepted condition associated with depression. I had encountered a few women who had it and used to think they were probably hypochondriacs for all their complaining. I certainly was not like that! I was a woman who was in control of her life and not given to self-pity or tolerant of whining in others.

But this illness now controlled and changed every aspect of my existence. It seemed the harder I fought it, the worse it got. The drugs were of little use. They only took the sharpness off the pain and left me feeling like a zombie, unable to think.

I had become close to two other women who had fibromyalgia and were diagnosed a few years before me. Both were fully addicted to the drugs the doctors had prescribed. The problem is that the body gets used to the medication and eventually demands more to kill the pain. I witnessed how these two women would beg their doctors to increase their medication. But the doctors had to answer to the regulations set for approved dosages and could not increase the amounts.

I decided at that point to use alcohol as my drug of choice. It was something I was familiar with and readily available. Having three whiskeys every evening seemed to be the answer to the pain-filled nights. I was careful not to increase the amount or take any medication with the alcohol. I also only drank at night before bedtime. But some days I simply had to take the morphine instead, which left me feeling doped out for days afterwards.

I confronted one doctor about this problem. He said, 'With fibromyalgia pain you have only two choices, either become a drug addict or an alcoholic. You take your pick.' I left his office in such despair. What kind of life did I have to look forward to? I decided to do without both, the medicines and the alcohol. My resolve lasted only two days before the pain consumed me. I gave in and poured myself a drink. By now my smoking had also increased to a pack a day.

The symptoms were insidious, slowly creeping up on me and changing my lifestyle. First I gave in and bought myself a cane. Though this helped for a few months, my loss of control over my legs became so severe that I had to resort to metal crutches, the kind that wrapped around my arms for support. I was no longer able to climb ladders to paint or plaster the walls in my home.

But the most humiliating symptom was when my body began to shake and tremble. At first it was frightening. It was like I was sitting in an alien body watching it as it jerked and twitched out of control. Facial tics would appear and last for minutes or hours. If I became stressed my body would go into a series of spasms lasting for an hour or more.

I forced myself into deep breathing and relaxing meditation and found that this worked well. But if I was in public, or with my family and I felt the trembling coming on, I would rush home; my pride wouldn't allow me to let them see me in that state, and I didn't want them to worry more, or have pity on me.

For six months I was able to get around with the crutches, but the pain became so severe in my lower back and legs that I rarely ventured out. It was humiliating to be seen in such a condition by my friends, family and the people I used to work with. I got tired of answering the inevitable question, 'What happened to you?'

On one visit to my doctor I reluctantly asked him for a temporary 'handicapped' sticker for my car, explaining that by the time I parked and walked into a store the pain was so bad that I had no energy left for shopping. The doctor filled out a form and told me to take it to the local vehicle department. When I got home I looked at the form and noticed that he had checked off the 'permanent' box for the handicapped plates. Thinking that this was a mistake, I telephoned him. When I told him of his error, he said. 'Janice, you have one of the worst cases of fibromyalgia I have ever seen. I must tell you that your condition will not improve, but will more than likely get even worse. The sooner you accept that, the better you will be.' He was silent for a minute, then added gently. 'Your condition *is* permanent, Janice.' I mumbled a thank you and hung up.

The word 'permanent' echoed in my head over and over. Until that moment I truly did not consider myself handicapped. I was just 'going through' a tough time physically, but eventually it would all go away. Was the doctor right? Was I in denial? 'The sooner you accept that, the better you will be,' I said out loud. For the remainder of that day I was in a sort of shock, vacillating between acceptance and denial. I asked myself, 'If I accept it, does that mean I am giving up?' Then, 'Just because *he* says it is so, doesn't mean it is!'

But it was my own body that told me the answer. It was my own body that would not respond to my efforts to move around like a normal person again. The pain told me the bitter truth.

∼

By April 2001, I was in a wheelchair. By this time I had seen no less than six specialists. Every imaginable test was done. They all seemed to be in agreement. I would never walk again.

It is true that I wept bitterly, that I wallowed in self-pity for a few weeks and I hated my wheelchair with a passion.

Even though it was electric and had controls, I banged into everything in the house. I screamed out in anger at God and asked, 'Why me?'

But there finally came a time when I accepted my condition. I woke up one day and said to myself, 'Okay, it is time to go on with your life, such as it is. It is time to make the best of a bad situation. This may be the end of your old life, but it is the beginning of a new one. Make the most of it!'

I began to learn how to do things differently, to work around the affliction, to get some sense of control back into my life. My legs were not working, but my upper torso did; my arms and shoulders were strong and worked fine. I bought a stool with wheels so I could do dishes and cook. I adapted my environment to fit my condition, allowing me more freedom to do the things normal people did

Unfortunately my husband, my family and friends just could not accept my condition. Rod became increasingly resentful and bitter the more I depended on him. From the beginning he had refused to go with me to the doctors. I had to depend on my parents to take me the many miles to specialists. His focus was only on what I could not do for him anymore. He reminded me daily how much of a burden I had become on him.

One of the most frustrating and unexplained things about fibromyalgia is that the pain levels vary and the pain moves from one part of the body to another. Though the pain in my lower back and legs remained constant, each day was a challenge depending on where another pain was focused. Then there were blessed days when I felt hardly any pain. On these days I could stand and walk a little.

The doctors had warned me that when this happened, I must be careful not to overdo anything. But it was as if heavy chains had been removed from my body and I was set free, if only for that moment, that day. I would rejoice and do a few of the many activities that had been taken away from me. Moving cautiously, I would clean the house, do some gardening, or visit my family. But I soon learned that those golden days were inevitably followed by days of excruciating pain and exhaustion.

But worse than this, those that were closest to me, those who saw me nearly normal one day and bedridden the next, began to doubt the reality of the disease. 'It must be psychological,' they would say. Or, 'She's just faking it to get attention.' I understood their feelings—after all, hadn't I thought the same of the women I had known who had been in the predicament I was in now?

How could this ailment be so unpredictable? I knew I needed to learn all I could about fibromyalgia, since I would have to live with it for the rest of my life. I bought books recommended by my doctors. I studied as if for a college exam. The more I read, the more confused I became. 'No known cause.' 'No known cure.' 'It affects different people differently.'

Some books said that exercise helped. Some said it did more damage. The only thing that everyone seemed to agree on was that it was an auto-immune disease that weakened the nervous system. It was the result of the body's inability to dispose of waste properly. This waste built up in the connective tissues of the body, the thin membrane that surrounds nearly every organ, every muscle in the body, even the brain, causing pain.

I learned that I was part of the 15 per cent of fibromyalgia patients that ended up in a wheelchair. I was also a lucky 5 per cent who exhibited Parkinson-like symptoms. Some people with fibromyalgia were able to function with regular naps and some painkillers, but not I. No wonder my doctor said that I had the worst case he had experienced. What made matters worse, was that it was an affliction that most of the medical profession didn't understand or had training for. Indeed, many denied its existence altogether. It was not even recognized as a disease. It was called a 'syndrome.' Somehow I felt insulted. What I was feeling, the crippling change of lifestyle, deserved to be called a disease.

But, no matter what the rest of the world called it, or what my family and friends believed it to be, this was my life. The pain was real. The damned wheelchair was real!

The doubts and rejection from them only added to the feeling of isolation, of being suddenly left out of the rhythm of life out there in the world. Somehow I had become one of those dreaded people in society who, when you see them, you say, 'There, but for the grace of God go I', and quickly walk away. I know, because I used to do that myself.

As if things were not bad enough, I began losing my hair. My teeth began to loosen and I was diagnosed with sleep apnea. This meant I was tied to a breathing machine all night long. I also suffered from 'chronic fatigue' that left me so exhausted that sometimes I would sleep for days.

In January 2002, Rod and I separated. My family and friends stopped coming by because they 'couldn't stand to see me in this condition.' I was no longer included in social functions or family get-togethers. My two children lived in different states and were independent. I stayed on in the fixer-upper, while Rod bought another, smaller mobile home a few houses away on the same street. I hired someone to finish the work in the house and tried to make it as comfortable as possible.

∼

The Secret Wife

In the beginning, after Rod and I had separated, I spent my days alone. I wheeled around the house aimlessly day in and day out. Eventually I began doing a little gardening. I bought bird feeders and set to task to create a garden that would lift my spirits. Wheelchair ramps were made for every exit which allowed me to get out of the house and the yard was lined with concrete pavers so I could wheel myself around most of the yard. I potted plants and watched the birds, which were of a rich variety in Northern Arizona. Quail families would wander in the yard. Red-crested woodpeckers, common sparrows, bluejays and so many hummingbirds! I researched each variety and what their feeding habits were, then created a feeding area. A neighbor even built me a few bird-houses and hung them in the trees.

Where I went was dictated by the miles that the charge on my wheelchair battery would take me, and good weather conditions. Fortunately, there was quite a lot within the radius of the twelve miles that my battery held. My parents lived two blocks away. Sometimes I would go there and play rummy or Scrabble with them. I was able to go to my bank or fast food restaurants, my local grocery store and even the movie theatre.

There were many obstacles along the way, such as heavy doors to open, especially for the toilets, and many areas had no sidewalks, so I had to drive on the streets dangerously close to passing cars.

Nothing humbles or frustrates you more than having to ask people to open doors, even to the bathrooms for the handicapped. I also learned patience as I sat outside a store waiting to get someone's attention to come and open the door for me, then repeating the process when leaving. How I loved it when a store had automatic doors!

The theatre was a double problem. If I managed to get inside the lobby, the doors to the theatre were closed if the previews had started. I had to hunt down an employee and ask him to let me in. Why hadn't I noticed these details before? Why hadn't I noticed people in wheelchairs before? I was daily reminded of all the things I had taken for granted. Had I been so self-absorbed that I didn't notice the suffering of others? I was not a bad person, but I could not remember when I had helped a handicapped person.

Yet every day that I went out into the world I was keenly aware of those who helped me, who noticed my struggles and reached out, without me having to ask. I was grateful on each occasion and sometimes surprised.

I was also surprised at the negative reactions, the judgmental stares, as if, somehow I was guilty of some terrible sin to be in a wheelchair, the 'how dare you appear before me and upset my day' sort of look.

The worst experience happened one day in the local grocery store. I wanted something in the deli section and it was one of those delis where you had to take a ticket with a number and wait for your number to be called. Unfortunately the ticket machine was too high for me to reach. There was a woman standing there and I asked her if she would please get a ticket for me. She looked down at me in anger. 'You people make me sick!' she said. 'Why don't you just stay home and quit depending on normal people to help you all the time. You are leeches on society!' I was too shocked to reply to her, but a man standing nearby suddenly came between us, grabbed me a ticket and said loudly. 'Some people just like being assholes all the time!' He winked at me as he gave me my ticket with a broad smile, and stayed by my side until the woman got what she needed and left.

'I was in a car accident a few years back,' he explained. 'I had to be in a wheelchair for six months. I'm glad you're not too prideful to ask for help like I was.' He talked with me until my order came, gave it to me, and then said goodbye. I thanked him as he walked away, and thanked God for bringing that man into my day.

There was another experience in that same grocery store that baffles me to this day. I had driven myself to the store in my car because I had to do some big shopping that my little wheelchair couldn't handle. This was always difficult because getting into my car and driving was excruciating, even with an automatic gear shift, and I had to walk with my crutches into the store. Once inside the store, there were electric shopping carts I could use, but I had to leave my crutches with an attendant while I shopped. But the pouches that my wheelchair was fitted with couldn't hold much, so I had no choice but to use the car whenever I had any heavy shopping to do.

I gritted my teeth in pain as I got into the electric cart, wishing that someone could do the shopping for me. I was feeling a little lonely and sorry for myself. I worked my way up and down the aisles. With each item, I had to get out of the electric cart and take it down from the shelf. This meant getting up and down several times, increasing my pain levels to a maximum. Almost on the verge of tears, I prayed silently, 'Lord, give me the strength to finish this task.'

I had just turned the corner and entered into the pet food aisle when I saw a little old woman coming round the corner at the other end of the aisle. She was talking to herself. 'Yes, yes, don't you think I know this?' she said, as she shuffled towards me and stopped. She put her hand on my shoulder and said with a gentle smile on her face, 'God has sent me here to tell you that He loves you very much and He has heard your prayers.' She then straightened herself up and left before I could say a word.

My immediate reaction was that the lady was probably senile and was going around the store blessing people. But after she left, I realized that my pain was gone. I felt refreshed! I immediately went looking for the lady. I knew she couldn't have gone too far. I wanted to ask her questions, to thank her for her message. I raced up and down the aisles as fast as the electric cart would go, looking everywhere, asking people if they had seen her. But she was nowhere. No one else had seen her. Had I gone mad? It all happened so fast, could I have imagined it? No, she did touch me and somehow my pain was gone, my energy level was so much better. I felt sure that I had had an angel encounter of the third kind, right in the middle of the pet food aisle.

But the loneliness still enveloped me as the days turned into months. The disease controlled every aspect of my life, with pain, fatigue, or shaking.

Some days I would wake up feeling good. I would make plans to get out of the house, but by the time I was showered and dressed (a major physical effort), I was too exhausted to go anywhere and crawled back into bed. Sometimes I slept for days.

I was completely alone, except for my nurses from the Catholic Social Services who came twice a week to help me around the house, and Varun, my online friend.

∼

I had made whatever adjustments I could in my surroundings to make life easier. But I had to find something to do in the many hours that I was alone.

I bought a computer. The day it arrived, I opened the box and set it up. That night I went online and for the first time in my life, I entered a chat room. In a few moment's time, just when I thought I had control of my life again, God set in motion events that would forever change me and introduce me to a whole new world.

That night I met a troubled young man in West Bengal, India, and we began to chat in a Christian chat room I was 'ladywheeler'—the name I gave myself. I told him I was a short, fat, old lady in a wheelchair. He didn't seem to mind, so we talked. I could tell he was troubled and set about giving him motherly advice. He told me he was twenty-eight years old and living a life that seemed to have no direction or purpose, in a big city in India. Over the next few weeks we shared each other's stories and pains. Soon we were chatting online at a set time each day. It felt good to be helping and guiding him as he left the city and returned to his home in a village in the Purulia district of West Bengal. I tried to encourage him and give him confidence to start life afresh. Soon he had a good job and began changing for the better.

I learned that Varun's father worked for TLM, the Leprosy Mission hospital in Purulia. There was a large Christian population in the village of Bhat Bandh where he worked. Varun's family too had converted to Christianity, and belonged to the Church of North India, or CNI, which was affiliated to the Protestant sect of the Christian faith, as opposed to the Catholic sect.

When Varun was a child, the family lived inside the Leprosy Mission compound. He told me of the many leprosy-affected people that he grew up with and who were a part of his life. Even his uncles worked for TLM. This was an important part of his life. I began researching leprosy so I could know more about it.

Varun was always there for me when I needed a friend, but equally, he made me feel needed and important in his life. That went a long way in helping me overcome the rejection I had experienced from my own family and friends.

The manager of the internet café that Varun used also became a part of our lives. He was put on alert to call Varun if I came online. Often the manager would ask me how I was feeling and joke with me until Varun arrived. Some days I was in terrible pain and needed to talk to Varun. More than once, Varun would stop whatever he was doing and rush across town to be with me online. His words comforted me, distracted me, until I was ready to go to sleep.

I maintain that if pain was a color, like blue, and we could actually see the pain in others, we would not only see a world of different hues of blue, but we would also have more compassion for those who are in great pain. But pain is invisible, like love, hope and faith. It is not a color, but a condition only seen and recognized by those in that same condition, in that same state of mind.

Varun and I were both in pain, which was our common connection. This condition that we shared bonded us beyond age or cultural differences. There wasn't an event in our lives that Varun and I didn't share. I came to know the many characters in his village and the personalities of his friends. He learned about my family and the things that happened in my life too.

That is how it began. Varun and I became fast friends and for the next four years we shared our lives together.

It was in the second year that I began to realize how much a part of my daily life Varun had become. I looked forward to our chat times and reading the emails that he sent me. Sometimes he would call me and we would talk about anything and everything.

I suppose it was inevitable, but I never even dared to think about it...Varun was the first to say it: 'Janice, I love you.'

'No you don't,' I told him. 'I am too old for you and I am just your friend.'

'No!' he said emphatically, 'I am not a child and I know what is in my heart. I want you to be my wife!' I hung up on him. I turned off my computer and didn't answer the phone when it rang all night long and for the next few days.

But the truth had finally been spoken. Once the words were said, there was no turning back. No matter how hard I tried, I could not deny that I had fallen in love with him too. 'Ridiculous!' I would say to myself. 'Impossible!' I would yell in my empty house as I wheeled around in that wheelchair.

Determined to stop this nonsense, I wrote a scathing email to him, telling him to grow up and find a nice Indian girl his age and get married. I didn't want anything to do with India or with him. I accused him of manipulating me over the years just to get a ticket to the US and his green card. I told him to stop calling me and writing to me. I told him, 'If a chicken and a fish fall in love, where are they to live? Ridiculous!'

But I missed him terribly. How could I be in love with man half my age, living on the other side of the world? I suppose it is like living inside a romance novel, I justified it to myself... it isn't real. What harm would it do to just love each other in a surreal world? It wasn't like we were hurting each other or anyone else...I finally sent him an email. I confessed my love for him too, fully confident that nothing would ever come of it from 10,000 miles away.

That confession changed everything between us. He began calling me 'Mrs Kashyap'—Kashyap was his surname—and writing me e-mails addressed to 'My wife' and signing them with 'Your husband'. It was a wonderful romance, full of everything a love story contains. He was my Prince Charming who came galloping up on his white horse to rescue me from the sickness, the wheelchair and the loneliness. He made me feel young and beautiful in our imaginary world. And like a good novel, the more time we spent inside the story, the more time we wanted to live there.

There was another element that had entered into our story…it was God.

I am not sure how it happened, but each of us had, without telling the other, begun reading the Bible and going to church. One night I happened to mention that I had been to church that day. Varun said, in amazement, 'You too? I went to church today as well! I enjoyed it, but was afraid to bring it up because we both said we weren't really interested in it.'

'I know…' I hesitated. 'But something has changed inside me and I have been reading the Bible.'

'I can't believe this!' he replied. 'So have I. Every night I have been reading until late.' There was a long silence between us as we both absorbed what was happening. Finally I said, 'Maybe God is trying to show us something?'

'Yes He is. He is showing us that He loves us and wants us to share our faith,' Varun said.

It was the tiniest of miracles…or was it just a coincidence? But no, over the next two years we shared scripture and even prayed together online. Our lives now included God in almost every conversation. Both of us were caught up in a change that neither understood, but it was powerful and it was wonderful!

It is true that I grew to love Varun deeply, but I also grew to love God more. Every waking minute of my life was filled with Him. I talked to Him constantly and was filled with the awe and wonder of what He had created around me. It was as if my eyes suddenly opened to a whole new world. I studied scripture and prayed, never seeming to be able to get enough of God. Somehow, I knew that God had brought Varun into my life for His purpose, though I did not know the purpose yet. I trusted that the Lord would show me when the time was right.

~

Once I had dusted off my Bible and begun reading, I had the desire to go to church, but I could not because I had no vehicle that could take me and my wheelchair. Many people knocked on my door from various churches and invited me to come. But none could offer me a way to get there in my wheelchair.

Then a neighbor invited me to her church. I said, rather sarcastically, 'Sure I will, if you can figure out a way to get me there.' To my surprise, the following Sunday, Tammy and her husband, Marc, showed up in their truck. He pulled out some long wooden planks to use as ramps, and pushed my wheelchair up onto the bed of the truck. I was going to church!

It was so refreshing to sit in the church and share fellowship with other Christians. I discovered that the church was just a few miles from my house and decided I could wheel myself there and back in my electric chair.

And that is what I did. No matter what the weather, you could see me wheeling along the streets each Sunday.

I had a hunger building inside me, a hunger to learn more about God. One day I said to myself, 'Okay, Janice, when you worked, you gave your job 110 per cent. Now is the time to give God that 110 per cent.' After that day I couldn't get enough of reading the Bible. My prayer time doubled. I bought albums of Christian music and turned the stereo up loud and danced around and around in my wheelchair. How wonderful it was to worship and praise God this way!

2. Visions and Healing

A strange thing started to happen. I began to have visions of myself in India. I could see myself quite clearly sitting in a chair, speaking to people who sat around me on the ground. At first I dismissed it as just a silly dream or a desire I had because I was in love with Varun. How could I get to India when I was so sick and in a wheelchair? It was impossible!

But our God is a God of impossibilities. He kept showing me this vision until one day I said, 'Okay, God, I have prayed for you to use me in this wheelchair, so if that is where you want me to go, I will declare it and claim it!' From that day and for the next two years, I began to tell everyone that I was going to India. From my pastor to my family, I boldly declared it...And everyone thought I had lost my mind.

I never asked to be healed. I suppose because I felt unworthy of such a miracle. It would be an insult to those who didn't smoke or drink and had lived their entire lives in a Christian environment. I had only dusted off my Bible a couple of years ago.

Though I had raised my two children in the Christian faith and took them to church when they were growing up, I had long ago given up on attaining the perfection of living like Christ. I abandoned the church, but hung onto my simple faith.

I hadn't yet begun to learn the language and catchphrases

that devout Christians used. I studied the Bible furiously, trying to catch up with those who quoted the Gospel with ease. But I also read the Bible with a hunger for more of God. The words jumped out at me and danced alive as the stories, the truth, unfolded my very spirit. I didn't understand what was happening to me, but I loved it! If I had to remain in a wheelchair for the rest of my life to feel this way, I was willing.

When I told Varun of my visions of being in India, he simply said, 'Then we should prepare for you to come here.'

Around this time, Varun got a job at a Leprosy Mission hospital in the town of Bankura that provided a house and a reasonable pay. We began making our plans to live together. Varun also had a vision one night that was very powerful. He said that God spoke to him and told him that he must prepare to be strong and ready for change, that I would be coming to India and it was Varun's job to protect and take care of me. This event had a profound effect on Varun and I could feel a change in him in our conversations after that.

I will never forget the reaction I got from my family.

Dad was against religion of any kind. So on that fateful day when I excitedly announced that I was going to India to be a missionary, dad's reaction was as though I had announced that I had decided to become a prostitute. 'How can you do this to me after the way I raised you?' he growled, with the familiar crimson color rising on his neck and face.

I boldly continued. 'I have been called by God to go to India...so I will be preparing to leave in a few months.' The reaction at the dinner table was a collective: 'She's lost her mind!' and 'Oh my God!'

In retrospect, I guess I don't blame them. There I was in that wheelchair and had been in that wheelchair for nearly four years. It really wasn't a logical thing for me to consider, let alone to do, in this real world of ours, this real world of doctors and tests and the diagnosis 'she will never walk again. She will only get worse.'

But I had long before entered into another world, a world where nothing was impossible, where my faith had grown to such a degree that I believed in the God of Abraham, Isaac and Jacob. God had shown me, in visions and dreams, that my place was in India. I believed that if God showed me in India, then God would pave the way for it to happen.

While my family was considering having me locked away in a mental hospital, God was opening and closing doors so fast that I watched in amazement.

At home, there was one other person who believed that God was using me, showing me to be in India—my nurse, Linda. She was Pentecostal and she had no doubt that God was working powerfully in our lives. Linda had the faith of a lion. She was a non-stop talker, but every word was uplifting and encouraging to me. She came three days a week to clean my house and help me with things I could not do. She also became my spiritual partner; often we would pray together and share scripture.

As I became closer to God and hungered for more spiritual food, my church became less satisfying. This is hard to explain, but it was like eating a meal with no seasoning. I came home feeling empty. I prayed for God to show me where I should be. I knew I needed to find another church, one that was close enough for me to get to in my wheelchair, but where?

Linda kept inviting me to her church, which was also nearby. But I had heard rumors about the Pentecostals and was reluctant to attend. Linda kept up her efforts until finally I agreed to wheel myself in and just stay in the back of the church and watch.

At first, I was uncomfortable with all the noise and method of worship. But gradually I accepted this odd behavior and began to worship more freely myself. One day, during the now familiar Holy Spirit movement, when everyone was speaking in tongues, wailing, shaking, crying, I felt a rush, like a wind blowing through me. I felt like I had been filled with love, a love like nothing I had ever experienced before. It was so profound that my eyes welled up with tears. I sat there quietly, not wanting to disturb the wonderful experience. Linda came over to me and asked me what was going on. I said simply, 'God really loves me.' She looked at me puzzled, like she didn't hear me amidst the noise in the chapel. I repeated it louder, with more emotion and a big smile on my face. 'God really loves me, He loves us so much!' Linda broke out laughing. 'Janice, I don't understand a word you just said,' she shouted back.

Frustrated, I shouted it again. I felt a hand on my shoulder and turned to find the pastor standing there, also with a big grin on his face. 'Janice, you are speaking in tongues!'

I just couldn't believe it! But Linda and the pastor both nodded in confirmation. They didn't understand me because I was speaking in tongues, not because they couldn't hear me. I sat there in shock, afraid to open my mouth...and the feeling left me as quickly as it had come.

This was the first time that I, personally, had felt the Holy Spirit inside me and definitely the first time I, without any effort or thinking on my own, had spoken in tongues... and yet, the experience was oddly familiar, as though I had experienced it earlier as well. I spent the next few days reliving that feeling, that event, and searching my memory banks for an answer. It never came...but I now understood why people tried so hard to bring on the Holy Spirit. It was like a drug high. I wanted more of it.

When Linda arrived the next day, as my nurse, she was still excited over my speaking in tongues. She explained to me, using the Book of Acts, that when a person speaks in tongues, it is a sign that they are saved. It was time for her to indoctrinate me in the rules of the church. I sat there and listened as she recited the requirements. Frankly I felt the urge to run.

No matter how hard I tried, I could not justify the strict rules placed upon women in the Pentecostal church. A woman was not allowed to expose parts of her body that might entice men. No makeup and jewelry or any kind of 'adornment', was allowed. A woman must never cut her hair, nor color it. A woman's head must be covered at all times, in church, but especially in prayer. A woman should be silent in the church. Though I began to let my hair grow and started changing my wardrobe according to their customs, I just could not imagine Jesus being so judgemental or setting such strict conditions.

Besides, the 'requirement' to speak in tongues really unnerved me. Though I was glad that I personally had experienced this, to me, this was just one of the many gifts that God had given me and not necessarily one I wanted to experience again.

But the one thing that being in the church did for me, for which I will be eternally grateful, was to teach me to worship openly and without reservation. My worship grew stronger as I whirled in my wheelchair to the music and praise. How my heart was lifted up!

It may seem odd in retrospect, but once I had accepted my

condition, and had asked God to 'use me' in the wheelchair, I expected to be used in that condition. Indeed, I looked forward to any opportunity I had to show Christ's love, not because of my condition, but in spite of it.

The pastors of the church laid hands on me many times, praying for a healing. I simply praised God for the healing and the changes that took place inside my heart. Each day that I was able to dress myself and go outside was blessing enough for me.

∽

One day, while reading the Bible, I came across the scripture where Jesus was telling the story of a farmer planting seeds: 'A farmer was sowing grain in his fields. As he scattered the seed across the ground, some fell beside a path, and the birds came and ate it. And some fell on rocky soil where there was little depth of earth; the plants sprang up quickly enough in the shallow ground, but the hot sun soon scorched them and they withered and died, for they had so little root. Other seeds fell among the thorns and the thorns choked out the tender blades. But some fell on good soil, and produced a crop that was thirty, sixty, and even a hundred times as much as he had planted.' (Mathew 13)

As I read on, the disciples asked Jesus to explain what the story meant. Here was His explanation: 'The hard path where some of the seeds fell represents the heart of a person who hears the Good News about the Kingdom of God and doesn't understand it; then Satan comes along and snatches the seeds from his heart. The shallow, rocky ground represents the heart of a man who hears the message and receives it with great joy, but he doesn't have much depth in his life, and the seeds don't root very deeply, and after a while, when trouble comes, or persecution begins because of his beliefs, his enthusiasm fades and he drops out.

'The ground covered with thistles represents a man who hears the message, but the cares of this life and his longing for money choke out God's word, and he does less and less for God. The good ground represents the heart of a man who listens to the message and understands it and goes out and brings thirty, sixty, or even a hundred others into the Kingdom of God.'

When I read this, it struck me that no one expects to be anything other than the seed in good soil. What a terrible fate it would be to become the seed that never took root or worse, the one who grew and died.

Yet I myself had turned away from the church once, because the message was difficult…or maybe because the message was wrong. Certainly what I understood now was like refreshing water to my soul. I prayed that I would not become the seed that landed on shallow ground, or amongst the thistles. How I wanted to be the one whose faith was strong enough to bring others into the kingdom.

∼

Linda and I spent more and more time together. She wanted me to get out of the house more often, but her car didn't have a way to carry my wheelchair. I had found, in an online store, a scooter that could be dismantled, folded and lifted into the trunk of a car. This scooter could be the answer to our predicament, I thought.

But my medical insurance had already paid for my wheelchair and I was pretty sure that they would not pay for the scooter too. I was right.

I began praying for God to show me a way to get this

scooter. I carried the picture of it with me everywhere and showed it to everyone. Christmas was coming soon and, like a child, I wanted this more than anything else. I imagined myself with it and being able to go wherever I wanted without the restrictions of my wheelchair. But the price of $950 was more than my budget would allow. This didn't stop me from believing that it would come...and it did!

As it turned out, Rod and my father bought it for me and it was delivered just before Christmas. I hadn't been so excited about a gift in years! It was shiny red and the most beautiful thing in the world. How grateful I was to both of them and I couldn't stop thanking them.

Linda suggested that we take the new scooter for a trip to have lunch at the local senior center. 'Casa' was a place for seniors to gather and have a good, inexpensive meal. It was also a place where they put together 'Meals on Wheels', a volunteer service that provided meals for those who were confined to their homes.

But on this particular day, the luncheon was attended by the mayor of Prescott Valley and a few of the people from the mayor's office. It was a special meeting to discuss what the city could do to help handicapped people.

I listened intently to the discussion and the suggestions put before the mayor. I finally raised my hand, holding my crutches aloft.

'As you can see, I am handicapped. I often have to travel though the city in my wheelchair and there are no sidewalks or ramps along the way. Often I have to drive on the edge of the road while cars are whizzing past me. It is very dangerous,' I said. 'In addition, the local businesses do not have automatic doors for the handicapped. I think this should be a requirement.'

Harvey Skoog, the mayor, listened intently to me. 'We are putting in sidewalks throughout the city,' he said.

'Yes,' I countered, 'in some areas, but there are no ramps for me to get down off the sidewalks, so again I am forced to ride in the street.'

'I didn't realize this,' Skoog said, his brow furrowed.

'There are many other problems for the wheelchair-bound person,' I continued, 'I challenge you and your people to spend just a few hours with me riding wheelchairs and I will take you on a different tour of the city!'

The mayor laughed. 'Though your offer is tempting, I think it won't be necessary. Can we call you in the future for your advice?'

'Anytime!' I smiled, and we shook hands.

After the luncheon Harvey came over to me, thanked me for my input and gave me his card. 'Please give me a call at my office so we can continue our discussion,' he said. Linda was very impressed. 'See?' she said, 'God brought us here today for a reason. I can't believe how brave you were telling him all of that.'

'Brave?' I said. 'Not at all. I was glad to have the chance to tell him what needs to be done.'

Little did I know that Harvey Skoog, the mayor of Prescott Valley, would become a significant part of my future.

∽

Physically, I was getting worse. The pain grew in intensity and my body was twitching and shaking so much that the smallest of tasks became impossible. Yet, the visions of India came to me larger and full of color and light, smells and sounds. I could *see* myself there. It was the strangest thing, but the sicker I became, the more I could see myself walking and doing many things. I held tightly to these visions and dreams. They had become my reality.

I was also diagnosed with diabetes. I had to ask the Catholic Social Services to send me a nurse everyday to help me. The disease had moved up into my shoulders and neck leaving me unable to use any part of my body without a great deal of pain and effort. Linda had arranged for the 'Meals on Wheels' to deliver me lunch so that I could have at least one good meal a day.

It was at this time that depression set in heavily. Not even Varun could bring me out of the darkness I was in. I tried everything to shake myself out of it. I read scripture out loud. I played my favorite music and prayed for God to help me. But the pain and the darkness enveloped me. I felt useless, abandoned and in great despair. After three days of this, I poured myself a large drink. I decided to end it all and hoped that God would understand. I wheeled myself into the bathroom.

I had a perfect plan. I would climb into the bathtub and slit my wrists. This way the blood could be easily washed away after I was dead. It wouldn't be messy at all.

I found a box of razor blades and pulled one out. It was a new one with paper wrapping around it. I was quite calm, but my hands shook as usual. It took my complete concentration to unwrap the blade. But as I unwrapped it, it flipped out of the paper and landed on the floor. Undaunted, I slid myself out of the wheelchair onto the floor. The blade had landed next to a metal grate. It was a floor duct for the heating and air-conditioning. I was sprawled out on the floor in a very uncomfortable position. I had to push myself up to reach for the blade, my hands trembling even more from the pressure. I lost control and instead of grabbing it, I accidently pushed it. I watched as it fell through the grate and down into the floor duct. There was no way I could retrieve it. I felt a rage build up inside me. 'Why God?' I screamed. 'Don't you know how much pain and suffering I am going through?'

All of a sudden, it seemed as though the room lit up. In my mind, the ceiling disappeared, and a vision appeared, strong and real. I was no longer lying on the bathroom floor, but at the foot of the Cross and looking up at Christ. I saw the nails in His hands and His face stained with blood from the crown of thorns. 'Yes,' He said gently, 'I know the pain and suffering you are going through.' He smiled a gentle, knowing smile and I felt a deep, wonderful love embrace me, consume me. Then the vision disappeared.

Guilt and shame rushed through me like a tidal wave. I lay on the bathroom floor sobbing and begging God's forgiveness. I felt ashamed for being so weak. Where was my faith?

'All right, God,' I said, 'I will abide in your love. I will do whatever you ask of me. I will suffer and endure this pain until you call me to be with you.'

I struggled back into my wheelchair, a new woman. I felt Christ's love so strongly that I was full of a joy that lasted a very, very long time. With this new filling of love and joy came a strong determination, a willingness to live my life to the fullest.

Oddly, my estranged husband began coming over and checking on me, to make sure I was okay. He offered help and encouragement too. But it was clear that we were both better off living apart. Our friendship was a welcome contrast to the many years of turmoil in our marriage.

Once a month, the head nurse from the Catholic Social Services came to visit me, to see if all was taken care of in my home and to monitor my condition. I received a phone call one morning that she would be arriving at eleven. It was a bad day for me, physically. My shaking was out of control. She asked me the usual questions and I tried hard not to shake as we talked. As her visit came to an end, she said, 'Janice, there is something I must tell you.'

She told me that my condition had worsened to a point where their services could no longer help me. In addition, they were running out of funds to pay for the visits. She told me that it was time for me to consider moving into a nursing home. I sat in my wheelchair staring at my shaking hands. For a brief moment despair flooded over me. It was true. I was in bad shape. I did need more help each day.

But I also knew that this was a situation that only God could change. I only had to believe and stay strong. Finally I said to her, 'I am not going into a care facility. I am not sure how, but God will step in and change this.' Then a little more boldly, I said, 'No! I am going to India! That is what God has shown me and that is where I will be.'

She was a kind woman. I liked her very much. She patted my hand and said, 'Then I will pray for you.' But I knew she did not believe me. The look on her face was one of loving kindness and pity, a look I had become all too familiar with over the years.

I cannot explain it, but I actually felt sorry for her and the others for their lack of faith in God's promises. I simply began preparing myself for a life in India, in the wheelchair, with Varun.

～

It was one week later that the most miraculous thing in my entire life happened. It was, for me, completely unexpected. It was on Sunday, 20 February 2005.

I was sitting in church listening to the music. A strange sensation began to come into my feet. It was as if small volts of electricity were tickling them. I thought it was just another symptom of my illness and began to wiggle my toes to relieve it. Then something happened to me that had never happened before. A loud voice commanded me, 'Stand!' At first, I looked around, searching for the source of the voice. But I realized that it had come from inside me. I grabbed Linda's hand and slid out of the pew. I pulled myself up on my weak legs and stood. The sensation that I had felt in my feet was now moving up my legs. A power I cannot explain was overtaking me. Then the voice came again, more forcefully. 'Go forth and walk!'

At that same instant the power surged like lightning up into my entire body and I stepped forward confidently. Linda, my nurse and friend, held my arm and smiling, said, 'Don't forget your wheelchair.' I smiled back at her and said simply, 'I don't need it.' I stepped towards the front of the church.

Strangely, the hymn we were singing was, 'I will walk with you.' And at the very moment that I stepped forward, the pastor announced, 'Let's all get up and walk around the church as we sing this song.'

I took a few more steps and shouted out loud, 'I can walk! Thank you, God!' The tears flowed down my cheeks. I was in my own world, completely unaware of anything but the great love and power I felt within me. I reached the back of the church and wiped my tears. As I looked around I saw that all eyes were upon me and everyone was crying and praising God for my healing. They had all witnessed it, about 120 people that glorious Sunday saw the miracle of Christ's healing.

I walked out of the church that day and have been walking

ever since. When I got home I threw away all the medications and put my wheelchair in a dark corner of my bedroom.

For weeks afterwards I was in a sort of shock. One minute I would laugh out loud and even skip around the house. The next minute I would cry with joy, thanking God over and over. I would wake up in the middle of the night and sit on the edge of my bed wondering if I could still stand and walk. When I did, I would break out into a smile and whisper, 'Thank you Jesus!'

I immediately made an appointment with my doctor, Dennis Little.

He had been so supportive and encouraging through my suffering. He was a warrior on my behalf as I struggled to understand what my body was doing and the pain I was suffering. In addition, he was my parents' doctor, so he knew my family well.

I couldn't wait to show him that I was healed and out of the wheelchair. I made sure that when he walked into the examination room, I was standing up. I went over and gave him a big hug. It was obvious that I had shaken him up. 'Umm, how are you doing?' he stammered. I could barely hold in the good news. 'I am doing great!' I said. 'I know it may sound crazy, but a few Sundays ago I was healed by God. My pain is gone and my legs are working. I have been walking for two weeks now.'

'I see,' he said, taking a deep breath. 'Th-that's wonderful news. I am so happy for you...but I must caution you not to be too optimistic. Janice, you have the worst case of fibro that I have ever seen. Maybe the medicines have finally kicked in and you are feeling the relief of all of it. But I am sorry to tell you that this is what we call "remission" in the system. It may be only temporary, or may last six months to a year, but I assure you that you still have fibromyalgia and will have it the rest of your life.' He was obviously upset.

'Look, I want to believe in this miracle, but I have had too much experience in this disease. I will swear in a court of law that you have it now and will always have it, in spite of this wonderful thing you are experiencing.' He sighed deeply. 'I wish I had better news for you.'

'It's okay, doctor,' I said. 'I understand what you are saying to protect me from any false hope. Perhaps you are right, but all I know is that I am walking and without pain. I also know that God stepped in and lifted me out of that wheelchair. Even if it is a partial or temporary healing, I am so blessed! If it comes back, then I am equally blessed to have you as my doctor. All I want from you now is to be happy for me. You are a Mormon. Therefore you believe in God. As strange as it may sound, I want you to believe in this miracle from God.'

Dr Little smiled at me and gave me a quick hug. 'I am happy for you. I hope the remission lasts a long time,' he said. He stood back and looked at me. 'Is there anything I can do for you?' I said yes. 'I am going to India to do some work for God and to meet an Indian man I have fallen in love with. I want to take some medical supplies with me, especially blood pressure machines and blood sugar testers. If you have anything like these, please save them up and I will come here before I go.' His eyes lit up. 'Yes, I will tell everyone to set these things aside. I think we already have some extra blood sugar monitors. Just let me know when you are ready to go.'

～

It was at this time that I began to have dreams and visions almost daily. I believe God was preparing me for what was to come. But the strongest and most persistent was a 'calling' to 'go out and tell the world.' Inside I was bursting with such joy. It seemed an easy task, at first.

The opportunity was there as I now *walked* out into the world. All who had known me in my wheelchair would be amazed and ask me what happened. I would tell them, 'God healed me.' If they asked me how, I would tell them all about that Sunday. I found myself sharing my testimony everywhere I went.

But there were those who would not accept my explanation. Sadly, even among my fellow Christians, there were doubts and suspicions in their minds. What rubbish, I could see them thinking. Couldn't it just be that the medication had finally worked? Or, maybe it had all been in my mind all along, and then one fine day I decided to get up and walk. I found that the harder I tried to tell people, the more they made me feel like I was some nutcase walking around.

But my friend Linda had no problem telling everyone she saw about my miracle. She even boldly went to the local newspaper office and told the religion journalist about my healing. Though I don't know what exactly happened, Linda came away disgusted and, of course, that bit of news never appeared in the paper.

Even my own church, the ones who had witnessed the sickness in me, and the healing, discouraged me from sharing my testimony. 'Let me go to other churches and tell them of the healing,' I said eagerly to the head pastor.

'No. We sent news to the head office and they will print it in the monthly magazine,' I was told.

'Well, then, let me at least give my testimony here, in my church,' I begged.

'Well, yes, I suppose we could give you five minutes in our Sunday program,' the pastor told me. 'It is not good for a woman to speak too much,' he said quietly. I was shocked and disappointed. I knew that the Pentecostal rules did not encourage women to speak in public, and this church was very patriarchal. I also knew it was a societal thing. Most of us don't want to appear like 'nutcases', claiming to have seen angels, spirits and healings. It is fine to talk about it in the context of Biblical history, but to speak of it as a real, present-day happening is a different matter. Even in Christ's time, there were those who believed but remained silent because they feared for their safety. But for me, it was a 'coming out' of my spiritual closet, and the more people tried to stop me, the more determined I became to go out and tell the world.

Inside I was raging. I took it to God. 'Lord, here you performed a great miracle right in front of their eyes and they will not allow me to speak of it!' I cried out. 'Five minutes indeed.' Then I added, 'If I were a man they would not stop me.'

The church tried everything to discourage me from going to India, to follow God's call. Everyone tried to instill some practical common sense into me. I knew that they meant well in their concern for me. 'It is a dangerous place. You don't know this man, Varun, at all. He could be just using you to get money, or his green card,' they said.

When I asked about becoming a missionary for the church they told me that I was too inexperienced. That only seminary students trained for the mission field were qualified...They only sent married couples. I was too old...I heard it all and indeed it sounded very 'practical' and 'of the world' wisdom. But it was not God's wisdom.

But just in case, I set about a 'Plan B,' which was to

contact other missionaries in the area and let them know I was coming. This was more to appease the doubters, but I also felt it would be a good idea to have fellow Christians for Varun and I to lean on for support. Unfortunately, these missionaries were not in India, but nearby countries. I wrote down their addresses and tucked them inside my wallet along with my passport.

When the church realized that I was going ahead with my plans to go to India, they had the church matriarch, who was also a friend, call me. She told me to stay and find another way to serve God, here, where it was safe. She talked on and on about it not being my calling. I listened politely.

'No, sister,' I said firmly, 'God has called me to go to India and that is where I am going.'

She flew into a rage. 'I tell you that if you insist on taking this trip against my wishes and the pastor's advice, you will never arrive there. That plane will crash!'

'Well then,' I said calmly, 'if that is the way the Lord wants me to die, so be it. But I will follow God's lead and not the coercions of you or the church. Thank you for your concerns. I will be praying for all of you,' I said, and hung up.

What, after all, is a calling? For me, it began as a passing thought, a sort of whisper in my mind. Tiny visions emerged interrupting my regular thought pattern, of serving God. A smile would cross my face and I would laugh it off. We all get silly thoughts like that now and then. Surely God would choose someone more holy and perfect than I was!

But then those interruptions became more frequent, more insistent as the months went by. My irritation mounted as I tried to convince myself and God that I was not fit to serve

Him. But those whispers became louder and my desire to serve became stronger...yet still doubts and concerns wavered in my mind.

Was it really God calling me at this late stage of my life? I had no way of knowing for sure, no one to talk to about it all...except God. So one day, after reading scripture and prayer, I decided to have a real conversation with Him. I imagined Jesus sitting in the chair in the living room. 'Lord,' I began, 'there is a lot going on in my life that I don't understand, and I really wish you would show me clearly what I am supposed to do.' I thought for a minute. 'Whenever I try to do things according to my own thinking, I mess it up. So what I want is for you to just take over. I want your will in my life, not my own.' I took a deep breath. 'All I can think about is the dreams and visions that I know have come from you. I feel that I can't take another day of not doing anything about this urge you have placed in my heart. I am most unworthy and have no idea why you would choose me, but I wanted to say this out loud, to declare it to you in my own voice.' And with another deep breath, I proclaimed, 'Lord, if you are calling me to serve you, please let me know and I will surely go.'

From the moment I said this, my heart leapt inside me. There were no bells ringing, choir singing or flashes of light in the room, but I knew that I had crossed into a new beginning of something that would change my life completely.

The calling became a shout, and the shout became an obsession written in my heart. Nothing or no one could stop what I knew was His will for my life. Unspeakable joy filled me and an extreme humbling of my spirit. I felt the need to say something, to express the emotions that I was feeling. All I could come up with was, 'How great Thou art!' It sounded a little corny, even to me, but I really felt the words. 'How great Thou art!' I said again, as tears fell from my face. Little did I know that this calling, this obsession, this declaration would be irreversible and no matter what happened, I was bound eternally to it and to God.

A few weeks later I was healed.

Though I didn't realize it then, I now see that God was closing doors in my world so I would be willing to step into another one. It was a painful process for me, but so rewarding in the end.

The church where I was healed decided that I was 'shunned' which meant that they were not allowed to speak to me. I ran into them now and then in the town and they would avoid me. I was sad for them, not for myself.

I ran into the pastor of my first church one day in Wal-Mart. He was obviously shocked to see me walking. I had heard that he had been recently diagnosed with fibromyalgia too. 'What happened? You are out of the wheelchair?' he asked.

'Yes,' I said. 'God healed me a few weeks ago.'

'But you haven't been coming to church lately,' he said disapprovingly.

'Yes, I am sorry, but I have been going to another church,' I said awkwardly. He looked at me disparagingly and walked away. It seemed no one could see the miracle or feel the joy I was feeling.

In my conversations with God, I would explain to Him that, just as in Jesus' time, no one wanted to listen to me. My 'good news' was falling upon deaf ears. He just kept telling me to 'Go out and tell the world.' And, oh, how I wanted to. I wanted to shout it from the roof tops. It was like an itch I could not scratch. It was no longer about me, but about the glory and grace of our living God.

In my naive mind I thought that my healing would bring people to the Lord. I now know that healings do not bring great faith. But it is great faith that brings healings.

When I told Varun about my wonderful miracle, he was overjoyed and told his family and friends. They were all amazed and overjoyed to hear of the healing. Varun told me to come to India and give my testimony. He arranged for me to speak in a local church as soon as I arrived.

'How long can I speak?' I asked him. He laughed, 'As long as it takes to tell your story.' How strange, I thought. My own world did not want to hear about God's miracle. But evidently Varun's world had stronger faith than mine.

There were many obstacles to stop me from going to India. But somehow each one of them crumbled away and I just watched as the doors opened for me to leave. I rented my house to my niece, my younger sister's daughter. I stored away the things that I wanted my children to inherit, but left everything else as it was.

When I was getting ready to leave, I jokingly said, 'Well if I don't come back, I guess everything here is yours.'

I gave my car to Kevin, my son. I got a six-month visa for India and a mass of shots at the health department. Every detail was taken care of. My soon to be ex-husband gave me the money for the plane ticket. He knew I had been healed by God and he believed in my calling, even though his own relationship with God was very distant. He jokingly called me the next Mother Teresa. He also gave me a generous sum of money which he called 'alimony payment.'

There was another battle going on within me, the smoking. It was an addiction that I had had for over thirty years. I tried and tried to quit, but could not. How could I stand before others and tell them of this great healing when

I still had this addiction? The answer came to me much later, but for now, I knew that I could not let it stop me from following my calling.

---

3. India, Finally

I arrived in India on 1 June 2005, three and a half months after my healing. I had two Bibles and many suitcases, one of which contained medical supplies given by my doctor. I had brought my wheelchair along, thinking I would donate it to a needy person in India.

I was full of conviction. For the first time in my life, at the ripe age of fifty-four, I was sure of my purpose and looking forward to the adventures that lay ahead. There was no doubt in my mind that I was doing the right thing, no matter how crazy it sounded to the world.

I did have one moment of fear, though, just before I landed in Kolkata. What if Varun was not there to meet me? What would I do alone in a strange country? What if all the warnings I had heard were to come true? What if Varun was a bad person after all? I gripped the seat as a wave of fear and doubt enveloped me.

Then my confidence returned. 'God has led you here and He will protect you, no matter what happens. You are here for His purpose,' I said to myself and kicked the fear off like a wet blanket.

Getting off the plane, collecting my luggage and going through security seemed to take forever. Inside the airport the air was humid and smelt of spices and mildew. As I slowly pushed my luggage trolley through the airport and into the corridor outside, my eyes searched for the face I had only seen a few times on a webcam and in one photograph Varun had sent me.

Would I recognize this person I had grown to love? I knew his heart and his soul, but not what he really looked like. Would he recognize me? I was still short and fat. Would he take one look at me and disappear?

I held my breath as I searched through the line of people standing on the other side of the gate. It was like a pool of Indian faces staring and searching. Then I spotted him. I would recognize that smile and those eyes anywhere! He pushed his way through the gate and rushed towards me. 'No hugs,' he said. 'My uncle is watching.' With that he took the luggage trolley and guided me swiftly out of the airport. I could not take my eyes off him as my luggage was loaded into a Leprosy Mission jeep and we got into the back seat. Varun introduced me briefly to his uncle but he barely returned my greeting. He probably doesn't speak much English, I told myself. Not that it mattered. It still hadn't sunk in that I was actually in India, sitting next to the man I had known and loved for so long, Varun Kashyap!

As we drove through the streets of Kolkata, I tried to take in the sights, sounds and smells of the city. It was all so alien and exciting. The heat and humidity was more than anything I had experienced. We sat in traffic with all the windows rolled down. Suddenly I felt a tap on my arm. I turned and saw a young boy, a beggar. He was tapping me with the stub of his arm and holding his one hand out for money. My first reaction was shock mixed with curiosity. I had never witnessed anyone with a stub for an arm, let alone been touched with it. I found myself staring at the jagged limb, trying to gather the scene in. Varun shouted something at him and the traffic finally moved. I felt a sense of regret that I didn't give him any money.

Varun and I soon discovered that our accents were difficult to understand. How strange that we could communicate so well on the internet but now we would have to learn to understand each other. Varun got frustrated repeating things to me so we sat in silence until we reached our destination, the guesthouse of the Leprosy Mission. Varun's uncle dropped us off at the gate and drove away while Varun and I carried my many pieces of luggage into the guesthouse.

There was a room for us with a bathroom attached, and a community kitchen. Varun left me alone while he went to find something for us to eat. I took a shower and freshened up. After we had eaten, we went into the bedroom and embraced each other for the first time. It was a surreal situation, knowing his heart and mind so well, having shared and endured so much that it felt as though we were one, but never having seen or heard him before. 'I love you, Mrs Kashyap,' he said. 'I am so glad you are finally here!'

I thought it was odd when Varun said it was time to sleep. It was in the middle of the afternoon. But I dutifully lay down and listened to the strange sounds outside as I studied the ceiling of this ancient building. It had obviously been built by the British and was once an elegant home. But years of neglect showed in every corner.

My mind was whirling with so many thoughts as I watched Varun sleep. He was young. Yet there was something about him that seemed much older than his years. His skin was darker than I had imagined, but he had a handsome face with big eyes and a smile that melted my heart. He was patient and gentle with me that day as I had hoped he would be.

Later that day we loaded my luggage into a taxi and

rode across Kolkata to Howrah station. There are no words to describe a taxi ride across Kolkata. I was both fascinated and terrified as we swung in and out of traffic barely missing people and vehicles. I knew there had to be a system to it all, but maybe that was hopeful thinking on my part.

We crossed over a great bridge that arched over a wide river. Varun told me it was the Howrah Bridge, one of the most famous landmarks in the city. Men carrying huge bundles of merchandise on their heads jostled each other on the pavements. Others were pulling wagons piled high and swaying precariously with bundles of cloth, utensils and all manner of things. Trucks, buses and cars competed for space on the bridge across the wide span of the river.

When we finally arrived at the station, we were surrounded by a gaggle of men offering to take our luggage. I was told to remain in the taxi, so I watched as Varun skillfully interviewed several of them. Finally two, very tall, skinny men were chosen. I wondered how they would be able to handle my six, yes six, large pieces of luggage. Back then, there weren't as many restrictions for extra baggage. Besides, two of the suitcases had been labeled 'For Leprosy Mission Hospital, Purulia, India' as they contained medical equipment and supplies, and British Airways was kind enough to waive the charges for these; my father paid the $75 they did charge for whatever was over the allowance.

I watched in amazement as they lifted the heavy pieces onto their heads and began rushing through the gaping mouth of the railway station. Varun grabbed my hand and pulled me along as we tried to keep up with them. 'Sit,' he commanded me when we reached a platform inside, then gave the men some orders, gesturing wildly. The luggage was lifted off their heads and dropped in front of us. I sat down breathlessly on the nearest bench, inspecting my suitcases for any damage.

I made a mental note to pack lighter next time. But then, I told myself, it was my first experience with packing for a six-month stay in a country I had never been to before. I thought of everything I could possibly need and bought it in every available color, times seven.

I had envisioned sleeping in tents in the Indian desert surrounded by camels and elephants. Such was my picture of India. Had I mistaken it for some other country I had seen in the movies? So far that vision was completely and utterly dashed. Perhaps the landscape outside the city would prove my mental picture was correct?

Sitting on that hard railway bench, I observed the strange world I was now in. It seemed as though entire families had set up camp on the platform. Mats and blankets were spread as mothers opened metal tins of food to feed the family. I was amazed at how many were sound asleep on the hard concrete.

I heard the sound of different languages chattering around me. The rich smell of spices mixed with sweat, assaulted my nostrils. Women in brightly colored saris with children in tow, passed in front of me as they followed their husbands. Everyone was bustling around as the loudspeakers announced the arrival of the next train.

The railway station showed signs of once having been a majestic architectural beauty that, no doubt, the British had built. But many years of neglect rendered it more of an ancient museum piece that was crumbling down. It seemed that all of Kolkata was like this, shadows of beautiful architecture and British culture in the many buildings throughout the city.

Suddenly the loudspeaker announced the departure of another train. It was ours. Varun jumped up, signaling to the men who sat cross-legged on the floor. Once again the coolies lifted the luggage onto their heads and rushed through the crowds almost knocking others down. Varun gripped my hand tightly as we followed them for what seemed like a mile before we boarded our bogey. I was glad when we finally got onto the train. I was also glad of the cool air inside the AC compartment. That dash had been a real test for my new legs!

With some difficulty, my luggage was lifted onto the racks above our seats. I sat down with relief as the compartment quickly filled up with passengers.

The train made many stops. With each stop, men would come on board selling everything from magazines to tea, to fresh coconuts, calling out their wares in sing-song voices. Varun bought me a coconut. It was a whole coconut with the top chopped off and a straw inserted inside. It was my first taste of pure coconut water and it was delicious.

I peered through the cloudy window trying to catch a glimpse of the landscape. No desert here. It was rich and green with ponds and rivers everywhere. We passed through villages that even had canals running through them. Banana and coconut trees filled the landscape.

Varun and I didn't speak much through the journey. We just kept looking at each other and smiling, letting the reality of our love silently settle in.

But soon it became dark and I began to get drowsy. I drifted off to sleep.

It was nearly seven hours later, at around 11:30 at night, when we arrived in Purulia. New coolies came rushing into the compartment and were hired and the luggage was soon on its way out the door. We had to climb many steps up and over a bridge and back down to the dimly lit parking lot of the station. I asked Varun, as we were climbing the steps, 'How could we have done this if I were in my wheelchair?' He just smiled and said, 'I would have found a way.'

There was a car waiting to meet us and drive us to our destination. Though I was tired, and it was dark, I didn't want to miss a single thing. I watched everything we passed until I was dizzy.

We checked into a hotel. It had statues of Hindu gods in the hallway and on the patio outside our room. I made a mental note to take a close look at these brightly colored statues later.

I was surprised at how spacious the room was. The bed occupied most of the wall across from the entrance. There was a couch and chair with a table next to the door. I went over to the bed and sat on it. It was very hard. As I reached for a pillow, I was surprised at how heavy and hard it was too. There was no top sheet or blanket. I didn't care. I was exhausted and this bed was much better than I had imagined. All I wanted was to fall asleep in Varun's arms for our first night together.

Shortly after we arrived, two young men came to meet us. Varun introduced them to me as Arun and Peter. Arun was dark-skinned and muscular. His build and his manner indicated a seriousness, as well as self-discipline in his life. Peter was smaller and thinner with a gentle smile and a handsome face. His skin seemed so much lighter compared to Arun's. They did not know a word of English, so I sat and listened as the three men talked in Bengali for what seemed like hours. I kept waiting for our two visitors to leave but to my surprise, they stayed and slept on the floor of the room that night. I was too tired to ask questions and fell into a deep sleep.

The next morning I woke up at dawn and knelt down by a window as the morning sun began to break across the room. I thanked God until tears flowed down my face. So much to be thankful for! The next few days many people came to meet me at the hotel. Varun had to leave for work—he had quit his job in Bankura and returned to teaching computers at a school in a small town outside Purulia—so Peter and Arun became my constant companions and, I soon learned, my bodyguards. At first, I found it odd that they continued to stay with us but then it dawned on me that this was probably to prevent Varun's family from thinking that we were sharing a room alone—and I also realized that it would take Varun a while to feel comfortable about staying alone with me too.

The first Sunday after my arrival in Purulia I stood in front of a large congregation in a church and gave my testimony.

There was standing room only, with Varun and his men guarding each door. How wonderful it was to finally share my miracle story with others! I was given all the time I needed as a pastor translated everything I said into Bengali. I thanked God for what I hoped would be the beginning of spreading hope in this new world in which I found myself. I quoted the verse about the ten lepers, whom Jesus had healed and how only one came back to thank Him. I told them that I had made a promise to myself that I would be that one.

The hotel room soon became even busier with visitors, but with each knock on the door, Peter or Arun would first open it and decide if the guest should be allowed in. One day I was sitting on the couch when a man came bursting into the room. His eyes were wild and he seemed panic-stricken. He wanted to speak to me alone, but he was told that this was not allowed.

When I saw the fear in his eyes I took his hands and sat him down beside me. In his broken English, he asked, 'Why you come here? I must know. Why you come to Purulia?' I smiled at him and kept holding his hands. 'I am just an old lady who has come to meet people and learn about Purulia,' I said.

'But you Christian, I Hindu.'

'Yes,' I said, 'but we are all brothers and sisters in this world, aren't we?' He took a deep breath and his whole body relaxed as if unloading a heavy burden off his shoulders. He gave me a weak grin. 'Okay, I go now,' he said, and left the room quickly.

It wasn't until a few years later that the same man approached me in the marketplace. I hardly recognized him, but as before, he insisted on talking to me. He had a confession to make. He told me that he had come into my hotel room that day to kill me. He had heard about this Christian woman who was boldly staying in a Hindu hotel and was talking about Christ and miracles. He was very angry and felt that I was a threat to his gods and it was his duty to kill me. 'But I see only love in your face,' he said. 'Your God protect you. I want to tell you this.' Again, he disappeared as quickly as he had come. 'Thank you, Jesus,' I whispered, wondering how many times God would protect me that first year and in the years to come.

---

4. Discovery of India—My Way

In those first few week, I often felt as if I had boarded a spaceship and landed on an entirely different planet. The plants, the birds and animals, were of a different variety than any I had seen before. Whenever I ventured out, my senses were assaulted with new sights, sounds and smells.

One morning, a week after my arrival, I woke up early in

the mood for a walk in a nearby park. I grabbed my camera, hoping for an opportunity to begin documenting the things around me, leaving the men sleeping in the room.

I felt invigorated and excited as I entered the park. How green everything was! Ponds and tall trees dotted the landscape. I snapped a few pictures as I walked along.

I heard a noise above my head in the trees and spotted a large monkey with a baby. As I scanned the treetops I discovered many more monkeys swinging from the branches. I decided to move away, not knowing how they may react to this strange white woman invading their territory.

As I walked along, I saw a group of boys playing a game in an open field. It looked a lot like baseball, as they had a bat they were using to hit a small round ball. I had never seen cricket being played before, so I had no idea that was what they were playing. I decided to sit on the grass and watch.

Soon a few of the boys came over to me. I smiled at them, but they did not smile back. Then a few women joined them, and stood in front of me, staring. Within minutes I was surrounded by people of all ages. They just stood and stared. I was becoming quite uncomfortable as they began to talk amongst themselves and point and nod at me. 'English?' I asked, hoping someone could speak to me. No response. A crowd began to form and seemed to close in on me. What should I do?

Then an idea came to me. I took out my camera and began taking pictures. This aroused their curiosity. It was a digital camera, and when I showed them their pictures on the small screen, they began to smile! They began to crowd around me even more. Though I was relieved to get a response, I was also unnerved by so many people pressing around me.

Suddenly I heard a familiar voice calling my name. Peter

and Arun were pushing their way through the crowd. They did not look happy, but I was so relieved to see them! They took me by the arm and led me quickly away from the crowd. No words were spoken as they marched me back to the hotel room. Now I understood why I needed them as security guards and I felt like a disobedient child as Varun scolded me for leaving the hotel alone.

∼

Varun and I had very little time alone together, those first few weeks.

One day, I was taken to his parents' house and introduced to them and his uncles and aunts who lived nearby.

Varun's mother, Sabita, and sister were busy preparing food. I was looking forward to eating a meal with the family, wanting badly to be accepted by them. I was surprised and disappointed that I was served the food separately on a tray, in the bedroom. Why wasn't I allowed to eat with them? Was I being punished? As a child, when I was bad, I was sent to my room to eat alone. What had I done wrong?

I watched from the bed where I had been seated, as Varun's father was also served at the same time but in the living room. Why couldn't I sit next to him so we could eat and talk together? Why didn't they all eat together as a family? I was puzzled and disturbed by this turn of events, until Varun explained that it was an honor to serve the guest first, and since there was no 'dining room or table', it was common to serve food on the bed. Also, it was the custom for the women to serve the men first, before eating themselves. Over the years, I found this to be true, nearly everywhere we went.

A short while later, we moved into a first-floor flat owned

by a Christian family that Varun knew. It was a new flat, and completely bare of any furniture. That night Varun and his men showed up with a mattress and put it on the floor in the bedroom. This, evidently, was our new home.

In the next few days Varun had a stove, similar to an American camping stove, set up in the kitchen with a large gas cylinder beneath it. Varun had made arrangements for his mother to make my lunch which Peter would deliver daily. But I had a terrible time with the spices and chillies, and the food also had far more oil than I was used to eating. I ended up only eating the chapattis and drinking tea. I began losing weight rapidly, and Peter was worried because I wasn't eating. Finally I confessed to Varun that the rich oils and spices hurt my stomach and gave me diarrhea. His mother tried to make my meals as bland as possible after that. Our dinner usually came from a restaurant, or Peter would cook. Back home, I was used to cooking for myself, but I had yet to master the art of Indian cooking.

Varun also had a Western-style toilet installed for me in the bathroom. He even brought home a roll of toilet paper. Varun seemed to know my needs and constantly asked me what I wanted. Since I could not drink the local water, he would buy five or six bottles of mineral water every day, but as the temperatures rose, this increased to nearly ten a day. A water filter was purchased. I had never seen such a contraption—there were two stainless steel cylinders, placed one on top of the other, with candle-shaped stone filters inside. Water was first boiled, then poured into the top cylinder. Slowly, it filtered into the one below, and was ready to drink. The bottom cylinder had a small tap through which one could pour out the water.

Though the flat had a separate entrance, we soon

discovered that it also had a back entrance that led down into the owner's house. One day after returning from Varun's parents' house, I walked into our flat and found the owners and their children sitting on the floor of the bedroom. All my suitcases were open and some of the contents were strewn around the room. I was annoyed, but before I had a chance to explode, each one of them took a Q-tip, an earbud, out of the box, and stuck it into their ears, smiling as they turned it round and round. It truly was a funny sight to see and I couldn't help but laugh. I sat down with them and tried to communicate in sign language.

I knew that Varun's mother was diabetic so I had brought a glucose tester and meter, as well as a large supply of needles and test strips. I had also brought anti-fungal creams, bandages, Q-tips, triple antibiotic creams and analgesic medicines as well as a blood pressure cuff to give to Varun's parents. All of this was strewn over the room and they were full of curiosity, especially about the glucose meter. I showed them how it worked by testing it on myself. They understood immediately about 'blood sugar' and wanted to be tested too. I obliged the parents. They both had slightly high glucose levels, so I told them to eat less rice, potatoes and fruits for a while. I had no idea if they understood any of it as they only spoke a few words of English.

This incident started a rumor that I was 'Dr Janice' and our landlords soon began bringing their relatives to have their glucose tested as well as show me skin conditions. I kept telling them, 'I am not a doctor.' But they would just smile, nod and return again seeking some medical advice.

After that Sunday when I spoke in church, news spread about my arrival and about my healing. People lined up outside our door, wanting to see me. They came from churches and organizations wanting to use me for their own projects, be it an orphanage, school or whatever. Each one was ready to give me whatever I wanted, if they could but use my name and testimony to increase their profits or credibility. I was like a celebrity and they all wanted me to endorse their causes. Even the large churches sent their representatives to speak to me. But I had no idea who they were, or how genuine their causes were. I had to depend on Varun's knowledge to guide me in this. I decided to tell them all that I would pray about it and let them know if I could espouse their cause. I did pray, a lot. But not one of these people, or their causes, felt right. Something was wrong with all of this fuss over me and it made me feel very uncomfortable. God remained silent.

It didn't take long before I realized that I was, for all intents and purposes, under a sort of 'protective custody.' Only a select few people were allowed inside the house and I was not allowed outside without Varun's consent. Varun told me that there were some Hindu groups that might be hostile towards me, believing that I had come to convert their people to Christianity, and it would be dangerous for me to wander outside alone. He was very busy with his job as well as arranging for his sister's wedding, and did not have time to be with me.

Day after day I found myself alone. Though all my physical needs were taken care of, the empty hours and loneliness enveloped me. There was no TV or radio to fill the hours. I prayed and read scripture and wrote in my journal in the mornings. But the hours ticked by so slowly. I thought my patience was tried enough when I was in the wheelchair, but now that I had a purpose and a goal, it was pure torture to just sit and stare out the barred windows every day. After a few weeks I knew that I needed to begin doing something productive or I would go crazy.

I began writing scripture on sheets of paper and pasting them around the house. I also made small notes saying, 'It's okay to pray here,' and put them up them throughout the house, even in the bathroom. Of course I knew that no one could read English, except Varun, but I hoped that these signs would spark a curiosity in others and would be a reminder of God's presence.

Now I admit that I am a strong and willful woman. Add to this the constant reminder of God's command to 'go out and tell the world,' and my spirit was restless. I would tell Varun, 'God did not send me here to sit on my butt day after day. Please arrange for me to give my testimony to other churches so that I can spread the message.' His answer was always the same. 'Not now. Trust me. The time will come after my sister's wedding.'

But I was impatient. The hours alone were getting to me and watching the world go by through the windows was no longer enough. I decided it was time to venture out on my own. One morning, with great determination, I showered and dressed and proceeded out the door, down the stairs, and into the courtyard where the well was. As I approached the outer gate, the woman of the house ran outside, babbling to me. She grabbed my hand and pulled me back towards the flat. I was insistent that I was going to take a walk outside the house. She gestured to me to sit on the stairs and stay until she returned. Reluctantly I sat and waited.

In a matter of minutes Peter came rushing into the courtyard and the woman came out to meet him. They had a discussion, which was obviously about me. She was more upset than I thought was necessary over me wanting to take a simple walk.

Peter came across to me and took my hand. 'Come,' he said, and gently guided me back up the stairs and into the flat. Peter remained with me for the next few hours until I convinced him through signs that I would stay inside.

It was that incident that confirmed to me that I was, indeed, a prisoner. That night, when Varun came home, he asked me why I tried to go out and cause such a commotion. I lit into him with a fury and told him that I refused to remain in the house day after day. I was, after all, a human being and I needed fresh air and sunshine and to be with people. I refused to allow him to keep me a prisoner!

'I am doing this for your own good,' he said. 'You are not a prisoner. But you don't know this country like I do and I am only trying to protect you.'

'Then spend more time with me and stop leaving me alone!' I shouted in anger. 'At least let me go to the market and buy things I want and need. Is this too much to ask?' He thought for a minute. 'Okay, you make a list of what you want and I will make arrangements for you to go to the market tomorrow.'

The next morning I was up early, ready and waiting to venture outside. It would be the first time that I would see the town and the marketplace since we had arrived.

To my surprise, Peter, Arun and four other young men arrived at the flat. Varun gave them instructions. I was escorted out of the courtyard and onto the main road. There a cycle rickshaw was waiting for me. I climbed in awkwardly as Peter joined me. Two other rickshaws were waiting for the men, but Varun had his own motorbike. After a few minutes of conversation, he and Arun rode away and we were off in our rickshaws. I was outside! I was riding in a rickshaw for the first time in my life! All my senses were alert as we took the long ride to the market center.

When we arrived, I was helped down out of the rickshaw. Varun was barking orders to the men. Soon I found myself surrounded by them. One on each side of me, two in front and two behind. Varun walked ten paces ahead of them all, looking from side to side. I felt ridiculous and unnerved by it all. 'So much for blending in,' I said to myself. Everyone was staring and moving aside in the crowded market. I felt like a dignitary, or the Pope descending upon these people and disrupting their lives.

We came to a halt in an open space in the center of the market. 'Okay,' Varun said, 'Did you bring your list?' I rummaged through my purse and brought it out. He snatched it from me, read through it and began barking orders to the men and giving them each some money. They all disappeared in different directions, leaving Varun and I standing alone. 'What is going on?' I asked angrily. 'I want to go shopping myself. I want to see all that is here and find out where things are!'

'Not possible. Too dangerous,' was his terse reply, then he added more softly, 'I really hate shopping, honey. This way is faster.'

I looked around at the many shops and stalls. So much to explore and see! Fabrics of every color and texture waved in the breeze in the shopfronts, copper pots and brass bowls gleamed brightly in others. There were tailor shops with old-fashioned peddle sewing machines whirring busily away as customers were being measured on the footpath. My mind and eyes drank in all the sights excitedly. The narrow alleys were jammed with people, dogs, cows and rickshaws.

I found myself drifting towards a gift shop with a display of shiny trinkets and battery-operated toys. Varun pulled me back abruptly. 'Stay with me and hold on to your purse,' he said. 'The guys will be back soon with your things.' I felt like a child with a parent. I resented this whole affair and was getting angrier by the minute. But I was also afraid. There must be a good reason for Varun to be so protective, I told myself. So many eyes were watching me that I felt vulnerable and on display. I kept silent as I realized that I knew nothing about this country or what impact I had just being there. Maybe I really did need all this protection?

The men returned, arms laden with the items on my list. We then marched back to the rickshaws and climbed in. 'I'll meet you back at the house,' Varun said, and zipped off on his motorbike. The rest of us lumbered slowly back home as the poor rickshaw-pullers struggled with the weight of all of us in the heat of the late morning. I marveled at their strength in spite of the thinness of their bodies. There was not an ounce of fat on them. Pure muscle and bone pulled us along almost effortlessly.

When we arrived, I watched as the rickshaw-pullers were paid fifty rupees each—less than 10 cents, but it seemed to satisfy them. But I wasn't satisfied with my one day out into the world. This wasn't what I had envisioned at all. I wanted to go and explore the marketplace and this new world without protective custody.

What I didn't know then, but came to find out over the next few years, was that there was good reason for Varun to be protective of me. Purulia, and indeed, most of the state of West Bengal, was the hotbed of Maoist territory. Not only was I the only white person living in the area, but as an American, I could easily become the target of kidnapping or a hate crime. Luckily, God placed me in good hands...sort of.

What I also didn't realize was that Varun was 'presenting' me to the general public in this manner as a warning to all. That show of bodyguards was for this purpose. News quickly got around not to mess with me!

5. Discovering Varun

There were many things I learned about Varun that could never have been discovered online. I learned that he was only twenty-four when we had first 'met' in the chat room, not twenty-eight, as he had told me, a smoker like I was, and a man who was used to controlling others and getting his way. He was also the leader of a group of men. They waited on him and seemed to obey his every command as if he were God. They hung around together, mostly playing cards and drinking and—I was told—at times got into fights and harassed people (though I myself never witnessed this). They were well known in the area as characters one shouldn't mess with. I knew Varun had gotten into enough trouble before I met him, to make his parents worried, but I never asked for details. I thought that if I were to bring about a change in him—and his gang—it was better to leave the past behind.

I knew that his left arm had been damaged in an accident as a child. This arm was significantly thinner and weaker than the right one, but I didn't know how much others pampered him because of it, especially his family. Not only was he the cherished only son, but he was given 'allowances' for his behavior because of his disability. To Varun's credit, he did most things independently in spite of his disability and his right hand more than made up for the lack of strength in his left.

When we used to chat online, he never seemed to run out of things to say. In real life, he was a man of few words, embarrassed by his English and his accent. In truth, he had never been with a woman before, much less an American woman, and had no clue how to handle it. I guessed that this was why he always kept Peter and Arun and the rest of the guys around us.

We never went anywhere without the guys and they were often at our house. They would sit on the floor around our mattress and laugh and talk in Bengali. I was hungry to learn their language and to be a part of their conversations. But whenever I asked Varun what they were talking about, he would brush me off with an impatient, 'I'll tell you later.' He never did. I felt isolated and ignored.

At this point, nothing was the way I had envisioned it to be, and far worse than I had expected. Varun would often come home drunk and obnoxious. It was obvious that he intended to go on with his life as if he were single, all the while privately calling me Mrs Kashyap. It was also clear that he was not used to being held accountable for his actions. He manipulated people with lies and promises that he had no intentions of keeping. He was arrogant, boastful and selfish. And his faith in God was far less than he had led me to believe.

But what Varun didn't know was that my faith was stronger than anything he could throw at me. Nothing could shake my conviction that God had healed me and brought me here for His purpose. Nothing would deter me from following this calling. But to say that I never doubted, never faltered or became discouraged, would be a lie. Twice I packed my suitcases, ready to fly home and forget the whole thing. But something always made me change my mind.

I often thought about the healing. I relived it over and

over again. It was much like pinching oneself just to make sure you were awake. And while that healing was the most miraculous, extraordinary thing that had happened in my life, I knew it came with a heavy responsibility. 'To whom much is given, much is expected.'

Life-changing events like this didn't happen to everyone, and yet I knew that I was not the only one to whom it had happened...there were others. Bizarre as it sounded, I couldn't help wishing that there was some sort of self-help group out there for 'living with oneself after being healed by God.' It really would be good to get some feedback about my experience from others who had been through something similar. I often felt completely out of my element in this new world, this new condition, and most of all, this new position as a missionary. I felt like I needed some sort of 'missionary training classes' but had no idea how to go about it.

I tried to analyze it all in my mind. Who was I to deserve such a miracle?

I didn't want to sound ungrateful to God, but really, couldn't He have at least made me holy in the healing process? I didn't feel holy yet surely holiness should be the number one requirement, shouldn't it? I lit another cigarette as I mulled over it all.

Okay, so I wasn't perfect, nor was I qualified. I was flying by the seat of my pants and taking every day, and sometimes every moment, as it came, trusting that God knew what He was doing. My apologies to all those who studied for years and knew every book of the Bible by heart. My apologies also to those who dreamed of becoming missionaries in a foreign land. The truth was, I had never in my wildest dreams, imagined becoming a missionary, and if I had, it certainly wouldn't have been in any part of Asia, let alone India. It just happened—yet instinct told me that when it came to God, nothing just happens. There had to be a purpose behind it.

All I knew was that I was given this gift, this position and this place to show the love of Christ and to glorify God. And since there were no self-help groups or classes for me to attend, I relied on the Bible and prayer as my guide. In my eyes, there was no room for failure. Self-doubt may come, but I knew that I was not alone. By myself I was nothing. With God all things were possible.

There were wonderful times when the man I had come to know on the internet shone through. We had shared the deepest of feelings and knew everything about each other beneath the surface and the pulls of our world. Our souls were united in great intimacy that absolutely nothing or no one, including ourselves, could tear apart. We didn't need words to communicate with each other. The smallest of gestures or eye movement was all that was required for us, almost like a secret language we both knew. Others could not help but see this connection between us and a few commented that we were true 'soulmates.' Varun did not seem to see me as the short, fat old woman who was physically in front of him. He was genuine about his love for me, and because he saw beneath the physical part of me, I felt young and beautiful in his eyes. I also looked at him as much older than his years. I knew that this was because we were looking with our hearts. I kept my eyes and heart on the man I knew to be inside, not on the man physically in front of me. I was not blind to the realities that were there. I knew only that our love could take away that outward man and bring forth the inward man I had come to know. This was why my determination increased with each challenge that Varun threw at me.

∽

It was a year of record heat in Purulia with temperatures reaching 53 degrees Celsius and the humidity at nearly 98 per cent.

I had never experienced such heat in my life. Though there were ceiling fans in the flat, the electricity was unreliable and would go off for hours at a time. The sweat poured off my body. As an American, I felt that sweating was embarrassing and should be controlled somehow. It was a very unnatural occurrence to be sweating to such a degree! It felt like living in a sauna with no door to open to escape and get some relief. I assured myself often that sweating would not kill me, but oh how I hated it! I found some relief by pouring water over myself, clothes and all, and lying still on the cool floor.

One day, when I was alone, I became very ill with the heat. I began to hallucinate. The heat was so intense that the ceiling fans blew only hot air. My skin felt wind-burned. I also suffered bouts of diarrhea.

In my state, I thought I was lying in the middle of the desert with hot winds blowing around me and the sun beating down upon me. I crawled under the bed for relief from the sun and wind.

I don't know how long I lay under the bed in this condition before the owners of the flat came in to check on me. The woman found me burning with fever. She took me to the bathroom and made me sit on a stool as she poured cold water over me. She also brought me mineral water to drink. I remember feeling like a small child as they patiently took care of me.

They called Varun at the school and he rushed home. He brought me medicine for the diarrhea and moved me into a local hotel with air-conditioning. I lay there for three days and nights, recovering. The hotel staff treated me like a queen, even though a very sick one.

How I loved to have a menu to choose from and fresh water and drinks whenever I needed them! There was a TV I could watch to pass the time. The TV introduced me to a completely different India from the one in which I was living. Though everything was in Hindi, it was obvious that it represented a richer, more modern lifestyle of the big cities. I enjoyed watching it, but I also realized that where I was, represented the 'real' India. This was where God had placed me and where much work needed to be done. This was off the beaten path of any tourist map. Indeed, anyone who came here from the outside world had to have a purpose other than just seeing the sights!

I was reluctant to return to the flat and leave the comforts of the hotel but I couldn't afford to stay more than a few days. But I sent Varun out to purchase a CD player, so I could at least listen to the music and sermons I had brought with me. This purchase, plus a small icebox, was the best decision I had made. We also decided to ditch the water filter system and purchase bottled water by the case. We discovered that the flat owners were bringing me filtered water but didn't understand that the filters needed cleaning now and then. The water I was drinking was extremely contaminated. The bottled water eliminated any further attacks of dysentery, and I learned to never drink water offered to me at other homes, unless it came from a sealed bottle.

Sitting all alone in an unfamiliar house, in a country I knew nothing about, was a learning experience in itself. The construction of the homes in Purulia fascinated me, after my experience of working at Home Depot and learning so much about construction in the US. I found these homes to be constructed like American homes in the previous century. The houses were built of brick and concrete with plastered walls and flat roofs. The electricity was put in after the home was built, so electrical lines ran on the outside of the walls. There was usually one electrical outlet per room and it sat high upon the wall. The main lighting was a tubelight, what we would call 'shop lights' in the US, with one or two smaller light sockets in each room.

All of the homes' gray waste water went out into concrete ditches and flowed into open drains in the streets. These drains were a breeding ground for mosquitoes.

Each home had a well, where all the laundry and dishes were washed on the concrete slab beside the well. The bathrooms had no showers, instead, plastic buckets and mugs were used for bathing.

The windows had no screens or glass but were covered with iron grills in creative designs. Wooden shutters were attached to the windows on the outside, and one had to reach through the grills to pull the shutters closed. But because of the heat, the shutters remained open day and night.

Nature enjoyed free access to the house, and I was often visited by hornets, bees, the occasional dragonfly or butterfly. But the most entertaining creatures that resided with me day and night were the 'house lizards' or geckos. It seemed each room had one and Varun said that they brought good luck to a home. The lizards kept busy chasing the insects that came into the house. They were particular about which insects they ate and much to my disappointment, they didn't like the mosquitoes that populated the house. They also chatted with each other with little clucking noises. The Bengali name for the lizards was 'tick-ticky' after the sound they made. I actually named a few of them myself and watched as they bred and tiny babies suddenly emerged on the wall. Such was my daily life.

In the evening, different kinds of critters fluttered in and out. To my delight, there were fireflies that twinkled and fluttered like stars in the dark sky. I had never seen these before, other than the fake ones in the 'Pirates of the Caribbean' ride at Disneyland. I was disappointed to discover that the bugs themselves were not as pretty as I imagined them to be. Somehow I thought they would sparkle like fairies or be as colorful as butterflies, not the little plain beetles they were.

The most dreaded of the nighttime invaders, for me, were the giant flying cockroaches. I could deal with spiders and other flying creatures, but cockroaches scared me to death. Silly, I know, but I had had a traumatic experience with a room full of cockroaches in my early twenties that left a lasting impression that these creatures were more intelligent than any other on the planet. When I discovered that, in India, they actually flew, my blood curdled. This fear was a source of entertainment for Varun and the guys.

6. Dress Like An Indian

At the end of four months in India I had lost quite a lot of weight and all the clothes I had brought with me had grown loose. I spent the hours alone with needle and thread taking them in. It was time to have some new clothes made. Another exciting trip to the downtown market was arranged by a few women in our neighbourhood. They were friendly and eager to help but spoke almost no English so we had to manage as best as we could with sign language.

When we reached the market, I was guided into a shop in a narrow alley. The walls of the shop were lined with shelves of fabric in a rainbow of colors and designs. There was a dais in front of these shelves, where the shop owner and his assistants sat. Opposite the dais were benches for customers to sit on. Each bolt of cloth seemed to be paired and color coordinated with another bolt. I was shown a pattern book and told to order the type of kameez I wanted. The kameez, I had learned earlier, was like a long dress with slits halfway up the sides. Under this was worn a billowy pair of pants known as a salwar. Evidently coordinating the patterns and colors of the pants and dress was how a woman reflected her taste and style. Traditionally, single women wore the salwar kameez, while married women wore saris.

With the advice of the women and the help of the shopkeeper, I picked out the materials for two sets of salwar kameezes. One of the shop assistants took my measurements, and I was told to come back in a few days.

When the salwar kameezes were finished and delivered, I was amazed to see the huge size of the pants and the long string that was used to tighten them around the waist. One of the women, with little English and much sign language, explained that the salwar was thus designed so that women could sit comfortably on the floor without revealing any part of their legs. All I could think of was the sitcom, 'I Dream of Jeanie', and how she looked in similar pants. The reality was quite different and certainly not flattering to a woman of my size and build.

But I was determined to fit in and become a part of this new culture, so I excitedly showed the new clothes to the guys that evening. There was a long scarf that came with each salwar kameez—the women called it a dupatta. I had seen how they wore it, folded a certain way across their chests, but I had no clue how to do this. It was Varun and the men, after some debate about the right way, who showed me how to do it. Safety pins were brought for me to fasten the scarf at the shoulders, so that it wouldn't slip off.

Nevertheless I found the scarf constantly in my way and quite a nuisance while bending over or sitting down. The kameez came down to below my knees, the standard length. I felt quite comfortable wearing it. But as far as the salwar went, using the toilet was a totally frustrating experience. All that billowy material had to fall somewhere. How in the world did the women do this without getting their pants soaked on the wet floors, I wondered. But I had no women to ask. I was surrounded by men who knew nothing of the intricacies of women's clothing, nor the bathroom complications. This was a problem I had to figure out on my own.

Eventually, I opted to wear the kameezes over my Western-style pants instead of the salwars. I also shed the dupatta, after getting it caught on things or, if I forgot the safety pins, have it slip off my shoulders or blown away in the wind.

I admit to having been a tomboy all my life, preferring pants and loose shirts over a dress any day. All this fluff and fancy just didn't sit well with me. Comfort was my style. Though there were times when I enjoyed 'dressing up' in a beautiful dress and jewelry, this was only on special occasions. Besides, I realized that no matter how hard I tried to look like an Indian, or dress like one, I was still an outsider, a foreigner in this world.

Another problem I had was my hair. I had lost quite a bit of it with the fibromyalgia and it had become grayer. Even though I let it grow long, it was thin. The hair color I had used back in the US had by now grown out. I needed to find a shop that sold hair dye. After several attempts, I realized that the only colors available were dark brown, black and red. I chose the dark brown. Little did I know that the hair color I had chosen contained henna. Not only did my hair turn almost black, but so did my hands, and anything else the dye touched. I looked a fright! I went out and bought a cap and a few scarves to hide my mistake. I also quickly learned that it was useless to wear any makeup, for the heat and humidity caused it all to melt off my face. It seemed that God was showing me how to accept and appreciate my own 'natural beauty' such as it was. Luckily Varun preferred me this way.

It took me months to convince Varun that I was perfectly fine with just the rickshaw puller, minus bodyguards. He assigned me one, but not without giving him detailed instructions on how to take care of me. So Abhoy became my own personal rickshaw puller. He was paid well, but earned every rupee that first year!

One day I needed toilet paper. Varun had always bought this for me, but he was busy and I was completely out of stock. I climbed in the rickshaw and told Abhoy that I needed toilet paper. He gave me a puzzled look and drove to the market. His first stop was at a stationery store. 'Paper' was what he understood. I smiled and said, 'No, toilet paper.' Again he gave me a puzzled look, but hopped back on the rickshaw.

Two hours later, Abhoy, with great determination, had taken me to every shop in the market that he thought had paper—wrapping paper at the gift shop, newspaper at the bookshop, etc. With each stop I would try with my hands to show him what toilet paper looked like, what it was used for, but to no avail. None of the shopkeepers seemed to know what toilet paper was either. We both returned home empty-handed and frustrated.

When Varun came home, I told him the sad story. He laughed out loud. 'Okay, I will go get you the toilet paper now. Tomorrow I will show you where to buy it. There is only one shop in town that keeps it for the foreigners that come to the Leprosy Mission hospital.'

True to his word, the next day he showed me the shop. I went in and asked for another roll. The owner called his employee, who brought out a tall stool. He climbed up and opened a panel in the ceiling and, reaching far inside, produced a dusty bag. Inside were a few rolls of thin, pink toilet paper. 'Old paper,' the owner said, matter-of-factly. 'New order coming.'

For the next few years, each time I returned to Purulia, that shop owner always had toilet paper available, and each time the same helper would get the tall stool and slide open the ceiling panel. He found better quality paper and even ordered some peanut butter for me, which was a rare find.

(Note: I tried to use the Indian method of washing oneself with water after using the toilet. Indeed, there were many times, while traveling, when I was forced to try. But with each attempt I ended up drenched and frustrated. I learned to carry toilet paper with me at all times.)

∼

The first time I went to take a shower, I noticed a plastic bucket under the water tap, with a mug hanging on the side. I wondered why they were there, when there was a shower head on the wall. I ignored the bucket and turned on the shower. Not a trickle of water emerged. I looked at the bucket, turned on the tap and started filling it up. The first thing I noticed was that the water was speckled with floating green debris. The second thing was a slight odor of something...

fish...yes, it had to be fish...like a fish tank that hadn't been cleaned for a while.

With great resolve and my American liquid soap, body scrubber and shampoo, I took my first bucket shower. I closed my mind to the green things in the water and to the fact that there was no hot water and began to lather up. Using the mug I poured the water over myself until the bucket was empty. I still had to condition my hair, so I filled it up again and saw that even more green things, like moss, were in the water. 'Just don't look at it,' I said to myself. 'It's wet and it's water.' With pictures in my mind of villagers bathing in murky ponds, I managed to convince myself of the blessing of having a private bathroom. I was proud that I had accomplished my ablutions with only two buckets of water.

Our landlords, though, were far from pleased. The landlady called me down to the well and signaled for me to look in. I gazed down into the dark hole, waiting for my eyes to adjust. There wasn't much water in the well, maybe four feet at most...but then something caught my eye. Something was moving inside the well...as a matter of fact several somethings were moving around. I couldn't believe my eyes. It was fish!

I pointed down and told the lady, 'Fish! Did you know that you have fish in your well?' She gave me an exasperated look and nodded, like, of course we have fish in our well, doesn't everybody? She called her son to come over and began talking to him. He knew a little English from school, so he became our translator. 'Mama says no more showers, water low. No more flushing American toilet too.'

'Umm, okay, but then how do I clean the toilet?' I asked.

'You only use one bucket for toilet and one for shower,' he said grinning up at me. I stared back down into the well.

'How did you get fish in your well?' I asked. He shrugged his shoulders, 'Don't know. Maybe fall from sky,' he said with a cheeky grin. I was trying to picture fish falling from the sky when his mother asked, 'Cloth? Washing cloth? I wash.' She was crouched down on her haunches and scrubbing clothes with a bar of soap, then rinsing them in a bucket from the well. 'No,' I said. 'Don't you have a washing machine?'

'Yes,' she said, tapping her chest, 'I washing machine!' Then she laughed and shook her head. I smiled and said, 'Yes and very good washing machine!' Her son said, 'Bhalo.' I looked at him blankly. 'Bhalo means good,' he said, giving me the look of a seasoned teacher. 'Oh! Then bhalo washing machine?' I asked.

He nodded. I had learned my first Bengali word!

---

7. A Big, Fat Indian Wedding

The time for Varun's sister's wedding was fast approaching. I received a formal invitation. Except for one brief visit to their house, I had not met them since the day I had had a meal with them. At first, I found it strange that they never came over to visit us, or invited me for another meal, but grew to accept it as another thing that was very different from my own culture. It was not until later that I learned that Varun had told them that I had come out to India as a foreign missionary and he was working for me voluntarily, so they believed that our relationship was a professional one.

I was told that I was also to attend a special ceremony the day before, for the bride and her family. My Western mind envisioned a bridal shower of sorts. I was given an already purchased and wrapped gift to take with me. To my surprise, Varun's father had arranged for a car to pick me up. When we pulled up in front of their home, I didn't recognize the house. It was completely covered by brightly colored tents. What used to be their front yard, was now a room covered by a cloth roof, a shamiana as I later learned it was called, filled with chairs and tables. The chairs encircled another small half-tent. Inside, sitting on the floor, was Juhi, Varun's sister. She was dressed in a bright red and yellow sari, looking so sad, I was sure she was about to cry. Another young girl sat with her, which I assumed was our equivalent of the maid of honor. I watched in fascination and wonder as a priest prayed over her and gave her communion. Then one by one, family members knelt down, dipped their fingers in a yellow powder and smeared it on Juhi's face. Then they would take a piece of cake, break it off and feed it to her.

~

I never learned the true significance of this ceremony, except that it was known as the mehndi, and the turmeric powder was smeared for good luck and the cake was given for good health. I also learned that Juhi was supposed to show great sadness at leaving her family. This ceremony was a chance for family members to say goodbye and bless her on her marital journey. What puzzled me was, this was a Christian family, yet the ceremony was a Hindu custom. It took me a few years to realize that Indian culture was intertwined with so many religions that the ceremonies endured inspite of the change of faith.

The following morning the wedding was held in the church in Bhat Bandh. The groom was an orphan who had been raised by nuns in the hostel in the church grounds.

(I learned that the word 'orphanage' was not used because many children had families, but were given to the hostel for a better life, due to the extreme poverty of the parents. This was a much better option to selling the children for slave labor.)

A British couple had befriended the groom and supported him through his childhood. They were invited to attend the ceremony. They were the first white people I had seen since my arrival.

The ceremony was beautiful and almost typical of a Catholic wedding in the US. A three-day celebration followed. The bride and groom seemed to be occupied day and night with visitors. On the second night we were invited to attend a party which, traditionally, would be held by the groom's family. In this case it was the groom's friends.

Varun's sister was a vision in a sari that was magnificent in both color and design. She was wearing large gold earrings and a matching necklace with a headpiece like a tiara that dangled down upon her forehead. Her hands were painted in an intricate design on both the front and back. This was set off by many gold bracelets on each hand. She was beautiful as she sat there with her husband, who was dressed in a fine silk kurta and pajama.

After meeting them, we sat down and watched as they greeted each guest graciously. But as I watched, I could see a fear in her eyes, a deep sadness that was not there before. I wondered to myself, did he hurt her? Was their wedding night a frightful experience for her? For a brief moment I wanted to grab her and take her away to protect her from whatever it was that caused her so much pain and sorrow. But when I mentioned this to Varun, in a whisper, he dismissed it. 'She is just overwhelmed. It is natural for a woman to be this way,' he said. 'But I will talk to her later.' The next day he told me that she was just scared and everything was fine.

∼

One month after my divorce was final in the US, Varun and I got married, on 8 September 2005. We knew that this was the right thing to do; in our hearts we were already married. We were Mr and Mrs Kashyap for several years now.

How could we put into words such a love that knew no earthly boundaries, such as our age difference, skin color or culture? We were connected in spirit, by God. It was time to perform the earthly ceremony. This was not an easy task in this culture where 'love marriages' were looked upon with shock and disdain. As usual, Varun took care of all the details and simply told me when it would take place. The ceremony had to be held in secrecy, in our flat. It was late at night; the shutters were drawn and the room was lit only by candles. The minister showed up and was obviously anxious. It seemed everyone was anxious. Whispered conversations in the corner of the room between the pastor, Varun and three of the guys went on for several minutes. Some agreement had been reached and money exchanged. Varun told me that it was time to do the ceremony.

My heart fluttered for a minute. I hesitated and told Varun to give me a moment to pray first. He smiled and said, 'Go ahead, but hurry.' I went into the bedroom and knelt down. 'Lord, I know you brought us together for a purpose. Our love for each other is strong because of you. I ask that you bless this wedding tonight and always. Keep our love strong and use us together for your will. Amen.'

Everyone was waiting for me as I came out of the bedroom. We all gathered together. Varun and I stood facing each other.

The nervous pastor didn't know English, and no one knew the American wedding customs, so I had written down what I could remember of the words in a normal marriage ceremony. We had no rings, so we exchanged garlands of flowers as was the tradition in Indian marriages. We recited our vows as we placed the garlands on each other's necks. The preacher said something quickly in Bengali adding a brief prayer. A friend took a few pictures with his cellphone. There was no marriage certificate so we wrote it down on a piece of paper and had our witnesses sign it. The preacher quickly disappeared into the night. That was it. A piece of paper and a few cellphone pictures. Our friend promised to have the pictures developed and the paper was hidden away. All were sworn to secrecy and then left us alone to celebrate together.

We spent the evening in a romantic glow wrapped in each other's arms. 'Hello, Mrs Kashyap,' Varun whispered to me with a smile on his face, gently stroking my hair. 'I will love you and protect you forever.'

I felt young and beautiful and just as I had always dreamed when we shared our lives on the internet. Our storybook love had become a reality. A magical and wonderful story that I knew was just the beginning. We had so many beautiful adventures to look forward to, so much to discover and learn. Life was beautiful.

In my heart of hearts, I did not want this secrecy. Varun reassured me that it was only temporary, that it was for my safety and to keep his parents' honor. He told me that I must be patient and that he would slowly introduce the idea of our marriage to his parents. 'This is India, not America,' he said. 'We do things differently here. In the meantime, we will continue to do God's work and show them that we are together.'

Little did I know how much this would impact our lives. My Western mind and my faith believed that one day I would be a part of their lives and that they would accept our marriage. I had no idea just how much we would have to suffer to remain married.

Quite contrary to the secrecy surrounding our marriage, no one had ever questioned our living together. When I asked Varun why, he told me that it was a custom in the country that no older woman should be left to live alone, and it was quite normal for a younger male relative—or in our case, a 'friend'—to live with her as her protector. Indeed, when the relative of one of the men in our group died and left a woman widowed, he was chosen to move in with her. I thought it was a wonderful custom that worked well in our situation—for once, the difference in our ages worked in our favor. But because of this, we were not allowed to be seen together outside the home unescorted, thus the constant companionship of the other men.

Outside, Varun behaved as my guardian, nothing more. Our home was the only place where we could relax and be like husband and wife, but even there we had to close the windows for a simple hug and kiss. Only our closest companions knew of our true relationship.

On a few rare occasions, Varun would take me to his parents' house. They treated me with the utmost respect. Varun's father was a thin, stern man. But because he worked at the Leprosy Mission hospital, he was familiar with foreigners and did speak a little English. Varun's mother, Sabita, knew almost no English, but she was a kind woman with a twinkle in her eyes as she studied me with curiosity. I liked her very much.

One day, as I was sipping tea at their house, Varun's father asked me why I was in India. They knew how God had healed me. My wheelchair sat in the front bedroom of their house, waiting to be given to the right person at the hospital. 'I am here because God sent me here,' I said matter-of-factly. 'The problem is, I don't know yet, what God wants me to do. There have been many churches and organizations wanting me to do something for them,' I added, 'but I don't think God wants me to do these things. It must be something else.'

He paced in front of me, then his eyes lit up. 'There is an abandoned hospital. It was closed a few years back,' he said. 'It could be a school or orphanage or anything. Perhaps you could use it.' I was thrilled at the idea. 'Yes!' I said excitedly. 'Can we go take a look at it?'

He sat down, silent for a moment. 'I can arrange a driver and get the keys,' he finally said. 'I will tell Varun to prepare the trip for this Sunday.' Outwardly, I sipped my tea silently. But inside I was praising God. Could this be the thing that God wanted us to do here? Was God using Varun's father to show us the way? But also, the excitement building up inside me was because this trip would be my first opportunity to see more of India, to expand my tiny world, to escape from the monotony my life had become.

8. Lessons in Leprosy

On Sunday, all of whom I now called Varun's men, showed up at our flat. I was escorted into a waiting car and we all piled in. As we reached the outskirts of Purulia, I felt as if a veil was lifted from my life. The sights were things I had only seen in a National Geographic magazine.

Huge black water buffalo pulling wooden carts, buses and jeeps tilting and swaying, loaded with people hanging on the sides and sitting on the roofs. Brightly colored saris flowing as the women walked along the roads carrying huge copper water jugs on their heads and hips. Women and children were bathing in murky ponds, shared by water buffalos, their heads floating above the water.

On either side of the rocky highway were miles and miles of paddy fields in different hues of green, divided in squares like a patchwork quilt. Palm trees and banana trees dotted the landscape...and the banyan trees. How I loved these trees. Large and majestic with thick roots hanging down and twisting around their trunks, it seemed each of them reached out to humanity and gave energy to all who lingered beneath them.

As we passed through the villages, I tried to get a glimpse of the life of these people in their mud huts. Half-naked babies were sitting on their mothers' laps, nursing at their breasts, small children, some not more than six or seven years old, carried babies on their hips as they wandered about with their friends, playing and laughing. Old women sat around in courtyards, separating fresh vegetables, tossing the unwanted ones to the dogs, chickens and goats. I made a mental note of each scene, promising myself that one day I would walk through these villages, meeting the people and taking pictures.

The landscape changed as we approached the village of Jhalda. Volcanic hills jutted up along the horizon, surrounding the farmland. Our car inched its way through the bustling market center and turned left, bumping across a field, dodging shepherds and cattle. Another left turn and past a local school brought us in front of the old hospital grounds.

We all climbed out of the car and stood at the entrance

gate. The sign that once boldly announced the presence of the hospital was now faded, the letters barely legible. The buildings were covered in a black mildew that was common in this area, due to the high humidity. The once majestic garden was now covered in weeds and vines that crept up the trees and into the windows of the hospital. Iron doors and windows were rusted and broken. It seemed as if the hospital had been closed for ten years, instead of three or four.

But I could still see the beauty of it, of what it once was, of what it could be again. Dedicated doctors, nurses and missionaries had treated hundreds of patients a day in this building, in spite of the heat, humidity and constant battle with mosquitoes. They were legends in the community. But they had had to vacate the hospital so suddenly that, as I peered inside the windows, I saw lab equipment, medicines, surgical tools and leaflets scattered on the shelves and floor. Varun had told me that the government had decided to shut down the hospital. The World Health Organization (WHO) had announced that leprosy was no longer an issue. Donations to TLM dropped dramatically, and many hospitals were forced to close. The locals protested and held all the hospital staff captive on the grounds until the police moved in and dispersed them, using brute force. Varun's father was one of the hostages. Once the hospital was closed, the local community was without not only medical care, but also a place to worship. The missionaries had done their job creating a strong Christian community.

The caretaker of the hospital told us about the Christian families that were left behind. Their numbers were too small for any of the larger churches to send a permanent pastor, so they still held church services inside one small room that had once been the living quarters of one of the workers. They had saved up money and purchased a plot of land across from the hospital. We politely followed him as he showed us the land they had purchased, but our minds were focused on the hospital, excited about the possibilities, and what we could do with the space.

I asked for a moment alone inside the hospital grounds. I found a concrete gazebo to sit under and prayed. 'God, if this is what you want us to do, if this is the place you want us to be, open the paths wide so we may do your will. Show us clearly what you want us to do.'

We sat in silence on the trip back home. I gazed out the window, still absorbing the sights and wonders of this strange new world. I was filled with a peace that told me I was on the right path.

When we got home, we all sat on the mattress and talked of all the things we could do with the hospital. We knew it would take a lot of work to clean it up and make it habitable again, but there was an excitement in the air, a sense of something big happening in our lives. But that night God showed us a completely different plan.

∼

Varun and I woke up to find that we had both had the same dream. It was not of the hospital at all. We both dreamed of the church that the Christian families were praying for. We both saw the church complete, with bells ringing and families coming inside. We looked at each other in surprise. But there was no doubt that *this* was what God wanted us to do.

'We must go back,' I ordered. 'We must look at the land again. I need to go there and pray.' Varun was more practical. 'We need to find out if the land is truly owned by the people. We need to measure it and calculate what it will cost to build the church.' He wasted no time in arranging for a car again. All the men were called and in a few hours we were on our way.

The sky was dark and cloudy, threatening rain. This trip was completely different from the first one. Varun and the men talked amongst themselves in Bengali. I knew, from the tone, that they were making plans, with Varun giving directions as to what needed to be done when we arrived. I, on the other hand, was focused on prayer and praise. Again I was praying for direction, a clear sign that this was what God wanted us to do. Men can make plans, but without God, I knew it would be pointless.

When we arrived this time, we were not expected. But within half an hour the groundskeeper was summoned and a rapid conversation began. I already knew what I had to do. I told Varun that I wanted to pray, first in the hospital grounds, then on the land where the church was to be built. Peter was sent to guard me from a distance.

I found my way back to the gazebo. This time I knelt down and prayed the same prayer. 'God, show me, is this where you want us to be? My heart wants to do something with this hospital, but I need to know your will.' I sat there gazing at the overgrown garden, picturing it as it once was and seeking some sign, confirmation of some sort. I felt a little silly for it, but God never ceased to surprise me. No answer to my prayer was forthcoming.

As I walked back outside the compound, I shivered. A cold wind blew as the skies above darkened. Surely rain would come soon.

I found the men standing on the vacant land where the church was to be built. A small wall of brick, about two feet high, had been built long ago. A sense of hopelessness prevailed amongst the weeds. The groundskeeper explained that they had begun construction, but ran out of money to continue. Threats from the local Hindu factions also stopped their work. A sort of stage, or altar, had been built with mud, at what I assumed was the front of the church. I whispered to Varun that I wanted to be alone there to pray. He quietly moved everyone back up to the road. Once they were out of sight, I walked over to the altar, and knelt down. This time my prayer was more fervent. With my eyes closed, and my face lifted up, I prayed out loud. 'Lord, you have brought me here to this strange land to do your work. I am willing, Lord! But I need to know if this is what you want. Do you want me to build this church? If so, I need you to show me, in some way, that this is your will and not mine.' I prayed and praised God until tears filled my eyes and coursed down my cheeks. Suddenly warmth enveloped me. Light penetrated through my lids. I opened my eyes to see a tiny opening in an otherwise dark sky and one bright beam of sunlight shone down upon me. I felt His presence within me. 'Thank you, Lord,' I whispered. 'Thank you for showing me, using me, loving me. I will build this church for you.' I was filled with peace as I wiped the tears from my face and rose to my feet. I walked up to the road with a new conviction and the knowledge that this was my purpose.

We began building the church. When I had arrived in India, I had nine hundred dollars in my savings, which I had earmarked as 'God's money.' It was a healthy start for the church.

---

9. The First Bible Study

Deep within me there was a sense of urgency, of time running out. I knew there was so much to be done. There was so much need everywhere I looked, but where to begin? Building the church was fine, but what about building souls? I hungered to begin reaching out somehow, but my world was confined to the house and the men.

I knelt down and went into a deep prayer. This is the kind of prayer that shuts out all the noises of your mind and the world and you dwell in a peaceful, spiritual place. I asked God to show me what to do, to send me the people whom I could help.

When I finished praying and was coming out of the trance of the prayer, I saw Varun and the men standing there. They had been quietly watching me. I didn't realize that there were tears in my eyes. I wiped the tears and stood up. 'I was praying,' I smiled.

'What did God tell you?' Varun asked with a grin.

Oddly enough, just as he asked that question, I knew the answer. 'He told me that we need to get into the Word together, all of us. We need to start a Bible study!' They all looked at each other with eyebrows raised. 'Us?' Peter asked incredulously. 'Absolutely,' I said. 'If we are going to do God's work we need to know what God says—and the way to that is Bible study.'

This was a Christian village and these men were born into Christian families, but they were without purpose, spending most of their time on the streets, playing cards and drinking. I was determined to not only have the Bible study, but to make it into a time of praise and worship. For this we needed music.

I was delighted to discover that one of the men was a musician and played the guitar. He was a Hindu, but assured me that he knew some Christian songs. Varun's mother provided songbooks and a few Bengali Bibles. I improvised a rattle to beat out a rhythm with an empty plastic water bottle in which I filled sand and stones.

I prayed all week and decided to use John 3:16 as the first lesson. On Friday night Varun went out to remind everyone of the Bible study. He returned with only Peter and Arun. 'Sorry, honey,' he said. 'They were the only men I could find.' I hid my disappointment with a smile. 'That's okay,' I said. 'We have to start somewhere.' I looked sternly at the two men. 'Where are your Bibles?' I asked. 'Next time, bring them.'

It was an awkward Bible study. Varun had to translate my every word. But Peter and Arun listened intently and participated in reading scripture. I would first read from my Bible in English, then Varun would translate it haltingly into Bengali. There was some lively discussion after each reading. I was encouraged by this, even though I didn't understand most of what was said—I knew I was getting through to them.

The following week two more men came, as well as our Hindu guitarist. I sat on the floor watching them all singing, while I beat out the rhythm with my plastic bottle. It was a wonderful sight and I thanked God for bringing them all to me. Six souls, including Varun was a good beginning.

Over the months I came to know each of these young men well, and they became like sons to me. I made it a point to visit each of their homes and meet their families. I prayed for them daily.

I began trying to teach them English as I struggled to learn Bengali. It soon became clear that learning another language was not one of my gifts. The men soon learned some English words and I began to realize from their mimicking that I repeated a lot of phrases, like 'Hello, how are you?' I said this so often that the men began walking into the room saying 'fine' before I could ask.

The one word that I said often as the men brought me things I needed was a polite 'thank you.' I had learned the Bengali word for this was 'dhanyabad.' But every time I used this word I got a surprised reaction. Perhaps I was saying it wrong? When I asked Varun about this, he told me that the men didn't expect it of me. 'It shows a weakness in you,' was his explanation. I puzzled over this but decided to continue doing what I thought was right. It was only after I had spent more time in India that I realized that Varun hadn't put it rightly, or perhaps he didn't want to hurt me by bringing up my age. It was part of the culture here to serve one's elders, and the men felt embarrassed to be constantly thanked for doing what they simply saw as their duty. Coming from America, where there is little honor or respect paid to the elderly, even one's own parents, it took me a while to understand this.

Peter was the one who spent the most time with me, bringing me the daily items I needed. One day he brought me my lunch as usual and I thanked him. To my surprise he scowled at me and shouted, 'No more thank yous!' I had never seen such anger in his face.

'I-I am sorry,' I said. Peter's face softened, 'I sorry,' he sighed, sitting down on the mattress with me, 'I friend, no thank you to friend.' I nodded, 'Okay, I will try.' And though it felt awkward and unnatural not saying it, I did try and reduce the number of times I used the word, especially around Peter.

The next lesson I learned was about smiling and laughing. By nature, I am a friendly person and smiling comes easily to me. Back home, I always smiled at strangers passing by, with a quick nod of my head. Here, I was especially full of the joy of the spirit and of the new life I was living in India and felt like smiling at everyone I met. It was Arun who said to me, with a frown, 'No smiling. Too much smiles.' I thought he was joking with me and laughed. 'No laugh too,' he said, still frowning. 'Why?' I asked, trying not to smile. 'Not good,' was his reply as he left the room.

I knew that Arun was the serious type and looked the part of my bodyguard with his dark skin and rippling muscles. He worked out at the gym and kept himself in shape. He showed glimpses of occasional humor when we were all gathered together, but mostly, he was a more negative thinker. Varun always asked him for advice because he could be counted on to think of all the angles. Still, I couldn't fathom his reaction to my smiling.

That evening I mentioned this to Varun and asked him why Arun would say such a thing. 'Smiling makes you look like a fool,' he said frankly. 'Only children and fools smile so much.' Then he told me a story of when he was a little boy. 'I was laughing and giggling with my friends at my house,' he recalled. 'My mother came out and slapped me. She told me that I was too old to be giggling like a schoolgirl. She said not to shame the family anymore and act like a man.' He looked at me. 'Our culture sees it as a weakness, honey. But I like your smile. You are a foreigner, so people don't expect you to behave like us.'

So I now lived in a land of no thank yous and no smiling. My Christian upbringing had taught me to 'Love your neighbor as yourself' and 'treat others as you wish to be treated.' Didn't this include saying thank you and smiling? I decided that this was one adaptation I would not make.

~

We made several trips to Jhalda to begin the building of the church. Before long we had a contractor and workers. Supplies were ordered and the construction began. Varun and the men handled all the details, but when money was needed, I insisted on being a part of it, of seeing the progress and meeting the people doing the work. We attended their Sunday services inside that small room at the hospital. I spoke and prayed at the service.

We learned that for nearly fifteen years the people had appealed to their church to help them build a place to worship, to have a pastor to marry them, bless the babies and pray over the dead. A pastor was assigned, but only came when necessary to perform these services. They wanted desperately to have a pastor of their own. In spite of this, they remained loyal to their church, and were concerned that I would want to start a new denomination. I assured them that we were only putting up the building. Once it was finished, it was up to them to decide the name and the denomination. Perhaps once the building was complete, their church would send a permanent pastor to them.

A week after the construction of the church began, we were wakened from our afternoon nap with an urgent knock on the door. A friend came to warn us that we were getting visitors, representatives from the main office of the church. I thought that perhaps they were coming to thank us for building the church, for helping the Christians in Jhalda. But I wondered why they had chosen to come during the hottest time of the day and when everyone was sleeping. What could this mean?

While I was freshening up, Varun was on the phone calling the guys. They showed up rather quickly, dressed as if for church. Judging from all the nervous gestures and talking, I realized that my instincts were right. Why were these people coming to see me? I wondered.

When the two men arrived, it was obvious that they were not there to thank me. They were there to deliver a message from the Bishop of the church. It was a warning. Either I stop the construction of the church or they would make sure that I was deported, for proselytizing, my visa revoked and I would never be allowed in India again.

At first, I was taken aback—this was a reaction one could expect from a group of Hindu militants, not from the Bishop of a Christian church, who surely should be pleased that I was building a place of worship for his people. Then it began to dawn on me that the Bishop was probably afraid that I was trying to set up a rival church that would undermine his authority. 'There is obviously a misunderstanding,' I said, looking them directly in the eye. 'I am only building the church for these people, which I understand your church refused to do. I am not trying to start my own church. They need a place to worship and God told me to build it, that is it.' There was an awkward silence. The men stood up. 'We will deliver this message to the Bishop. Until then, all construction must be stopped.' They said their polite goodbyes and left.

We were all infuriated. 'How dare they!' I kept saying, as I paced the room. 'Who are they to tell us to stop construction? That land belongs to those people, not to the church!' I paced some more. 'You would think we were trying to steal their people from them, people they don't seem to care a bit about anyway. What kind of Christians are these?'

There was a heated discussion among the guys, as we all

sat on the mattress on the floor. We were all in agreement. We would not stop construction. 'God told us to build that church. I believe this with all my heart. So if God wants this church to be built, He will help us to build it, in spite of the Bishop! If they want to deport me, then let them!'

So the construction continued. For a while I waited for some sign from the church, or to be arrested, but nothing happened.

There was opposition from the Hindus in the area as well, who showed their unhappiness by trying to destroy what was built. On one trip we discovered that a few windows had been broken. The altar was strewn with empty liquor bottles, trash and evidence that sex had been performed. The mud altar had been hacked at, leaving a gaping hole. None of this deterred us. Instead it increased our determination to continue. A few guards were assigned to watch the construction site.

I jokingly called our group 'the God Squad' as we all were fighting for one purpose, our 'God job.' This, of course, brought us closer together. It also eventually became our official name.

∼

The newness of 'the American foreigner' eventually wore off as I went often to the market and had, with Varun, shared meals with the families of our men. I also attended a women's Bible study that Varun's mother held. But still, wherever I went, people would stare and point. The beggars saw me as an easy target and children's eyes would light up when they saw me. My rickshaw puller became protective of me and would shoo away the beggars and loiterers with harsh words.

On my route to the market, riding high on the rickshaw, I was able to observe the everyday life of a Bengali village.

It was full of sights, sounds and smells that assaulted my senses. Everything, from brightly colored clothing to fish and snails, was on sale in the market. Some sold their wares on carts, others sat on the ground displaying fresh vegetables that came from neighbouring villages. Everywhere there was dust flying as people plied their way through the maze, on foot, on bicycles, rickshaws and motorbikes. Buses shoved them all aside as they lumbered slowly down the road, their horns so loud that they pierced my ears.

There were a few beggars I watched on my route to the market. One was a man, possibly in his fifties. It was obvious to me that he was autistic. He bounced back and forth on his feet, as if running on the spot, repeating the same phrase over and over again. His feet were minus most of their toes, but seemed quite healed. This told me that he was once a victim of leprosy. He was also completely blind. When I first saw him, I wondered how he managed to get to that same spot every day. One morning, I watched as a tiny older woman guided him to it. It was his mother. She must have been in her eighties.

Sitting directly across from this autistic man, was a leper. His feet were wrapped in gauze in an attempt to cover his oozing sores. His hands had several fingers missing. Every day, as I passed, he smiled at me and placed his hands together, raising them high above his head in a respectful namaskar. I made it a habit to give some rupees to these two beggars whenever I passed them and soon, in a small way, we became a part of each other's daily lives.

More than the beggars, it was the street dogs that affected me most, the most pathetic-looking dogs I had ever seen, mostly hairless and almost always limping, skin sagging and oozing from the effects of mange or injuries. Having worked in veterinary clinics in the US and owned a pet grooming shop for several years, they broke my heart. I tried not to look at them.

The downtown marketplace was quite different. The shops here were mostly permanent structures. The roads were in better condition and wide enough for cars to drive through. On one corner, at an intersection, was a general grocery shop. I learned that this store had most of the products that I needed and the owner was a pleasant man who knew English and tried his best to get me whatever I wanted. If he didn't have it, he would send one of his boys out to find it for me. Often, I would use the time spent waiting for the item to arrive to buy a cold drink or ice cream for myself and Abhoy, much to his delight.

Across the street was a large temple. Most of the time people sat on the ground in front of the temple selling spices, flowers, fruits and vegetables. But if there was a special puja, people gathered in front of it as the priest rang bells and chanted. I also observed that many people would pause, face the temple and bow, others would make a motion with one hand, similar to the sign of the cross that Christians made, whenever they passed by the temple. They would first touch their foreheads, then their lips, chest and then the lips again. What I didn't understand was why people often did this when they saw me, or passed by me. What did this mean? Was it a bad thing, or good?

One day a woman walked up to me, cursed, made that sign and spat on the ground near my feet. It was quite shocking, but quickly answered my question. Evidently this white foreigner woman oddly clad in pants and kameez, induced some sort of fear in them, or worse, anger. I prayed that God would teach me how to show them my love.

10. Unexpected Danger

The year that I arrived, 2005, was election year in India. It was a battle between the Communists and the Congress in the state of West Bengal. I understood nothing of the politics and had no desire to do so. My job was souls, not politics.

One of our men, Rajat, though, was deeply involved in the elections. Often he would miss our Bible studies because of some meeting or protest. We would hear stories of riots between the parties and people being seriously injured or killed. Evidently politics was a very dangerous business in this part of the world. I prayed for Rajat's safety every night.

I saw signs posted throughout the marketplace promoting one political candidate or other. Red hammer and sickle signs also sprang up overnight, appearing on every blank wall or building. Varun warned me to be careful when I was outside and not to encourage strangers to come near me. He told me to keep a low profile and do my shopping quickly.

A few weeks passed and everything seemed to be normal in my daily routine. I was proud of myself that I was able to do many things alone now.

Without any help, except from Abhoy, I had learned to navigate the marketplace, make friends there and even bargain with the shopkeepers. I had even managed to learn a few more words of Bengali, especially the names of vegetables. Abhoy developed an instinct for what I needed and where I wanted to go. He still didn't know any English, and I knew very little Bengali, but we communicated fairly well.

I had found a tailor to help me take in some of my clothes that had become too big for me. He had a small shop hidden in one of the many narrow alleys in Purulia. One day, when I needed to go to the tailor, we took a back route to the marketplace. As I was giving him the clothes to be altered, we heard a loud chanting coming from the direction of the main road. Loudspeakers blaring were a common occurrence, and there were always marriage processions and celebrations of one kind or another taking place, so we didn't think anything of it.

I hopped back on the rickshaw and told Abhoy to take me to the main market area. But as we got out on the main road, we could see a long line of men marching towards us with sickles in their hands. They wore bands with the red hammer and sickle sign on their heads. The leaders of the group marched in front. Behind them were four young men carrying Communist flags. Behind the flags were hundreds of men. Policemen were posted around the perimeter, trying to stop the marchers from entering into the marketplace. We were stopped in the middle of the road by a policeman and ordered to turn back. The angry shouts of the marchers grew louder as they drew nearer.

I felt a cold chill down my spine and prayed for protection. With fear and confusion in his eyes, Abhoy kept looking at me and back at the policeman, at a loss about what to do. My own fear gave way to a strange calm and curiosity as I watched the crowd.

Two of the leaders gave me an angry stare as our eyes met. There was a gap of just thirty yards between us, and I thought it was because we were in their way. A line of policemen moved across the road, blocking the marchers.

Suddenly, shots rang out and I saw one marcher fall to the ground. Within seconds, the marchers became a mob, pushing and shoving. More shots were fired and the screams and shouts became deafening. Sickles began swinging and I watched in horror as a bloody battle began. People ran in all directions, trying to find cover, and shopkeepers hastened to down their shutters. I could see the fear in people's eyes as they rushed past us.

Without wasting a second, Abhoy pushed the rickshaw past the policemen and carried me away from the scene. I had never seen him pedal so fast! We whirled through the narrow alleyways with Abhoy shouting at people to get out of the way. He was constantly looking over his shoulder, as if someone was chasing us. I hung on for dear life as we hit potholes and bumps along the way. I had no idea where we were going, or even where we were. He had taken me into parts of the town I had never seen before. The reality of what had just happened had not fully registered in my mind, but the scenes were replaying over and over.

Before I realized it, we pulled up in front of the Akash hotel, where I often stopped for breakfast or tea. Abhoy, breathless and still in a panic, nearly yanked me off the rickshaw. I obediently followed him into the lobby and further into the restaurant. Abhoy was chattering to the hotel owner about what had happened. Within minutes, Varun came running into the restaurant, concern and fear in his eyes. 'Are you okay?' he asked. I laughed nervously. 'I may have a few bruises from that wild ride I just had, but other than that, I am fine.'

'Didn't I tell you to be careful?' he shouted angrily. 'You are like a glowing target out there!' I was shocked and angered at his tone. 'I didn't do anything but go shopping! It is not my fault that all this happened.'

'But you could have been killed,' he said a little more calmly. Then, with a sigh of relief, he added, 'Thank God you are okay.'

'Yes, we must thank God,' I said firmly. 'He is always protecting me.' Varun threw me an exasperated look.

We both sat down at a table and ordered cold drinks. In a short while, every single one of our 'God Squad' team came rushing in to see if I was all right. I smiled and told them how Abhoy was my hero, even though he almost lost me a few times on the road! I don't think Varun translated it to them correctly because none of them laughed. So much for lightning up the moment, I thought.

It wasn't until later that evening that Varun told me what had happened. 'Communists recruited Maoists to do the march,' he said. 'They both hate Americans. And there you were sitting on that rickshaw right in front of them! If it weren't for the distraction of the shooting, they could have come straight after you.'

My mind flashed back to the scene. Those two men, the leaders, were looking directly at me. Perhaps it was hatred I saw in their eyes. I dismissed it at the time, thinking that it was the moment, and not me, personally, that had brought forth their hatred. My mind could not grasp the concept of someone hating me just because I was an American. Surely this could not be. But the reality of what happened that day slowly slithered into my being and changed me. A small piece of my naivety, my innocence in this new world, disappeared and was replaced with a more mature caution.

But I was also fully aware that God had been there that day. I remembered praying for protection and trusting in Him. A shield of protection did indeed surround me. I had been a sitting duck in the middle of that road. Yet I felt calm and at peace through it all. The course of events had changed within seconds. If that first shot had not been fired by the policeman, would I still be alive? I didn't want to think of it. I praised God for His love and presence in my life. I also thanked God when the elections were over.

It was not long after that, when Varun had just gone out the door on his way to work, that I heard a commotion downstairs. He and the landlord's brother-in-law were talking rapidly, using many hand gestures. Varun took out his mobile and made a call, and soon Peter and Arun appeared. I quickly got dressed and went downstairs to see what was going on. When I appeared, they stopped talking and stared at me. 'What's happening?' I asked.

'I'll tell you later,' Varun said sternly. 'Go back upstairs!' I didn't like his tone of voice, nor did I like to be ordered, but somehow I instinctively knew that something was wrong. I went back up the stairs, but stood outside on the landing, watching. Varun looked up at me with concern in his eyes. 'I have to go to work,' he said, 'Peter and Arun will be staying with you and you cannot go to the market today. We will talk when I get back from the school.' I simply nodded, but I felt a tinge of fear run through me. This must be serious.

The day was long. I tried to find out what had happened, but neither Peter nor Arun knew much English. The three of us sat on the mattress staring at each other. Finally, I got out a deck of cards and, with some difficulty, taught them how to play American rummy. Throughout the day they took turns leaving and returning with thin mattresses and snacks. This raised my curiosity even more. Evidently they were planning on moving in with us.

That evening, when Varun came home, there was an animated conversation between the men. Two more guys showed up, Rajat and Nitesh. More conversation ensued. My attempts to understand what was going on were ignored until finally I got angry. I looked Varun in the eye. 'You need to tell me what is going on and why everyone is here. I have waited all day to find out. You promised that you would tell me tonight.'

'Okay,' Varun sighed, 'I just didn't want to worry you.'

'Worry me?' I asked incredulously. 'I am going out of my mind with worry from not knowing!' Finally he told me the story, as we all sat on the mattress.

According to the landlord's brother-in-law, the night before, he surprised an intruder trying to scale the wall and break into our flat. He insisted that it was a man from a strong anti-Christian Hindu group. He and the entire family were worried that they would attempt to break in again. 'But,' Varun said, 'This brother-in-law is the nervous type and I think he is exaggerating the situation. But for the next few days the guys will stay with us.'

'Well, that's a relief,' I joked. 'I thought it was something serious.'

I prayed quietly for protection, but in truth, I felt no fear, I was at peace.

That night the men took shifts in sleeping and guarding the house, as well as walking the grounds outside. After a few days, things settled down for us. There were no signs of further intrusions, but it was obvious that the owners of the house were nervous about me staying there. We had to find another place to live.

---

11. A Home of Our Own

One of Varun's colleagues offered us a house that was still under construction, but habitable. It was on the other side of town, near a large lake named Saibhon. To my disappointment, I was not included in the house hunt. We simply moved, bag and baggage, to the new place one rainy afternoon.

It had two bedrooms, with a small kitchen and a stairway leading up to the roof. As was typical, the windows had metal bars, no glass or screens, and wooden shutters that could only be closed by reaching through the bars. But, to my dismay, it had an Indian toilet.

In my efforts to come to India fully prepared for any eventuality, I had packed a 'camping toilet,' a folding metal contraption with a plastic toilet seat. It fascinated the guys and had, in the past, been the subject of a few conversations, followed by laughter, as they passed it around among themselves. But now I had to use it. Though my legs had been healed, and were getting used to sitting and rising from the floor, I was still unable to squat over the ceramic hole of an Indian toilet without falling on my butt. However, I soon learned that the camping toilet was not built for use by an adult, or at least not one with my weight. Each time I tried to use it, it would collapse, landing me on my butt anyway. This was an embarrassing, but serious dilemma.

A meeting was held. Once again the toilet was passed around and examined, but this time the men were quite serious, studying the design and trying to figure out a way to solve the problem. They came to some sort of consensus and I watched as thick twine was wrapped around the toilet seat and the legs. This prevented the seat from detaching from the legs, but the aluminum legs still protested against my weight by wobbling and splaying whenever I sat on the seat. I felt like I was going into a dangerous battleground each time I used the toilet! To make matters worse, there was nothing to grab onto in case of a total collapse. I decided it was much safer to figure out a way to use the floor model, which I eventually did.

Once again, I found myself alone much of the time. Varun would leave for work early in the morning and return home around six in the evening.

I spent my time trying to make our new house into a home. We chose the darker, cooler bedroom for our sleeping quarters. New sheets were purchased for the mattress on the floor. The second bedroom was quite hot and sunny. I bought a rope and strung it from one window bar to another, thus making a sort of closet to hang my clothes. I quickly learned that clothes hangers were almost as rare as toilet paper where we lived.

I then tackled the kitchen. I bought some more pots and pans and a few plates. Since the entire house was raw concrete, I bought some rugs to brighten up the rooms. A few plastic chairs and a table were also purchased for the living room. I had grown tired of sitting on the floor all the time. Eating and having tea on a real table, even if plastic, seemed like luxury!

All of this gave me more experience and knowledge of the marketplace. Abhoy and I had become fast friends as he imitated my English and tried to teach me a few new Bengali words as we wandered around each day.

One day, when we arrived home, I walked into the bedroom and saw a huge centipede crawling across our bed. Without thinking, I blurted, 'Oh my God!' Abhoy came rushing in and quickly threw it out the window. But from that day forward, Abhoy began using this expression every chance he got. At first, it was quite amusing, and the guys began calling him 'Oh my God,' but it started bothering me and I felt guilty for having taught him to use the Lord's name inappropriately. The next time he said it, I corrected him and said, '"Not, oh my God," Abhoy, it is "Oh my goodness."' I made sure that I also used this expression a lot too. 'Oh my goodness,' I would say, 'What a beautiful morning,' 'Oh my goodness, I love this ice cream,' and so on, until he got the message.

One very hot and humid day, I had all the windows and the front door open. I had already been to the market and had purchased some fruit and put it in a bowl in the kitchen. I decided to pass my time crocheting and got out my yarn and what was now a huge blanket I was working on, and put them in the living room. I went into the bathroom before settling down to the project. While in the bathroom I heard noises in the house. Thinking that one of the guys had come to visit, I hollered, 'Be right out,' but got no reply.

As I opened the bathroom door I came face to face with a large male monkey, about the size of a five-year-old child. He stood in the living room with a banana in one hand and an apple in the other. He took a big bite out of the apple, giving me a clear view of his fang-like teeth.

I had already been warned of how dangerous monkeys were, especially the males, so I stood frozen, watching. He bounced around and began approaching my yarn and blanket. He dropped the apple and picked up my ball of yarn, his dirty fingers wrapped around it. That was a liberty I could not tolerate. 'Put that down,' I said firmly. 'Go! Get out of here!' I waved my arms and stamped my foot. 'Shoo! Leave!' The monkey looked at me curiously, dropped the yarn, picked up the apple, and bounced out the front door. With a huge sigh of relief, I quickly ran and shut the front door behind him.

I then went into the kitchen to find the fruit still sitting neatly in the bowl, minus an apple and banana. But another monkey was holding on to the bars of the window from the outside and trying to reach for the fruit. I grabbed a banana and threw it out the window. Once the monkey chased after it, I quickly reached out and closed the shutters. But when I returned to the living room I discovered a baby monkey outside the window, shaking the bars and shrieking. I began to panic. The shrieking sounded like twenty monkeys. I was surrounded! I grabbed my cellphone and dialed Peter. 'Come quickly!' I said, 'Monkeys!'

'Close windows. I come now,' Peter said.

Close the windows? I thought, how can I close the windows with monkeys hanging on them? The baby monkey was baring his teeth and shaking the bars violently. I managed to close the windows in the two bedrooms, and then I remembered the door upstairs that led out to the roof. I ran up the stairs. The door was open. As I looked, I saw two monkeys on the neighboring roof. I slammed the door shut. When I came back to the living room, I breathed a sigh of relief. The wild baby monkey was gone. I slowly reached outside the bars to grab the handle of the shutters. At that moment, the baby monkey jumped up, bared his teeth, shrieked, and pinched my cheek so hard that tears came to my eyes. I screamed as loud as he shrieked. That startled the baby. He released his grip on my cheek and disappeared. I was able to keep my wits about me and closed the two windows before collapsing on the floor.

A few minutes later I heard voices shouting and a banging on the front door. Still shaking, I went to the door and opened it. Peter was standing outside. He took one look at my face and his eyes widened. Then Abhoy came rushing in. He saw my face and blurted, 'Oh my God!' So much for teaching him the right way, I thought, as I rubbed my cheek. 'It's nothing,' I said, glaring at Abhoy. 'Just a pinch. Baby monkey got me.' When I looked in the mirror I was surprised to find a large red welt on my left cheek. It remained there for a week, gradually turning into a purple bruise. But I thanked God that it was not a bite, as monkey bites could be quite serious. I had also learned a great deal of respect for wild monkeys. Thereafter, I did my best to avoid any further encounters with them.

∼

I was getting tired of eating the typical food in Purulia. I had always had a history of digestive disorders, from acid reflux to diverticulitis and ulcers. As a result, eating fresh vegetables and fruit always gave me terrible indigestion. But I was a new creature in a new country and I was determined to eat like the natives...for a few months. It seemed my digestive system didn't know I was a new creature and rebelled violently at my change in diet.

All of the food I had tasted thus far was boiled, fried and covered with spices and chilies, making it unrecognizable either by sight or by taste, and everything was yellow and sitting in pools of oil. In addition, the chicken was always chopped into small pieces, bones and all. Eating it was a real challenge for me, picking out the tiny slivers of bone. I was surprised to learn that the locals didn't bother. They chewed away at the bones, reducing them to pulp and spitting out the remains.

Purulia is famous for its fish head curry and its sweets. People actually traveled for miles to come and eat the fish head curry. I had two thoughts about this: one, I won't eat anything that is staring back at me, and two, I had seen the ponds where these fish lived. The ponds were used for washing clothes, bodies and water buffalo. I would not risk swimming in those ponds, let alone eating anything that came out of them! Varun thought I was being unreasonable, but I refused to budge from my convictions.

One day I decided that I would go on a search for food that I could eat and then I would surprise Varun with a home-cooked dinner, American-style. I chose a dish that was always received well at home—coconut fried chicken. I knew both the chicken and the coconut were readily available in the market. I only had to show the butcher how to cut the chicken the American way.

After a very long and frustrating day, I ended up with skinless chicken and powdered coconut. The dinner was a disaster. The kind of pans they used here were not conducive to making golden fried chicken. The coconut powder was old and had become bitter to taste. In addition, I had decided on corn on the cob for the vegetable...I didn't know that the corn was not sweet or soft after boiling. I also didn't know that Varun hated corn. (After tasting it, I could understand why.) After that one attempt, Varun decided that he would learn to cook. I was not allowed in the kitchen...which was fine with me!

12. Prayers and Battles

Prayer. A highly underrated activity, more like an afterthought for many. I know it was for me, for many years. I was born with an awareness of spiritual activity around me, but I never really understood it until I came closer to God.

One of the wonderful things that the Pentecostal experience taught me, was to 'pray into the spirit.' For many, this was a time for emotional outbursts. But for me it was an indwelling of peace and quiet, a sense of His presence within me. I learned that prayer was more than words spoken from my lips. It was a communion, like slipping into another dimension and waiting there for His presence before uttering a word. Then my heart prayed, sometimes louder than the words that followed. It was the most extraordinary life-giving, life-changing experience I had ever had, a deeply personal relationship between me and my Father. I in Him, and He in me. We were as one. I finally understood how important my prayer life truly was, not only for those for whom I prayed, but for me. I needed that connection, that communion with Christ in order to serve Him. My very survival depended on it.

It was then that I came to see it as a gift and understood the importance of prayer to battle against the trials and tribulations that permeated daily life in this part of India. I was also keenly aware that this entire area was pervaded by an underlying current of violence and, dare I say it, evil, encouraged by black magic and worshipping of the dark world. Was this why everyone lived so cautiously behind barred windows and high fences? Sometimes I wondered if this area was not the gateway to hell. At other times I was quite sure of it. How could such a beautiful place have such a dark spiritual presence?

There was another side to this, though. As the days and months went by, I had observed the worship and rituals of the Hindu community. It was hard to ignore, since we were surrounded by temples and our lives were interrupted by the many pujas that took place. Every morning, at sunrise, and all through the day till evening, I would hear the azaan, the Muslim call to prayer, echoing across the rooftops, its haunting melody calling out to Allah.

The temple bells would ring three times a day, calling people to prayer. At first, in a sort of religious snobbery, I was offended. 'Why do they have to pray to idols all the time,' I would say to myself, praying for God to give me the opportunity to show Him to these infidels.

But as time went by, I began to admire their dedication. If Christian people prayed like that, three times a day, what wonderful things could happen! In the Old Testament it was written that the Jewish people did this. His chosen people, following the laws of Moses, stopped everything they were doing and prayed. So why didn't we, modern-day Christians, do it? More importantly, why didn't I? Was this too much to ask, to spend ten minutes, three times a day, praying for others? I was already dedicating a half hour or more in prayer, in the mornings, but what would happen if I did this, pardon the pun, 'religiously' three times a day?

I set about the task of creating a prayer area where I could pray undisturbed. I drew a cross on a sheet of art paper and hung it on the wall in the corner of the room I used as my 'closet'. I got a stool and placed it under the cross. Though I was not Catholic, I had seen in movies how they lit a candle before praying. Not a bad idea, I thought. So I set a candle on the table, under the paper cross. I had decided that I must dedicate this time to praying for others, so I made a prayer list.

Every day, I waited for the temple bells to ring. When they did, I stopped whatever I was doing, took my list and knelt down before the cross. I lit the candle. After that, I began my list. My own family, Varun's family, the men in our Bible study, and finally I ended with the same prayer I had said while in the wheelchair. 'Use me, oh Lord, to glorify you.'

When I finished, I felt refreshed in the spirit and encouraged with my new commitment. As the days and weeks went by, I watched in unceasing amazement as answered prayers unfolded in our lives.

∼

Our little group became quite busy. Many trips were required to the village where the church was being built. Yet, I never stopped thinking about the old Leprosy Mission hospital that sat abandoned near the church site. I prayed about it constantly. What wonderful work we could do in that community if only we could acquire that land. We did everything we could, contacting the organization and the many people involved, but to no avail.

One man began coming to our house and joining in some of our Bible studies. His name was Sujan. There was something about him that disturbed me, though I couldn't figure out what. He was different. When he heard that we were building a church, he was excited and wanted to be a part of it. He told us that he had his own Bible studies at his house and invited us to come the following Sunday.

On the preceding Friday, he asked to speak with us in private. The room was cleared and we sat down on the plastic chairs to talk. He wanted money. He told us that he owned a few rickshaws, which were bringing money in to support his wife and child. But he needed to buy another rickshaw, a second-hand one that was quite cheap. Varun asked how much he needed. It was Rs 1,800. While this was not a large sum, every rupee that we had was being put into the building of the church and for our own expenses. We were on a tight budget. Varun and I went into the bedroom to discuss this.

I told him that I didn't feel good about this man. It was

against my better judgment to loan him the money. The proverb, 'Neither a borrower, nor a lender be' came to my mind. 'Instead of asking him to pay us back,' I said, 'Let's ask him to contribute to building the bell tower for the church. This is the last thing we will build so it will give him plenty of time to raise the money.'

'Good idea,' Varun agreed. So we made an agreement with Sujan. He enthusiastically agreed to our request. I told him that I wanted the bell tower to be high and lit up with lights. I took a paper and pencil and drew my vision of the bell tower and gave it to him. Varun gave him the money. He thanked us profusely and swore that he would pay us back by next year

That Sunday, we went to his house for the Bible study. Varun and I were given chairs to sit on, but as people arrived, they came and sat on the floor.

We were both surprised to discover that their worship was Pentecostal. Varun had never seen anything like this before, but of course, I was very familiar with this method of worshipping. However, when people began falling on the floor, speaking in tongues and twitching, I could see Varun staring in disbelief. Even for me this was a bit too much to witness. We left as soon as the service was over.

'What the hell was that?' Varun asked as we rode back on the rickshaw. I laughed. 'That, my dear, was Holy Spirit Pentecostal worshipping. That is what was done in the church where I was healed.'

'Well, while I am glad that you were healed, please promise me that you won't be doing things like that!' I smiled. 'So far the Lord hasn't caused me to do that sort of stuff, but I have spoken in tongues.'

Varun gave me a stern look. 'Do me a favor, please, and

don't do it when I am around. It would scare the hell out of me!'

'Can't promise,' I retorted, 'but I'm pretty sure that if it were to happen, God would have done it by now.'

Our own Bible studies continued. Our hymns and music were truly beautiful. How I loved it when all the men sang together, really getting into the music. We were becoming more like a family. Sometimes the guys would come just to share their troubles and ask advice. Varun was their leader, but now the two of us had become like second parents to them.

We began going on monthly fishing trips or picnics in the country. I loved this special time out by a lake or river. The men were very well organized, packing the pots, pans, firewood and food. Peter became our chef, but everyone chipped in to cut onions, peel garlic or watch the fire. I never had to do anything but enjoy the experience.

No matter where we went, it was inevitable that people would begin to gather and watch. They were simple country folk who had never seen a white person before. Most of them would watch from a distance, but there were others who would walk right up to where I was and stare at me unblinkingly in a manner that was quite unnerving. My American upbringing was unambiguous about staring. 'It is impolite to stare at people,' my mother used to say sternly. Initially, I felt offended. It took me a while to accept that it was just natural curiosity and a break in their humdrum lives. Even so, I never felt comfortable being the center of attraction. The men were very protective of me and would quickly send away anyone who came too close.

There was one incident though when the guys left me alone in the car and I found myself surrounded by the villagers. I was on the verge of panic because the windows were down to let in the breeze, and hands began reaching inside. I felt like an animal in a zoo. I breathed a huge sigh of relief when Varun and the others returned and shooed them away. After this, I learned to carry a large scarf with me to cover my head and face whenever we had to stop somewhere in the remote villages. If we stopped to eat at a roadside hotel, I always preferred to sit in a far corner or a back room to avoid the stares while I was eating.

I was braver, though, than the two German women who came to Purulia to learn about the local dance forms. They planned on staying for a month to make a documentary film on the subject. But after a week, one of them left abruptly. Her partner told me that it was the staring that she couldn't handle. It drove her crazy.

I was thankful that the local people in Purulia, especially at the marketplace, were used to seeing me. It was the one place where I could walk the streets and not be followed. I felt almost like a normal person there.

I began making morning trips to the Akash Hotel for breakfast. I had come to know the owners and the staff when I spent a few days there recovering from heat exhaustion. Most of them spoke English, so I didn't have to worry about having someone with me to translate. It was a nice quiet time for me, as I ate my breakfast and read the newspaper. Often I would spend this time reading the Bible and setting up my Bible studies. The staff made sure that I was not disturbed.

As I began reading the local English newspapers regularly, I was able to get a better, more rounded picture of India. It seemed that the big cities were more like my world in the US.

Men and women went to night clubs and danced and drank alcohol. Their style of dress was more modern with fewer restrictions. What a completely different world these cities were from the world of Purulia and the village life I knew. This world was, to use their own terms, more 'backward.' Sometimes being backward was a good thing, I believed. I would rather term it 'unaffected by modern culture.' For instance, I loved to watch the furniture makers. They used only hand tools, not electric ones. Wood was a precious commodity here, so they collected scrap wood and fashioned the most beautiful furniture I have seen out of it.

I often felt that I had traveled back in time as I wandered through the countryside, that I was seeing the way of life of my great-grandparents. The most amazing thing to me was there was no air traffic, no planes or helicopters buzzing around the skies. Oxen still ploughed the fields. No sign of modern tractors or motorized farming equipment. Cows were still milked with hands and a sturdy bucket. Readymade clothes had only recently become available in the area. Before that, everyone had to have their clothes stitched at the local tailoring shops, or travel to the big city to buy these new items. Yes, there were a lot of advantages to being backward...but I realized too, the many disadvantages.

People were dying of diseases here that could be easily cured or controlled by modern medicine. Limbs were amputated when they could have been saved. Fires engulfed entire villages because of the want of simple pumps and hoses to put the fire out. Bicycles could be made with lighter materials and equipped with gears, instead of the heavy cumbersome ones I saw around town. The use of insecticides, asbestos and leaded paint was prevalent. Evidently this world hadn't heard of the dangers of these things. As a consequence the ratio of deformities and deaths from exposure was greater.

But the most pernicious aspect of the backwardness was the old traditional ways of governance and meting out justice. I soon came to realize that each village, each district and state had its own ways of dealing with justice...or the lack of it. Misfits or rebels were dealt with quickly and without mercy.

As I read the papers, I began to notice a disturbing pattern throughout most of India—one terrible incident after another labeled 'honor killings.' One young couple in Uttar Pradesh fell in love. They were from different castes—and intercaste marriage was forbidden in their community, something that brought dishonor to the entire family. So the boy's family slit his throat. The girl's family threw kerosene on her and set her on fire. Honor was restored to both families. No one was arrested.

Another young couple from different castes got married without their families' approval. They moved to a faraway village unhindered by their families for two years. They had a baby and were expecting a second child. One night the two families appeared at their house, murdered their own children and grandchild and set the house on fire.

I was shocked at these reports, one after another, with no arrests being made in each instance. For a young girl to become pregnant out of marriage was a death sentence.

Another frequent occurrence I learned about from the newspapers, and from listening to our group talking, was what happened after an accident. This was so incomprehensible to me that, at first, I thought it must be a joke, but it obviously wasn't. Whenever an auto accident happened, and especially if someone was injured or killed, people pounced upon the driver, beat him severely and often killed him. Often, the injured would lie bleeding and dying, ignored, while the mob beat up the person believed responsible. As a result of this, any driver involved in an accident would quickly disappear from the scene to save his own life.

My mind could not grasp the rationale behind the senseless violence, especially against one's own family. When I asked Varun why, he simply said 'Just like that,' which was his standard reply when he had no answer.

Then I asked him a pointed question. 'What would have happened in your family if one of your sisters had become pregnant before marriage?' He looked down at the floor for a minute, and then said, 'As her brother, it would be up to me to kill her in order to restore the family honor.'

'You would kill your own sister?' I asked in astonishment.

'Yes I would, because if I didn't, my father or my uncles would. For me not to do it, would add further shame to my family. As the only son, it is my duty.' I looked at my husband, trying to imagine him doing such a thing. I shuddered at the thought. 'Well praise God that didn't happen!' I said, attempting to lighten the conversation.

'Well, this is India,' he said. 'You can't survive here unless you are willing to defend yourself, your honor and your family.'

～

There were other social mores I had to absorb in order to survive in my new country. Abhoy, as my rickshaw puller, always sat on the floor in the corner of the room, no matter how often I would invite him to sit with me to have tea. This bothered me. I was determined to treat everyone as equal. Abhoy saw himself as my servant.

Varun warned me not to encourage him to sit with me, because then he would treat me with disrespect. How could this be? Surely he would appreciate this and become my friend. It wasn't until a year later that I discovered Varun was right and that there were some cultural things I needed to accept, no matter how much I disagreed with them. Part of this was understanding the 'caste' system and how it worked within the society. Even after several years, this was a difficult thing for me to understand.

I also had to get used to being called 'Madam' by everyone. Even Varun referred to me as madam when discussing things that I needed. 'Madam needs to have water bottles delivered by ten this morning,' 'Make sure that madam is home before dark, ' and so on. I was introduced by adults to children as 'Aunty.' I rather liked the idea of being an instant family member!

There was another occurrence that I had to get used to, which always made me feel ill at ease. As the story of my healing spread from village to village, people came into town asking my whereabouts. They wanted to see this woman that God had healed. Sometimes, while riding in the rickshaw, a man or woman would rush up to me, speaking in Bengali. Desperation in their eyes, they would want me to lay my hands on them and pray for them. Of course, I was willing to pray for them, but though I did as they asked and laid my hands on them, I always felt a sense of unease that I wasn't qualified to 'bless' them. Afterwards, they would kiss their fingers and touch my feet, which was a sign of great respect. People would stop and watch and begin to point. Not wanting to be a spectacle, I always left as quickly as I could.

One day, when I was meeting a couple of pastors from a church in Delhi at the Akash Hotel restaurant, a shabbily dressed man came hesitantly up to our table. The hotel staff came chasing after him, trying to get him to leave. I saw the look in his eyes, one of desperation, and beckoned to him to come forward. 'What does this man want?' I asked the pastors. 'Please ask him for me.'

After a short conversation with him, they said, 'He has come from a distant village to see you. He has heard of your great healing and wanted to see you with his own eyes. He asks only if you will lay your hands on him and bless him.' I looked up and studied the man in front of me. He was weather-beaten and had the look of a poor villager. But his eyes shone with hope as he smiled at me. He suddenly knelt down and kissed his hand, then touched my feet. I laid my hand upon him and prayed for him. Strangely, it was I who felt blessed to witness such a faith. The man rose up, bowed and put his hands together in the traditional way. 'Dhanyabad,' he said. 'Namaskar.' Then the hotel staff escorted him out of the hotel. Just before leaving the room, he turned back and gave me a look I will never forget. It was one of triumph and joy.

The two pastors sat in silence for a few minutes. 'It seems that the news of your healing has spread far and wide,' one of them said finally. 'It is obvious that you are an anointed woman. Not many foreign women would come to this part of India, let alone remain here to do what you are doing. This is why we came from New Delhi. We wanted to meet you and offer you our assistance in anything God leads you to do.'

'I am blessed very much that God is using me here,' I said. 'At the moment we are trying to finish the church and are praying to reopen the Leprosy Mission hospital in Jhalda. I am so grateful for your offer and will discuss this with Varun and the men.' We finished our meal, exchanged numbers and e-mail addresses and left.

When I came out of the hotel, I saw the man who had asked for a blessing, chattering away with a group of rickshaw pullers. When they saw me coming out, the man and the rickshaw pullers all placed their hands together lifting them high above their heads, in a mutual sign of respect towards me. I am not sure, but I think I blushed as I climbed onto my own rickshaw and sped away.

---

13. Spreading the Word

I was invited to speak at Varun's family church, St Barnabas. It was during the festival of Durga Puja, which was as important as Christmas back home. The schools were closed during this time, so a Sunday school was arranged for children from Christian families. I was to be the guest speaker.

I was apprehensive about my speech. What could I possibly say to a group of children and their teachers? Even up to the moment that we arrived, I didn't know what I was going to say. Varun was going to be my translator, which made him even more nervous than I was. But the words flowed easily as I talked about making wishes upon a star and how God was in the heavens and heard their wishes, like prayers. So all the children had to do was believe. Believe that God heard their prayers and wishes and that one day, in His time, they would come true.

When I came to the end of my talk, I got a big round of applause from the children and a little ceremony took place where they placed a garland of flowers around my neck and sang songs.

Afterwards, the group split up into classes to begin their Bible study. The pastors asked me to come to each class and talk to them. I enjoyed it very much as we wandered around the open-air classes in the large tree-lined grounds. But it was when we came to the oldest group, that we were given chairs to sit on and I was asked to share my testimony of the healing.

That vision I had had for so long, the one of me sitting in a chair talking to people on the ground? This was the moment, the vision! I realized it in the middle of my testimony. It took my breath away and I sat speechless for a moment. Tears came to my eyes. Joy filled my heart as I continued my testimony. Inside I was praising God for fulfilling His promises to me. What a wonderful and awesome thing, to know that He had used me for His purposes!

Just beyond the church was the village of Uffmanpur and beyond this village was a leprosy colony called Simonpur. I was invited to visit these two villages after the Sunday school.

Most of the homes in Uffmanpur were made of brick and mud. I was surprised at how clean and beautiful they were. The mud floors were hard and shiny from years of bare feet walking across them. The doorways were narrow and the windows were tiny so that the homes would stay cool. In spite of their simple homes, many of the families took great pride in their gardens, which were beautifully laid out with flowerbeds and trees. Our guide, a man from the church, told me the story of a missionary and his wife who had moved to this village and raised their family there. This man did many great things, including translating the Bible into Bengali. The village was named after him.

We visited three homes in Uffmanpur. In one home, we sat and drank tea as the owners brought out their picture album to show us their family photos. I was asked to bless their home and to lay hands on their children to bless them too. Though I still felt uncomfortable about 'blessing' people in this way, I also felt honored and humbled.

The next village, Simonpur, was a short distance away. I wanted to walk along the road, but the sun was ablaze in the sky and they insisted that I ride in a rickshaw under the shade of an umbrella. The dirt road led us along the lush countryside, past ponds and trees, to the village.

The Leprosy Mission hospital in Purulia was a large establishment covering many acres of land. At one time it was full of missionary doctors and volunteers from all over the world who worked hard to eradicate leprosy. But the stigma of leprosy was never eradicated. Often curing their disease was not enough, for even after being healed, these men and women were not welcomed back by their families. So this village or leprosy colony was established to provide them homes and rehabilitation. Over the sixty-odd years since it was established, it had grown into a good-sized village with the third generation of families now living there.

It was the first time that I had a chance to meet the leprosy-affected and their families. I was amazed at how well they had adjusted to their missing limbs, but I was equally amazed at how contented they seemed to be. Here they were accepted and loved and had established themselves as productive members of the village community.

As I wandered through the narrow winding alleys with my guide, I heard stories of many of the patients and the missionaries who had worked there. This place had a sense of history. There was no doubt of the presence of a merciful God, who had, in years past, instilled a desire to serve in the hearts of so many. I felt sadness too, as if somehow I had come too late. Once again I felt deeply humbled and blessed for having come to Purulia, never forgetting the wheelchair that once held me captive.

∽

When we arrived at the church grounds, I said goodbye to everyone and went on to Varun's parents' house.

Varun went out to do some errands and left me alone with them. It was always awkward because of our language barrier, and it was obvious that they didn't quite know what to do with me. But also, I was very uncomfortable about not being able to be honest with them about Varun's and my true relationship though I trusted Varun that this situation was only temporary, and he had his reasons for keeping our marriage a secret, for now. They offered me tea and then sat down with me. It was clear that they wanted to discuss something.

Varun's father, Tapan, broached the subject. 'Can you help Varun to go to America?' he asked.

I didn't know what to say. 'I...I don't know, but I will try,' was all I could think of.

'He needs a new start,' Tapan continued, 'nothing but trouble here for him.'

Their eyes spoke more than words. There was a pleading, a sort of desperation. Then Varun's mother spoke in what little English she knew. 'Varun is a very bad boy!' she said emphatically. 'No good here.'

I was startled by the strength of her words. I felt the pain of a mother who knew that her son was not what she had hoped he would be. Though Varun now had a respectable job teaching computers at the school, I knew he had been in enough trouble in the past, and even now, sometimes drank too much when he was with his group, lost control and acted wild and possessed. I also thought that, now that we were married, it should not be too difficult to get him across to America. 'I will do everything I can to get him to America,' I promised. 'It might take a long time, but I will try.' It was not a false promise. Though I myself wanted to stay and work in India, I also wanted to do the right thing for Varun and his family. I had no idea then how many trials lay before us as I said these words.

But there was another matter that I wanted to talk to them about. Something I had noticed in Varun. He had ADD, attention deficit disorder. I realized it almost from the first week that we were together, but I silently observed and studied his behavior. Since I had struggled with this disorder in my own son, I knew the signs quite well. The internal struggle in making the smallest of decisions, the frustration when important things were forgotten and the constant reminders of how he had let others down in his forgetfulness were all signs of ADD. I knew that there was always a sense of failure that permeated his daily life.

So I talked to Varun's parents about the symptoms and frustration of ADD.

Mental disorders were almost never dealt with in this part of the country, but I could see in their eyes that they recognized the symptoms I described. I told them that I knew of a drug that would help him. They agreed, hesitantly, that I should try to get Varun to start taking the drug.

But I also knew that Varun himself had to be ready to accept his condition and be willing to try the medicine. This would take time and many conversations and another year before he was ready.

---

14. A Surprise Homecoming

Six months after I had arrived in India, my savings were gone, and my visa had expired. I had to return to the US to try and get a new visa, and raise more funds to finish building the church and continue our ministry. I decided that I would sell some of the furniture and other stuff I had left in my house in Arizona, and go on a fund-raising campaign.

How difficult it was to leave! The guys threw a party in my honor and gave me a gift of my first sari. We all had fun trying to figure out how it was to be worn. Each time I tried to drape it, it would fall off, making them all laugh. They had brought a live chicken to the house, which I immediately ordered to be killed far away from me. Feathers flew everywhere outside in the yard.

Several of the men came with Varun and me on the long train ride to Kolkata. We stayed together in a hotel room that evening as my flight was early the next morning. We talked about my return and what needed to be done while I was away. I made them promise to continue the Bible studies. There were so many hugs and a few tears that night.

At the airport, an awkward silence and sadness overtook us, as we sat together watching other passengers arriving. The goodbyes had already been said and we had all prayed together early in the morning at the hotel. 'Don't forget that you are my wife, Mrs Kashyap,' Varun said to me, squeezing my hand. 'This is where you belong. You are 50 per cent Indian now. We still have lots of work to do here.'

'I know,' I replied, 'I will try to get more money and support for us and return just as soon as I get a new visa.'

When my flight was called for luggage check in, I knew I

had to go and join the line. This was the point of no return. Once I passed that railing, it was the last time I would see all of them—for how long, I didn't know. Varun and I both broke down as I stepped inside the outgoing passenger area. While my luggage was being inspected, the men stood on the other side of the barrier watching, waving and saying goodbye over and over. I could see the tears running down Varun's face. My heart broke. I ran back to Varun and hugged him over the barrier. 'I'll be back as soon as I can. I love you so much!' I whispered through our tears.

I will not say that my first beginnings in India had been easy. It was one of the toughest challenges of my life. But each day, when I got up and walked, I was renewed in determination and spirit.

I returned to the US a completely different person. I was also nearly half the woman I was, weighing in at 172 pounds. I had lost over sixty pounds in India. But more than this, my experiences in India had changed my whole perspective of the world. I saw my own country in a completely different light. I was also very much in love with Varun and did not want to be away from him for a moment longer than necessary, but I knew there was much to do before I could return.

Since my niece was living in my house, I let her know a month in advance that I would be returning, so she would have time to find another place to stay. I also told her she was welcome to stay with me until she was able to move.

But when I finally walked into my house, I was in for a shock. It was completely empty! All my furniture, the fridge, the TV, even the pictures on the walls, were gone. Why? How? So many questions whirled around in my head.

Suddenly the phone rang. It was my niece. 'How do you like your clean house?' she said mockingly. 'You told me I could keep everything in your house when you left. So I decided it was all mine!' She laughed and hung up.

Over the next few days I discovered from friends and neighbors that she and my sister had taken everything of mine that they wanted, and sold, or even given away the rest. I was devastated. It was true that my sister and I had always had a difficult relationship, but I had trusted her daughter with my house and just could not imagine she would behave in this way.

I could have filed a complaint against them and had them arrested. But that would only cause pain to my parents. My sister and niece lived directly across the street from them. My mother's health was not good and it was my sister who took care of them.

My son, Kevin, and I met inside my parents' motor home that was parked in their yard. He had been living there temporarily. I didn't hold back my rage and spoke bitterly about what my sister and niece had done to me as the tears flowed. Kevin was sympathetic and shared my anger. It seemed they had lied to everyone and told them I had called and asked them to get rid of everything in my house. That was why no one had informed me as my things disappeared.

After we had finished venting our anger, Kevin said, 'Mom, we need to pray about this. Maybe God will give us an answer.' We bowed our heads and he began to pray. Kevin always had a gift of praying. His words seemed to say exactly what needed to be said, what I wanted to say myself. As he prayed, a peace filled me. Then we opened the Bible. What was the scripture to tell us what to do?

It was Kevin who found it. 'If a man steals your cloak, give him your coat also.' It was a very clear message...let it go.

But more important, I had to forgive them. Again we prayed to God to show us how to forgive. I will never forget that day, my first morning back in America, when my son and I prayed together in my parents' home. It renewed my strength and determination to carry on with what I had set out to do.

As we walked across the yard and up onto the front porch, we discovered that my sister and niece were sitting across the street, waiting for us. They began shouting obscenities. 'Go back to India where you belong,' they said, 'you're not welcome here anymore.' They began to laugh. 'We figured since you like to live without things in India, you would enjoy living in an empty house here!' More laughter.

My son and I looked at each other and smiled. The anger and need to retaliate was gone. Only sadness and pity remained.

∼

It was a difficult time for me. So many things were gone that I had accumulated over the years. So many memories are connected to 'things' in our lives. It is those things that define who we are…or do they? I walked through my empty house with a sense of loss, but strangely I also felt relief.

What an odd thing to feel, I thought.

Then, like a 'light bulb' moment I realized that my sister and my niece had done me a favor. I thought that I had done enough by leaving behind my home and all my possessions to go to India and spread the story of my healing. In truth, there were still many things that made me cling to the old life—and now I was free of them. My most valuable possessions, that I had wanted to pass onto my grandchildren, I had put in storage before I left. At least I had that. I knew that my place was in India now, with my husband.

My focus now became that of raising funds for the church and the ministry. I had no idea how to do this, but I began by contacting churches in the area and telling them my story, hoping for an opportunity to speak and have a special collection for our ministry. I was met with polite rejection and a sense that I somehow didn't know 'the system' in America, the rules for acceptance as a legitimate missionary. What a stark contrast to India, where I was asked frequently to speak and tell of my healing. I had forgotten what American churches were like.

On one occasion, I was asked, 'Who are you accountable to?' I was puzzled by the question. This was our own ministry that we had worked so hard for.

'We are accountable to God,' I finally said. This was met with a frown. 'That is not enough. You must be accountable to some organization or diocese to show you are a team player, a legitimate ministry. We're sorry, but we can't help you.' I was seeking a church to sponsor us, but evidently, unless we were a part of a larger church organization, we couldn't get sponsorship. How ironic.

I soon learned that trying to get an American church to support us was like applying for a bank loan. No church would consider us unless we were already a member of an organization, just like a bank won't give you a loan unless you have the money to pay them back, or something to offer as collateral.

I really didn't have a church in Prescott Valley anymore. The church where I was healed had not supported me when I followed God's call. There was the first church I attended, however. Though the pastor was not happy about my having left his ministry and had been skeptical about my healing, perhaps things had changed in six months. In an act of bravery I called the pastor. I told him about India and the ministry and how we were trying to build a church. I told him I just wanted the opportunity to share my story with the church.

'Let me get this straight,' the pastor said. 'You left our church and joined another one. Then you were supposedly healed and went to India and now you are asking me to allow you to speak at our church? That is not going to happen. I suggest you go back to your Pentecostal church and ask forgiveness for not obeying the pastor and maybe, just maybe, they might let you back in.' He hung up the phone with a loud bang, leaving me stunned. Evidently, he didn't like losing a single member of his flock and I was like a traitor to him.

Kevin was attending a very large church in Prescott Valley. I went with him a few times, but found it too impersonal for my tastes. But Kevin urged me to call them and tell them about the needs of our ministry. I did call and spoke with the man in charge of foreign missions. But the response was no different. 'I'm sorry, but we can't allow every missionary who comes into town, to speak at our services. Nor do we encourage a 'passing of the plate' for these missionaries. You must be recommended and be a legitimate non-profit. Each year we choose the foreign missions that we donate to and we have already decided on these for the year. I wish you good luck and our board will pray for you.' I said a polite goodbye and hung up.

I was close to giving up...but then Linda came by one day and as we exchanged news about everything that had happened in our lives in the six months that I was gone, she told me that the mayor had been asking about me. Linda had told him that I was healed by God and had left for India. Evidently he had been very moved by my story. 'You really must call the mayor, Janice,' she urged. 'He would just love to see you now!' With that, she reached into her purse and pulled out his card. I called him immediately and he invited me to his office the following morning.

As I walked into his office, Harvey jumped up from his desk and came to me. 'Praise the Lord,' he said shaking his head. 'You are healed and walking!' He gave me a big hug. 'I heard about the miracle and I just couldn't believe it,' he said, still shaking his head and staring at me like he had seen a ghost. 'I want to hear the whole story and I want to hear about India. Let's go get some coffee and you can tell me about it all.'

As we sat in a café and talked, I told him everything. I lamented that no one really believed about my healing or was willing to help me in my ministry in India. 'I know, it is sad that Christians today don't want to believe these things anymore, but I do,' he beamed. 'I can't wait to tell my wife and family that I met you today!'

Harvey drove me to my car in the parking lot of the town hall. He urged me to keep in touch with him and let him know if there was anything he could do to help. 'We will be praying for you,' he said as I drove away.

In my heart, I admit, I was hoping that he would offer some kind of support to build our church. As I drove home I looked up at the sky and said, 'Well, I guess it's just you and me, Lord. You started this church and I know you will see it finished one way or another.'

15. Letting Go

When I was growing up, God was not allowed in our house. The mere mention of God or religion would spark immediate anger in my father.

My sisters and I were allowed to attend the Mormon church 'primary school' at the urgings of our Mormon relatives, but we all knew that it was against dad's will. Dad tolerated it, grumbling that we might as well find out for ourselves what God was like.

Over the years, any attempts to talk to him about God were met with anger and hostility. My mother remained silent and as far as we could tell, quietly agreed with my dad.

The irony was that while dad was denying anything Christian in our lives, he also demonstrated the very principles of the Bible. He was a kind man, always helping others. He gave generously of himself, shared what he had with others. He was known for his honesty, integrity and generosity. He was also extremely loyal in his dealings with others. His word and a handshake were as good as a contract.

Dad always said, 'I don't believe in God, but I believe in people,' and he showed it. Our home was an open house for all our relatives and friends, so much so that it was dubbed 'The Campbell Hotel' by neighbors and friends.

One time when our house was broken into and some things were stolen, Dad simply said, 'Well I guess they needed it more than we did.'

Everyone liked my dad, especially the women. It was no small wonder, because with three daughters and a wife, dad knew all there was to know about women! We always joked that dad was a ladies' man, but 'a chaser, not a catcher.' He often said with a wink, 'I never met an ugly woman.' His other statement that exasperated my mother was, 'I want to die getting shot by a jealous husband.' He thought it was funny, but mom did not!

My mother's health was deteriorating rapidly. She had suffered from congestive heart failure for a long time. After a couple of strokes, she was confined to a wheelchair and was put on oxygen. Her mind was still sharp and I would often go over to my parents' house to play rummy or Scrabble with them.

Dad began complaining of pain in his right leg. After a few X-rays, it was determined that his hip needed replacing. While he was in the hospital recovering from surgery, my mother was rushed to the same hospital with chest pains. After a few days in hospital, dad returned home. His recovery was very quick, but mom never recovered completely.

The drugs that she was on seemed to be causing hallucinations. She would tell me stories of strange visitors in her room. But there was one particular story that she shared with me that lifted my heart. 'You have to hear what happened to me last night,' she said, very seriously. 'Two men in white coats came and lifted me on a gurney and wheeled me down the hall and into the elevator. I asked them where they were taking me and they just said, "You'll see." The elevator kept going down, down, I couldn't move, and it was getting so hot in there. I looked at those men and they were glowing white, even their faces were so bright that I could hardly look at them. I was scared and I asked again, where are you taking me?' Tears were forming in her eyes. 'They simply said, together, "You know! You refuse to believe!" Mom was talking faster. 'I did know. All my life I followed your dad as he hated God. But at that moment I did believe.

I told them, yes, I do believe! And then the elevator began moving slowly up. I don't remember how I got back in my bed.' Mom grabbed my hand. 'I just wanted you to know that I believe in God and over the years I have prayed. I think those were angels giving me one last time to accept Jesus… and I did.' Then she pleaded, 'Please don't tell your father or he will kill me!'

I promised to not breathe a word of it to dad, but I was filled with joy. Together mom and I said a short prayer, and she fell peacefully asleep.

The doctors and nurses had warned us that mom might not make it but she surprised everyone and stabilized enough to come home. We enjoyed a few weeks with her, but it wasn't long before her condition deteriorated again. The tough decision was made; she had to go into a care home. For a few days, she seemed to be doing well, even eating with us out in the dining room. But then she suffered a sudden relapse. The whole family was called to her bedside. We watched helplessly as she struggled to breathe.

She died that April. My parents had been married for fifty-nine years. It was a terrible blow for all of us, but for my father, it was a life-changing event. Dad and I had always been close and it tore at my heart that I had to leave him again and return to India.

'How can I leave now?' I asked him a few weeks after mom's death. 'Because life must go on,' he said matter-of-factly. 'You have to continue what you started over there. That is what I want you to do.'

∼

All my efforts to raise funds had come to nought, and I was left with only one option. I decided that I must sell my house.

I contacted a realtor friend. She didn't hold out much hope of getting a good price as the realtor market was slow and prices had dropped.

While I was discussing this with my father that night, the phone rang. It was my ex-husband. He and dad had remained friends even after our divorce, and kept in touch. Dad told him about my problem. I heard dad say, 'Really?' then he handed the phone to me.

'I think I have a solution to your problem,' Rod said.

'Oh really?' I joked. 'Do you have a buyer for the house?'

'Actually, yes,' he said. 'I want to buy the house from you.' I was surprised into silence. He went on, 'You tell me what your asking price is and we will negotiate. I can give you a good down payment and I will take over the mortgage.'

'Are you serious?' I asked. 'Do you want to live there again after what we've been through?'

'Of course I do,' he said in a business-like tone. 'It was a good investment when we bought it together and it still is. I don't care what the market is now, I want to buy the house.'

Within a few weeks we negotiated the price and the conditions. Rod made the down payment and agreed to pay the balance amount in monthly instalments over the next three years. I now had money for my return to India and a little left over for the ministry. What a blessing it was! Rod found tenants for his own house and began moving his things over to mine.

Rod and I were better friends now than we ever had been when we were married. Though he never said so, I suspected his true reason for buying the house was because he wanted to help me.

One evening, at my father's house, the three of us had a barbecue party. After a few drinks he told me that he was sorry that he had treated me so badly when I was in the wheelchair and in the years before that. 'I want to try and make it up to you,' he said, then added quickly, 'don't get me wrong. I am glad we are divorced and you have Varun. I had no business being married to you, or any woman, if you understand what I mean.'

I did understand. Rod was gay. He had spent years denying it to himself and to me. He dealt with it by isolating himself from people and surrounding himself with beautiful things, too many things. He became a hoarder, an addictive shopper, living his life looking for the next 'great deal' he could find. We had shared twenty-two years together, the last ten of them living as brother and sister, and mostly fighting.

Rod still worked for a large warehouse store as a greeter. He loved his job and was well loved by his co-workers and customers. He had a quick sense of humor and real compassion for those customers he came to know well. But the Rod at work and the Rod at home were two very different people. I kept his secret well and we pretended to be a happily married couple. It must have been a good act, because all our friends and family were shocked when we separated and filed for divorce.

Rod was true to his promise. He was always at hand to help me and Varun and the ministry. He also offered to pay off all the credit card bills I had run up while I was in India, telling me that, 'You never know when you will need a good credit standing.' I was extremely grateful, and all the years of bitterness between us melted away.

Another phone call from Rod came one morning. 'Why don't you try and get Varun over here?' he asked.

'Well, our marriage hasn't been registered yet in India, so I can't file for a spousal visa,' I told him.

'So what about a tourist visa?' he asked. 'Surely he can come as a tourist for a few months. Why don't you look into it?'

I did look into it but immediately ran into a snag. A sponsor was required. Someone who had a large bank account and would promise to support him while he was visiting, as well as provide medical insurance for him.

Again Rod came through and said, 'I fit all the requirements, why don't I sponsor him?'

'Don't you think that would look odd?' I asked, 'I mean, having my ex-husband sponsor my new husband for a visa?'

'Perhaps, but what do they care as long as I am willing to do it and I meet all the criteria?' I saw that look of determination on his face. 'Well, if you are willing to do this, then I guess it is worth a try. I will talk to Varun about it,' I said.

Varun was surprised that Rod was willing to help him, but agreed. We set about completing all the paperwork and putting together all the documents the visa department needed—Varun's birth certificate, medical history, property ownership, job history and so on. Within three weeks of sending the documents, our answer came back. He was denied. Reason: He was too much at risk of becoming an illegal alien. That is not what they stated, but it was what we were told later. Evidently he was not rich enough, and didn't have enough family ties in India.

∼

All the churches I had approached for help with fund-raising had turned me away, but I still had an overpowering need to find a church where I could worship. I went to several churches in the area, and eventually found my way back to the old Pentecostal church where I was healed. I wanted to go back to that place where I had begun to walk again and kneel at the altar and pray. The pastor and his wife greeted me and asked me what I had done in India. I told them about Varun, the church we were trying to build and the Bible studies. I think they were pleasantly surprised. There were many familiar faces in the congregation, and they all met me with warmth and affection. I was no longer 'shunned'; I was accepted back into the fold.

Another church I went to was one recommended to me by a friend. It was a huge building with a large stage in front. I was amazed at the richness of it all and the modern equipment that was used during the service. What a contrast it was from the churches in India! This church had a full band and a drummer who sat behind a glass screen. It had an overhead projector displaying the words to the songs and I never had to open my Bible during the sermon because the scripture was up on the screen above the pastor. I was given a schedule when I walked in and an envelope to drop my donation into. This was the most organized and modern church I had seen.

Everything went according to schedule. When it was over, we were urged to leave quickly because their next service was beginning. There were ushers to make sure we moved along swiftly. It was very entertaining and there is no doubt that I was impressed…but I left feeling like I had just walked out of a movie or concert, not a church service.

But the best thing that happened was that I ran into some old friends from the first church I had attended in the wheelchair. They told me about a home fellowship that was starting and invited me to come the next Sunday.

I did go and was surprised to meet a few people from the Pentecostal church. The pastor joked about all of us being 'recovering Pentecostals,' believing in the importance of the Holy Spirit, and the many gifts of the spirit, but not in the business of 'speaking in tongues.' We were a small home fellowship and over the months that I was in the US, we became like friends and spiritual partners. We took turns holding our worship in each other's homes. There was always plenty of food and laughter, but more important, we shared scripture and had wonderful discussions afterwards. To this day I am in touch with many of them and I will be eternally grateful to Pastor Enrique for his encouragement at a time when I needed it the most.

16. Back to India

A wise man once told me, 'Many countries will steal your heart. But only India can steal your soul.' I was beginning to understand what he meant. India was in my blood now.

It was time to pack and say my goodbyes. I stored what was left of my things at what was now Rod's house.

I visited my doctor for a check-up before leaving. He was glad to see me still walking, but warned me again that it could be just a remission and that with fibromyalgia anything can happen at any time. He gave me a prescription for a new drug and strongly recommended that I take it. I admitted that, at times, I still suffered from complete exhaustion and would need to sleep for days. On rare occasions, my hands would begin shaking without warning. This would always put fear inside me that the disease was coming back. But the symptoms would leave as quickly as they came. When I told Varun my fears, he said, 'When God heals, He heals permanently. Your faith, your God, is stronger than this disease.'

The doctor was not as encouraging. 'Just be careful and watch for any signs of it returning,' he said, as he wrote out the prescription.

~

I returned to India in August 2006, full of confidence. Purulia was no longer a strange place to me. I felt I knew what to expect and what my goals were this time. I felt renewed 'in the spirit', refreshed with the fellowship I had received back home. I also came equipped with missionary materials I didn't have before. Kevin had put hours of Christian music on a CD and gave me a player as a parting gift. A few friends gave me a daily devotional and a journal in which to write down my experiences.

Varun and I had kept in daily contact by e-mail, enforcing our love and commitment to each other. When we finally embraced again, it was with so much strength and love!

We lived most of that year in a hotel room. Houses or flats were hard to find. The 'under construction' house we were living in before was completed and the owner had rented it out to someone else. Varun had moved in with his parents while I was away. The computer scool where he was once a student, offered him a job as manager, and since it was very close to Bhat Bandh, he took it. He had built a reputation as an expert on viruses in computers and was called by banks and other businesses to fix their company computer problems. While I was in the US, he had landed a contract with a large hydro-electric project to train employees on the new software. It was a major project and won him laurels with his employers.

It was exciting to return and begin working on the church again. Not much had been done in my absence. The biggest expense we still had to face was putting on a roof. Windows and doors needed to be designed and installed. Plastering the walls and laying the floors, building the bell tower and altar, painting the interiors and exteriors...so much more than I had funds for. Though Rod had made the down payment on the house, the monthly instalments would kick in only four months later, once he had paid off my credit card bills.

A chunk of our money went on the hotel. We were constantly looking for a cheaper place to live, but nothing was available. Eating in the hotel was limited to our dinner and that was expensive enough. Bringing food from outside was frowned upon, but we managed to sneak in some fast food and snacks.

My old rickshaw puller, Abhoy, decided that he didn't want to work with us anymore. He had struck lucky and won a good amount in a lottery, which changed his perspective on work. Plus, after the many things that happened the previous year, I think he decided I was too much to handle!

I was sorry to lose him. He knew my habits and where I did my regular shopping. We often enjoyed afternoon tea together. To me, he was like a member of our family. He had also become fiercely protective of me over the many months we traveled together. Replacing him would be difficult. I didn't know much Bengali or Hindi, and finding a rickshaw puller who knew a little English would be a miracle.

It looked like I was not going to have my personal rickshaw puller this time round. But I soon learned the ways of dealing with different rickshaw pullers every day. I knew the going rates and was able to negotiate prices, knowing full well that many of them would test me by asking for outrageous amounts. I was always generous, but firm. They also knew that I treated them with respect.

I did respect them. I had never seen such a hard-working group of men who, no matter what the weather or the temperatures outside, hauled people of every size, sometimes for miles at a stretch. The condition of most of the rickshaws was shabby, with worn seats and tyres. Most of them didn't own their own rickshaws, but had to pay a daily commission to the owners. Often I had to get down from a rickshaw while flat tyres or broken chains were repaired. I learned to check the condition of a rickshaw before climbing onto it. It wasn't long before I knew many of the rickshaw pullers and they would call out greetings as I traveled through Purulia.

I also now knew my way around the marketplace. The shop owners were familiar with me, and usually knew what I needed to buy. Some assumed that I was a doctor working at the Leprosy Mission hospital, while others had heard, through my testimonies, about how God had healed me. But wherever I went, I was treated with respect, and, occasionally, indifference, which suited me just as well. I enjoyed my independence and was able to move freely around the marketplace. What a far cry this was from the first year.

∼

The church in Jhalda haunted me. I felt guilty for not raising more funds.

One of our men created a beautiful iron window design shaped like a cross. The windows had to be measured and then the iron grills welded together. We ordered a door for the front entrance. Because of our limited funds, we had to be careful of the costs and try to spread the expenses out over a few months.

The weird thing was that we never heard from the church congregation that year. These were the people that wanted us to build the church for them, but there was no offer to help or expressions of interest in the progress of the church, with the exception of the church secretary, a man chosen to lead the church in services and prayer. He would show up at regular intervals for a few minutes and talk to Varun, but for the most part, we were on our own. This disturbed me.

The other annoying thing was that the larger churches were always asking me for donations but never once asked if we needed help. It would have been nice to gather a group together for a picnic and to work on the church building as Christians united…but that never happened. Because of my meager funds, the only progress we made that year was to get the windows installed.

The previous year, we had given some money to the man, Sujan, to purchase a rickshaw to earn an income for his family. The agreement was that, within one year, he would build the bell tower for the church. But when the men approached him and reminded him of his promises, he made excuses. I was not surprised, but was disappointed, especially because we really needed this addition to the church, for progress to be seen in the eyes of the believers in Jhalda.

I prayed daily about all the hurdles that confronted us. I questioned if God was still behind us in this work. I searched for signs, some sort of guidance.

I did have a few people in town tell me to give up on the men I was teaching. 'They will never change. They are nothing but trouble,' they would tell me.

I was discouraged to find that while I had been away in the US, the men had gone back to their old ways of hanging around and drinking. Though there were some Bible studies, they were few. I had been gone six months and it did seem like starting all over again with them. But I had new material for 'discipleship training' and was ready to start new classes again.

When the first Bible study was called, they all came, ready to begin. I required them to make new commitments of two days a week for this new course. I told them to think about it first and let me know. They all immediately agreed to attend and said they didn't need to think about it. Their enthusiasm gave me hope. We agreed to have the studies on Wednesday and Friday evenings.

Trying to hold Bible studies in our hotel room proved to be impossible. The hotel was a strictly Hindu one that frowned upon such meetings. We needed to find somewhere to hold the Bible studies.

Varun's mother came to our rescue by offering their house. I was delighted because this gave me an opportunity to spend more time with her.

It was a joy for me to watch as we praised God with many songs and then shared scripture with Varun's mom participating. She had never seen these wayward young men before in such an environment, praying and singing and opening up their lives to God. I was so happy to see the smile on her face and her eyes gleaming in the candlelight. I was also surprised to hear her singing. What a beautiful voice she had! I knew God was there with us in that room as we all stood, held hands, and recited the Lord's Prayer.

God had given me these young men, numbering only six, a small group to be sure, but tough as nails. I saw the sacrifices they made as we all worked together as a team to get the church finished.

Sometimes we would call them without notice and announce a need for another trip back to the village. They all dropped whatever they were doing and came. Often we would meet them, with the car, at a designated area, and they were standing in a group, waiting for us. Sometimes one or two young men, not of our group, would want to come too. Somehow we always made room in the car for everyone.

To be sure, the entire village was aware of our project and was amazed at what was happening. They had never seen this group doing anything useful before, so eyebrows were raised and questions were asked as the locals gathered each evening for the daily gossip.

I had visions of increasing our numbers and having a profound effect on everyone in the area. One by one we would make a difference.

∼

Shortly after returning to Purulia, I began to notice that my hair was falling out in chunks. I showed Varun one morning after a shower, the handful of hair I pulled out of the brush. 'We've got to get you to a doctor,' he said. By late that afternoon I was on my way to a woman doctor. I later learned that she was a specialist in leprosy and skin diseases and had worked with the Leprosy Mission hospital for years.

Her clinic was attached to a pharmacy and was located just outside the big bus station in Purulia. I was shown into her office immediately.

After a nice conversation about my hair problems, she asked me, 'Are you on hormone pills?'

'Well, I was,' I said, 'but there was this big scare in the US about it causing cancer so I stopped taking them.'

'Well, I think you need to start taking them again, and I will give you some hair growth medicine too,' she said.

Dr Kiran Sarkar and I got along well. She didn't know that I had no female friends and was hungering for someone

I could talk to. What I instantly liked was she seemed to be 'Westernized' and didn't treat me like I was a strange white woman. She invited me to dinner at her house and I gladly accepted.

She and her husband gave me inspiration, for she was a Christian and her husband a Hindu. This was rare and totally against the social norms of this country thirty years ago, let alone today. Normally, in such a marriage, one converts to the other's religion. But somehow they had managed to live together all these years, respecting each other's faith. They told me of their struggles in the beginning, that they had to move away from Purulia for a few years, until things calmed down, but eventually returned. She, being a well respected doctor at the Leprosy Mission hospital, and him making his name in the banking industry, they were able to be accepted back into the community.

In addition, their son and Varun had been playmates growing up and Kiran worked in the same hospital as Varun's father, Tapan. So there was a history of the two families sharing moments of life together.

Kiran and Prajit's son lived in Australia, so they frequently visited the country and were very familiar with Western culture. I could be myself with them, knowing that they were accepting and understanding of my culture. I told them about my miracle healing and how God brought Varun and me together, about the church being built in Jhalda and our Bible studies. They were both very encouraging, giving me advice and a little history of the community.

It was a wonderful evening. I didn't realize how much I missed socializing with people who had no hidden agenda. By this I mean that they didn't want or need anything from me.

I had learned from the first year that, almost without

exception, everyone wanted to be my friend...for money or social status or some charitable contribution. On the other side of the coin, there were those who might want to hurt me just for being a white American, let alone a Christian. I did not live in fear, not at all. I wore my large silver cross boldly wherever I went and was always friendly to everyone. But I became very suspicious of anyone who was over friendly, and learned to avoid getting too close to people. This led to a forced isolated existence where I attended public events, but avoided too much interaction with individuals and always had Varun and the men with me.

Varun was really over protective of me and often the men had to tell him to back off and let me do things alone. I was surprised that Varun approved of me going to Kiran's house for dinner though he called me several times during my visit. When I got home, he was moody and wanted to know all the details of the evening. This was one quality in him that I didn't like at all and was told that all Indian men were like this with their wives. But was it a cultural thing or just the way Varun was? I began to realize after some time with him that it was a bit of both. When I complained to Varun about this, he said, 'God showed me in that vision that you were coming here and that my job was to protect you. He healed you and brought you here for His purpose and I am bound to make sure nothing happens to you!'

17. Sin or No Sin?

I saw the subtle changes in each of the men during our Bible studies. They began to have prayer requests for others less fortunate than themselves and sometimes, tears would flow as they shared their own testimonies one by one. No, I would not give up on them.

But somehow I had to reach them, connect with each of them, a little more.

I spent more time in prayer about this, asking God to show me what to do. I truly believed that God could use this small group to light up this area and that it could grow into a larger ministry.

It was not their drinking that bothered me so much, I enjoyed a couple of drinks now and then too, but it was *how* they drank. I watched in total amazement the first time I witnessed their drinking. They drank extremely fast! It was like they were in a race to get drunk.

This group had no concept of social drinking as I had known it in the US, slowly sipping your drink and mingling with others. I watched horrified as they poured one drink after another, gulped it down quickly and set their glasses down ready for the next one. Within less than half an hour a large bottle of whiskey and a few bottles of water were empty. It wasn't until later that I learned the reason for this habit.

Throughout the region there were small country bars hidden away, where the locals would come and enjoy 'country wine' or what we would call 'moonshine.' This country wine was made under the worst sanitary conditions, using the nearest source of water that was available. Sometimes this was the local murky pond water. But the drink was powerful, cheap and seemed to please the locals.

These bars used empty plastic water bottles to store and sell the liquor. If you brought back the empties, you could get a discount on your next purchase. It was the only alternative for those with little income to indulge in drinking. But because of the taste and the look of these bottles (they often had debris floating in them), it was best to drink it down fast before the eyes let the stomach know what was coming. Not surprisingly, there were some who died from this and others rendered paralyzed for days at a time. This didn't seem to stop these bars from doing a booming business.

I knew that telling them to stop drinking was a waste of time. But I trusted that God would eventually convince each of them about it. My daily prayers for them always included this. I studied scripture trying to find God's words on this subject. I was surprised at what I discovered. I wanted to share it with everyone. Varun and I discussed it at length and he agreed that we needed to talk about this openly with the guys.

We called a meeting one evening. I sent Varun out to round up the guys. We had never done this before, and they were curious enough to attend. I also told Varun to purchase a large bottle of whiskey. When everyone was gathered, I asked them to come and join me on the floor. I had arranged the glasses in a circle. Varun brought out the bottle of whiskey and all eyes lit up in the room.

'In the Psalms, scripture tells us that God made wine to make the heart glad,' I said. 'I have spent the past few days looking up scripture about drinking. Of course you know that Jesus' first miracle was to turn water into wine.' This got all the guys smiling.

'However, scripture does speak repeatedly against drunkenness.' I paused and looked at each of them. 'I found many scriptures telling us not to get drunk.' I opened my Bible and read a few passages to them while Varun translated. Their smiles left the room. 'So, the way I see it, it is okay to enjoy a drink or two to celebrate together.' The smiles returned. ' I have prayed about this a lot and I have thought about how God has put us together and how we are so blessed that God is using us to glorify Him.' I waited as Varun translated. 'But I have some questions for you. Do you think it is right for you to be seen outside drunk now? Do you think that something inside you has changed just a little bit? Don't you want others to see this change?' I asked. 'All I am asking you is to act like you are "The God Squad" team. Be kind to others and set an example that would make me proud.'

Then I got serious. 'I am also going to ask you to limit your drinks to three. Count what you are doing and be aware how much you are drinking.'

Then I added, 'If you slow down, you can make those three drinks stretch over a few hours.'

They all looked at each other and then burst out laughing. Evidently they all thought this was a funny idea. 'Okay, we try,' Peter said. 'We try hard for you.' With that, I gave the bottle to Arun, and said, 'Now let's enjoy a few drinks together, but just a few!'

I almost laughed myself, while watching each of them trying to 'sip like Americans do.' The three drinks each were consumed and all went well, at least in our home. Only God knew what they did later!

∾

There was no doubt that we were all the most unlikely group of people to be considered by society as 'good Christians,' smoking, drinking and plotting to save Purulia from the Sadducees, my nickname for the churches in the area who enforced rules on the people, just like the Sadducees did in Biblical times. They were elitists who wanted to maintain the priestly caste, and believed in enforcing the written law. They felt that Jesus was a threat to their positions and constantly sent spies to try to catch him in breaking a law.

From the day we began to build the church in Jhalda, the Christian community became silent. I had no desire to fight against them, in fact, I attended each of the churches in the area, trying to understand their ways of worship and to get to know the church pastors.

I also had a strong desire to be 'filled with the spirit' with praise and music. I hungered for the church music and fellowship I had in my country.

But sitting through a two-hour church service in a foreign language and listening to songs that I didn't know, did nothing to my spirit. I left feeling empty. Varun refused to attend, saying that they were all against us and he knew their history as so-called Christians.

Of course, it didn't help that we had offended the most visible and influential pastor in the area by refusing his offer to join his ministry. And it didn't help that the bishop of one of the main churches in the area was extremely upset at us for continuing construction after he had ordered us to stop.

Yes, we were different. We were rebels, a motley group of misfits. But we were faithful. We were, after all 'The God Squad.'

As I read about Jesus, and studied scriptures, I could see a strong comparison with us and his chosen disciples. Everything Jesus and his men did, went against the religious leaders and people of his time...just like us. Nor were they all saint-like in their behavior, just like us.

Though nothing in the Bible mentions smoking, I was quite sure it wasn't a sin—an unhealthy habit maybe, but not a sin. Still it bothered me and I prayed daily to God to take away my desire for smoking.

I had heard stories of people, who, once they accepted Christ, would suddenly lose their desire for habits they had.

I believed that one day this would happen to me. I just had to keep trying and keep praying.

In the meantime I kept my smoking private. Only those close to us knew of my habit.

I had been studying Watchman Nee's books and in one of them he said to simply stop trying to get rid of a habit on our own, to trust and let the Lord do it for us. So after my daily prayer, I would leave it to the Lord and not worry about it.

I remember telling my son how unworthy I felt because I smoked. He said, 'Mom, God used a donkey to change Baal and stop him from worshipping money. If God can use a donkey for His purposes, he can certainly use you too!' I remember looking at him puzzled for a minute, then bursting out laughing. 'So now I am a donkey for Christ?' Kevin grinned. 'Better to be a donkey for Christ, than a tool for the devil!' he said.

I don't pretend to be an expert on scripture or religion. All I know is that God is with me and has called me, not as a perfect person, but as one who believes with all my heart. I will not say no to God just because I feel I am unworthy, or because others say I am not a good Christian. Who is to know where my heart lies, except for God? Who can declare me unfaithful because I smoke? 'For if God is for me, who can be against me?'

Perhaps this is the true 'thorn' in my flesh that makes me humble. Perhaps it is the one thing that shows me that just because I was healed by God, I am still not perfected in Christ. But I am still running the race!

---

18. Alien—or Indian?

Purulia is not a small town, nor is it a city. It is many villages connecting together until they blend seamlessly across the landscape. Those who live there know when they leave one village and enter into another, but for strangers, it appears as one.

There are Muslim villages and Hindu villages. The village where my husband was raised, the village of Bhat Bandh, is a Christian village.

Most villages have their own little market areas, but the main market is the largest where everyone goes to shop for most of their needs. From what I could see, they all lived in harmony with respect for each other's religion and territories.

The unemployment rate in the area is high. There is no industry and few jobs available. So when the youth graduate from school, there is little for them to look forward to. After a few years of trying to find decent work, most of them fall into a sort of hopeless acceptance of their fate, and like many in the US, end up connecting with street life in a gang mentality. Territories are defined and protected. Anyone who unknowingly wanders into the wrong area at night is meted out harsh treatment.

I learned very quickly that the young men in this culture lived with intense pressure from their families. A son was expected to marry a woman to take care of his parents. This woman was chosen for her lifelong vocation as a good house cleaner and cook, as well as her looks and social status or caste. Choosing a wife was a very serious business arrangement. This was usually done while the men were in their twenties or early thirties.

The marriage ceremony was a strong reflection on the status, or caste, of the family, so much expense and care was taken to project the right image in the community. More often than not, a family would find itself at the mercy of moneylenders and incur a huge debt to give their son a wedding befitting their status.

The young man would then usually become the sole provider for the entire household, including his younger brothers and sisters.

After the first son was married, plans were set to get the next son through school and then get him married as well. With each marriage, often a house was built next door. The houses were usually built in a circle with a common well in the center where all the women would meet to wash and cut vegetables, do laundry or dishes. Once, when I was in a plane flying over the Indian landscape, I was amazed to see all these circles interconnecting into large villages.

The one thing I admired about this culture was their closeness as a family and their tolerance of one another's shortcomings while living in such tight confines. They seemed to have an in-built acceptance of life. For instance, if a young couple were fighting, they would all smile and say 'when you put two dishes together, they are bound to make noise.' It was a natural occurrence and expected in a new marriage.

For the woman, or young girl, marriage was what she was born to do. Her entire upbringing was a training ground for teaching her how to care for her husband and the household. After the wedding, she had to leave behind everything she knew as a child and move in with her husband's family. Sometimes this was very far away from her world. Often the in-laws put her through many trials in the first few months as a sort of training ground to teach her their ways and test her emotional strength. For her to fail, would shame her family and leave her branded as an unwanted woman. The same held true if she did not produce a baby within the first year. If the baby was a girl, she was expected to produce a boy or risk being sent away.

But for many, the transition was not difficult and the husband's family was patient and understanding, wanting their son to be well taken care of and to hopefully fall in love with his new bride.

∼

For Varun's sister, Juhi, all seemed to be going well, for she was very pregnant and the baby was due any day. Several weeks earlier, she came to stay in her parents' house, where she could have the help and comfort of her family when the baby came.

We finally got the phone call to come to the hospital. Juhi was in labor! This was my first glimpse into what happened in this world when a baby was born. It was also the first time I entered a local hospital. This hospital was considered one of the best in the area, but when we walked in, the first thing I noticed was the dirty walls and dusty floors.

This was my Western critical eye that was looking and I sternly told myself to turn it off. There was no place for that anymore, not in this world. We climbed up a flight of stairs and spotted Varun's parents standing outside a room. I could tell by their faces that something was wrong. It seemed that the embryonic fluid was almost gone inside the womb. The doctor had ordered a C-section. They were waiting for the doctor to arrive.

Within the hour, Juhi was taken into surgery. Not one to sit around idle, I decided, while we were waiting, to wander through the maternity wing. The grandmother in me wanted to see some of the newborns. I found the large room where the new mothers and babies were. There must have been twenty beds lined up against the walls.

By now I was accustomed to being stared at everywhere I went, but here, many of the mothers and their families came from other villages and had never seen a white woman before. Wide eyes and curious glances greeted me as I walked into the room. A few young nurses came to me smiling. 'I just wanted to see the babies,' I said. One nurse turned and shouted something in Bengali. I had no idea what she said, but happy nods and smiles filled the room.

I always wore a cross around my neck and today was no exception. As I approached the first bed, the mother eagerly handed her baby to me, asking me to bless it. I held this precious life in my arms, and laid my hand on the baby's head, praying to God to give me the right words to say. I prayed for the baby to grow to know Christ and have a healthy childhood. I gave the baby a kiss on the forehead and handed it back to the mother. The nurses took me to the next bed and again I laid hands on the baby.

This went on from one bed to the next and I felt God's presence with me as I prayed over each new life. What a wonderful blessing it was for me to have the privilege to do this!

We were interrupted when Varun's dad came into the room to tell me that Juhi was out of surgery. I put my hands together in the customary 'namaskar,' thanked the nurses and left.

I followed Tapan down the hall and back into the room where we were before. Poor Juhi was just coming out of the anesthesia and smiled weakly at me. 'Well,' I asked with a smile, 'Is it a boy or a girl?' Varun answered for her. 'It's a boy!' he said grinning.

'Where is he then?' I asked.

'Nurses cleaning him. They bring him soon,' Varun's mother, Sabita, said. And at that moment the nurses came in. One was carrying the baby and the other was pushing a metal baby cot into the room.

Juhi was given her baby to see for the first time. I remembered my own babies and how I felt when I first saw them. A lump formed in my throat. She gazed down upon him in wonder, touching his cheeks and stroking his dark hair. The nurses urged her to feed him and rushed us out of the room.

A few minutes later we were allowed to come back in and found both mother and baby sound asleep. But the nurses began fussing and Juhi opened her eyes. Tapan went over to the bed and said something to her in Bengali and she nodded and smiled. He spoke to Varun and Sabita and they all nodded.

Then Tapan picked up the baby and gave him to me with a solemn look on his face. I looked at Varun, trying to figure out what was happening. 'We have all decided that you should name the baby and bless him,' Varun said. 'So give him a good American name.'

Word failed me. To be asked to bless the baby was honor enough, but to name him, the first grandson, was overwhelming! Names were swimming in my head. All of them were standing there, waiting, staring at me. I took a deep breath. 'Charles,' I blurted out. 'Charlie actually!' I said more confidently.

Varun's father smiled. Varun's mother smiled. I looked at Juhi. She smiled too and nodded. 'Now bless the baby, using his name,' Varun instructed.

I don't know why, but suddenly 'Lion King' came into my head, where the father lion lifted his cub up in the air to present him to all the animals.

It was a moment of inspiration. I held the baby out and lifted him up, and said, 'Father God, I present to you Charles. I ask that you fill his life with your presence and protection. Please make him healthy and strong and use him Lord to glorify you.' I brought the baby close to me, made the sign of the cross on his forehead and kissed him. The room was filled with smiles and I was filled with relief!

A few days later we went to Varun's parents home to visit Juhi and the baby again. We arrived at a time when the baby was being massaged with mustard oil. Two nurses were hired to take care of the mother and baby. I watched amazed as one nurse gently massaged every muscle and joint of the newborn, stretching and bending the arms and legs.

Varun explained to me that this was a tradition and that they believed that the mustard oil had medicinal effects on the baby. Both mother and baby received these massages to help overcome the shock of childbirth. Mustard oil was commonly used for cooking and applying to the body after a shower. It seemed that every household used mustard oil. I learned to recognize the scent though I never got used to its odor or taste.

Another tradition that Varun told me about, was giving the baby local water. I was quite shocked at this, because the local water was so dirty. But Varun said, 'Who can afford bottled water all the time? We believe it is best to give him the local water immediately, this way his body gets used to it.'

'But what if he dies from it?' I asked.

'Then he dies. He is too weak to survive in this world. Best to have it happen now.' Varun said this matter-of-factly, but to me it seemed unbelievably harsh. I was also surprised at the baby's bed. A small wooden cradle was in the room with Juhi. There was no mattress or pillow, just a thin blanket on top of the wood. I was told that the baby had to get used to sleeping on the hard wood because this would make his body tough for the future. 'Life here in India is hard,' Varun said, 'We don't believe in pampering our children.'

I now understood why I saw so many people taking naps on the ground, some using a rock for a pillow. This was their life, the way they were raised. As time went by, I discovered that even the thin cotton mattresses were removed from the beds in the summer time because they caused more heat to the body. The only thing on the bed was a sheet over the wood and pillows stuffed with heavy cotton. I was grateful that at least we had a regular store mattress to sleep on.

19. Living in a Man's World

As an older white American woman, I was allowed to do many things that were unheard of for an Indian woman. I often ate in the hotel alone and traveled around unescorted, sometimes in the early evenings. The one thing that became clear to me was that the evenings were the time for all men to gather. The few women I saw out after dark were escorted by a male family member or were 'ladies of the night'—sex workers. All decent women were at home with their families preparing dinner for whenever their husbands returned home.

But how strange it was to be out in the evening for a ride

in the rickshaw and see nothing but men and young boys gathering everywhere. They would walk along holding hands or with their arms around each other. There were clusters of men sitting on the roadside playing cards and others standing outside hotels with drinks in their hands. The older men gathered at small tea shops, sipping tea and sharing their lives with one another. I also saw men, young and old, carrying babies and toddlers on their evening strolls, but no women. This was when the stark reality of a patriarchal society became so clear to me. No women anywhere.

As I observed the men in our group, I was surprised at how close they all were with each other. There were no physical barriers as they interacted. They would lie on the floor with arms intertwined, often massaging each other's hands or feet or head. The idea that this was unnatural never crossed their minds because in this culture it was perfectly acceptable. To my American eyes though it was not, and I admit to feeling uncomfortable about the way they openly showed their affection to one another.

One night I even asked Varun if any of the guys were gay. 'What's that?' he asked looking puzzled. 'Gay,' I repeated, 'You know, men who like other men.' I watched as his eyes opened wide. 'No way!' he exclaimed. 'That would never be allowed here. I did read about it happening a lot in the US, but it is very rare here.'

Over the next few years I did realize that the men were a complete unit in themselves. Everything that they needed, they provided each other. There really was no need for a woman, except to take care of their homes and their physical needs and to bring their children into the world. But even the physical needs were taken care of by the many houses of prostitution spread throughout the area.

Indeed, after his marriage, if a man spent too much time with his wife, or displayed too much affection, he was ridiculed. Loving a wife had its own strict boundaries. No signs of public affection were acceptable, not even in front of visitors in their homes. Both the husband and the wife were expected to show their love by being dutiful to each other in their respective roles. The man must treat his family with honor and provide for their needs. A woman with beautiful saris and lots of gold jewelry was a sign of how well loved she was and the mark of a good husband. Some women showed off their huge bellies with pride as a sign that they were well taken care of instead of going on a diet to lose weight!

The roles that Varun and I played were the opposite of these norms. That first year he would often lament, 'Why can't you be like an Indian wife and treat me with honor and respect?' I would just grin and say, 'Because I am an American wife, which means we are a team.'

One day I realized, with a kind of loneliness in my heart, no women were in my life either. I had come to accept the young men of the God Squad team as our little group, a family. But it did seem odd that, though I invited women to our Bible studies, no one came. It was the young men who approached me with questions. Children too, were bold enough to approach me. But the women stood away and simply watched.

When I was invited into their homes, I was treated with the utmost respect, given the place of honor and always served refreshements first. The women would be very cordial and polite, but would always serve me with heads bowed and then leave.

I thought about this for several days and asked Varun why they did so. This was his reply. 'You are an American woman. To them you are far above them, like a queen who has honored them with your presence. They only wish to be where you are.'

'But I am not a queen. I am just a regular woman. Just because I was born in America doesn't make me better than they are,' I protested.

'Yes it does,' he said matter-of-factly. Then he added, 'Which is why you have got to stop smiling so much at people when you are on the rickshaw. You must hold your head high and behave like a queen.'

'That is ridiculous! How can I show them the love of Christ if I place myself above them? No. If I have to, I will walk with them.' Varun gave me his now-familiar exasperated look. 'You cannot change the culture, honey. This is my India. I know my people and trust me, you don't want to be considered equal to them. You must maintain a distance or you will find yourself in trouble.'

Over the next few weeks I began to understand what Varun had said. No matter what I did, I could not be real friends with the women, because their conditioning didn't allow it. It made me sad and dashed my visions of a women's fellowship. Though I knew it was possible, somehow, I realized that the very fact that I had white skin, that I was a foreigner, put a barrier up between me and them. I realized that no matter how much I dressed like them, or how many years I lived among them, I would always be looked upon as 'the foreigner woman.' I also began to understand why indigenous pastors were much more effective, in the long term, to leading people to Christ.

So where did I fit in? How could I be the most effective? I prayed often about this over the next few weeks.

∽

It was Peter who, in his broken English, enlightened me about the history of white Christians coming to India and his own tragic story.

It all began when I asked him if he had ever been in love. I watched as his eyes drifted into a memory of a time long ago, a wistful smile on his face.

He told me that there was a time in his life when he became aware of Jesus. He decided that he wanted to learn about Christ. There was an advertisement about a new Christian ministry in Kolkata. A group of American evangelists were coming to teach people about Christ and how to preach. To him this was an answer to his prayers and with great difficulty he raised some money, went to Kolkata and joined up with this new school of evangelism. It was there that he met a girl who was equally eager to learn to teach others about Christ.

They all slept in the same building and ate together and listened eagerly to their teachers. After about a month, he and this girl had fallen in love. They went everywhere together. Then the day came when the American evangelists told the students that it was time for them to go out in the streets and preach. They were sent out in groups of four and assigned street corners.

Peter, his girlfriend and two other young men began to approach people, handing out tracts and declaring the love of Christ. One of the young men was very excited and full of enthusiasm, approaching everyone who passed by. He came upon a man who pushed him away and told him to leave him alone. But this young man kept talking about Christ and pushing the tract at him. Peter and his girlfriend stood just a few feet away.

Soon other men came up and started shouting at this young man and some punches were thrown. Violence broke out and a policeman arrived on the scene to break it up. Suddenly a shot rang out, the bullet hitting Peter in his knee. He fell and shouted at his girlfriend to run fast as he writhed in pain on the ground.

Peter's eyes filled with tears as he told me this and what happened afterwards. He was taken to a government hospital where surgery was performed on his knee. Luckily the bones were intact, so only soft tissue surgery was required. But he lay in the hospital for a month in recovery. A few of his fellow students came to visit but he never saw his girlfriend again. In addition, the school of evangelism had promised the students graduation certificates and referrals to churches in their communities to preach the gospel. But one day the Americans simply left and the school was closed, leaving the students empty-handed and minus their tuition fees. The love of his life had been taken away to her village and quickly married. Peter came back to his village broken-hearted and bitter. He never again picked up his Bible or prayed until the day we started our Bible study.

Peter told me that foreign missionaries and so-called evangelists had often come to churches in India. They took pictures and preached for a few weeks, and then they left. They didn't understand that they left people alone and that many who had turned to Christ after listening to them, were beaten or even killed for leaving their family's religion when they returned home. Some struggled with their Bibles alone for a while, but eventually gave up on their faith. Some, very few, found a local church and continued in their faith.

'Then why do the local churches allow this to happen?' I asked.

'Because foreigners always bring money and donate to the churches,' Peter said. 'We are poor. No money without foreigners.'

My heart was filled with sadness as I heard Peter's story. I was also filled with anger at the stupidity of these Americans. Preaching and trying to convert people on the streets is strictly forbidden in India. They didn't do their research or they would have known that sending these students out on the streets was illegal and dangerous. I suspect that they were driven out of India by the authorities.

'Peter,' I said, 'I am so sorry that this happened to you. But Jesus didn't abandon you. God sent me here to show you this, I am sure of it! Each one of us is here for a purpose, to build that church in Jhalda and to make a difference in each other's lives. Do you believe this?'

'You already make a difference,' he said quietly. 'Now I read Bible and pray again. Now I believe.'

∼

Over the many conversations that the men and I had, I came to know that there were three main churches in Purulia. These were the Catholics, the GEL or German Lutheran, and the CNI or Church of Northern India. While there were small groups of other denominations in the area, these by and large kept to themselves.

All of these churches were established by missionaries in the past century.

Because of the strict laws against conversion or proselytization in India, there was a time when many lost their lives and were martyred for their faith. This still happens today in some states.

In order to reduce the tension between the Christians and the Hindus, the churches often met together with government officials to set some standards and arrive at a mutual understanding of the laws. This did help to some extent and the incidents of violence against the Christians decreased.

While this was well and good, what happened was that these churches, at one with the system, became powerful and in control over vast areas.

I now realized why, when they were told that this American woman was building a church, they felt I was invading their territory and felt threatened by my presence there. In addition, there were those who had come to me with offers to join their pet causes within the churches. I had rejected all of them, choosing to build the church instead.

I unintentionally offended all of them. As a result, they kept a close eye on us and our activities. I began to feel like we were the 'hole in the wall gang'!

My visits to these churches showed me that their worship was similar to the Episcopalian church I had once attended, with the repeating of prayers and conservative music. I soon also learned that they had taken the Ten Commandments and added a few hundred more rules to them. Christians in this area were kept under tight control just like the Pharisees in Jesus' time. Not a marriage, death or birth happened without following the rituals and rules prescribed by the church.

Probably, these rules were necessary a hundred years ago, in a country full of ritualism. Converts, who left Hinduism or the Muslim faith, were raised with many rules and rituals, so maintaining strict rituals as Christians was easy and natural for them.

But, it was obvious to me that Jesus, the real Jesus that I had come to know and love, was not present. What was present was the old teachings of the old school of missionaries, the kind that puts a heavy burden of guilt on all believers without the grace and mercy of Christ. How I wanted to show the other Jesus to them! Varun and I talked about this quite a lot, even before I came to India. I remember him saying, 'Forget about evangelizing. What is really needed is to show the existing Christians the love and forgiveness of Jesus, without all the rules that oppress them.'

20. The 'Other' Wife

Varun's and my lives slowly slipped into a routine. I had become accustomed to the heat and the frequent power outages. While he worked and ran errands for his parents, I would work out at the gym and prepare for our next Bible class, as well as make frequent trips to town. I was again a 'regular' at the Akash hotel for breakfast or a cold drink. It was the only decent restaurant in Purulia and it was air-conditioned. The hotel where we lived was owned by the same family, so they got to know us quite well.

A situation had arisen though that we found difficult to navigate. Sharing a house together hadn't aroused any suspicions in my first year, but when I returned the second year and Varun and I took up residence in the hotel, people began to talk. Soon the whispers made their way back to Varun's parents. While we hoped no one would notice, it was obvious that we were sharing the same room and the same bed. Something was bound to happen...and it did.

One day Varun came home with a serious look on his face. 'I don't know what to do,' he said. 'You are not going to like this, but my mom and dad have chosen a wife for me.' I looked at him speechlessly.

He knew that I didn't like keeping our marriage a secret.

We had argued about it many times in the past—I wanted him to tell his parents the truth but he would say each time, 'Not now, trust me.' The fact was, I *didn't* trust him on this subject and I felt that it was because he was embarrassed of me and our age difference. He always denied it and told me it was not time yet, that was all. This always followed with lots of affection to reassure me of his love.

But it always played on my mind as I waited for him to have the courage to tell his parents. I hoped now that this sudden turn of events would push him into confronting them with the truth. Varun continued, 'They want to take a trip to Bankura to meet her and her family.' I was still silent. He struggled to say what he had to next, pacing up and down the room. 'Ummm, dad wants you to come along and take pictures.'

'What?' I was incredulous. 'You've got to be kidding me!' Varun sat down beside me on the hotel bed. 'Honey, I can't refuse to meet her. It would make the girl look bad and cause all kinds of problems for her. Dad wants you to come along too, so you can give him your opinion of her.' I sat quietly, staring at him. He went on. 'Look, after we meet her, I will tell mom and dad that I am not ready for marriage. The girl can then go ahead and marry someone else.'

'Do you realize what you are asking me to do?' I said, looking directly into his eyes. 'To act like it doesn't matter to me when your parents show me your chosen wife?'

'I know, it will be difficult,' he said soothingly. 'But with you there I can be stronger and my parents will be happy too. You are my beautiful wife and one day they will know this, but for now we have to play this game. Please, do this for me.' I gave in and reluctantly agreed.

We left early on a Saturday morning. Varun's mother sat

in the back seat between Varun and I, while his dad rode up front for the two-hour journey. I kept telling myself that all this didn't matter, that I was his real wife and one day they would know this. It was important to me that they accepted me. I was as charming as I could be, hoping that they wouldn't see my nervousness.

We stopped at a roadside hotel for breakfast and a short while later, we reached Bankura. It was a small but well-kept house. As we walked up to the entrance, the family was waiting for us. The younger children bent down and respectfully touched our feet as we entered.

We were all escorted into a small living room with a couch and several chairs. So far, I hadn't seen the girl who was chosen to be my husband's bride. We all sat and made polite small talk. I decided to get my camera out and go search for the girl. I found her and her mother in the kitchen, preparing tea. I was surprised at how young she was. She looked like she could be Varun's sister, with the same round face and big eyes. I began to take pictures as if I was a professional photographer.

I went back to the living room and sat down as the tea was served by the chosen bride. She was nervous and very quiet, sneaking glances at Varun. All the while, the parents were watching for some spark in Varun's eyes, a hint that all was going as planned. That never happened. Varun remained polite, but distant. Since the conversation was in Bengali, all I could do was guess what was being said. By now I had learned to read gestures and facial expressions, rather than try to understand the words. It was obvious that they were having a serious discussion without consulting Varun. He sat there nervously shifting in his chair.

I decided to take more pictures, this time of the younger

children. For a moment, I was overcome by jealousy, not of the young girl, but of her being accepted as a potential bride for my husband. I knew that Varun's parents were sending me a loud message that I was not acceptable. I went outside fighting tears, all the while taking pictures of anything and everything.

What did you expect anyway? I asked myself, God didn't bring you here because it would be easy. God didn't bring Varun and you together because it was normal...it isn't normal at all, not by the world's standards, especially this world, but it was God's plan!

The tea had disappeared when I made my way back into the house, and was replaced with sodas or what they called 'cold drinks.' I never drank sodas, but I sat down and sipped politely as the conversation ended. I had never experienced such relief when we rose to leave. It was over!

The ride back was quiet and uneventful. We rode into the sunset and watched as the darkness enveloped the world. I was dropped off at the hotel while Varun and his parents went home to discuss the day's events. How I wished I could have been a fly on the wall that understood Bengali!

I settled into the room and opened my Bible, hoping for some words of encouragement. Though I didn't find that, I found peace as I read the gospel of John. Then I prayed, asking God to give my husband courage and wisdom during this night and the days that followed.

Varun was true to his word. He told his parents that he just wasn't ready for marriage yet, to give him a few more years. They weren't at all happy, but at least the pressure of them pushing him to get married stopped. But again I was disappointed that our truth didn't come out. I was sure that, with all the work we were doing for the Lord, they would see that this was a union of God, and would gradually come to accept me as family. How naive I was!

∼

Varun and I had agreed that we wouldn't talk about our pasts. After all we were new creatures in Christ and therefore washed clean of everything that once was. Becoming a new creature is not easy, neither is avoiding the past.

I knew that Varun had been in a very dark place. He was haunted by things that had happened, things he had done. He had told me bits and pieces of his story when we used to chat on the Net but living with him was quite different. He was convinced that he was no good. He told me that he sometimes went crazy and became violent. Though I never saw this part of him, I did see the potential for it and prayed for him constantly.

Varun did start going out less often and drinking less, but if he completely stopped going out with the guys, they would talk and ridicule him. Fortunately our Bible studies seemed to have an impact on them as well and they started following Varun's lead and drinking less too.

But this was puja season, and the biggest puja of the year, Durga Puja, was round the corner. To try to ignore this holiday would be like trying to ignore Christmas in the US. Add fireworks, music blaring from loudspeakers and brass bands to the mix and the picture would be complete. Everyone was in a festive mood. The marketplace was crowded with shoppers buying new clothes and gifts for their families.

Massive silk tents, resembling colorful castles, were erected in every village. Inside the tents were intricately carved statues of gods and goddesses. People came to Purulia from distant villages to celebrate this holiday—and the next one,

Diwali, the 'Festival of Lights' when every home was strung with lights and those tent-castles were beautifully lit up. People walked across the town with their families to visit one another.

In my first year in Purulia, I was escorted around the town on a rickshaw to see these celebrations. I marveled at the artistry of the statues of the gods. No one really explained the stories to me, but from what I saw, it reminded me somewhat of the Greek myths and their gods, perhaps with an elephant and monkey god thrown in. I vowed to one day learn more about them and this religion. I greatly admired their dedication to their faith, something I saw less of back in my own country.

This was the time of year when it was difficult to be a Christian, and have all your Hindu friends celebrating the pujas. For Varun and the men, this was a temptation never resisted and they joined in wholeheartedly. Though I tried to keep up our Bible study through the puja season, I knew that the lure of the festivities was stronger than my lectures.

I also came to expect many evenings alone during this period. In my second year in Purulia, Varun was teaching a computer class at night at Durga Puja time, and I was pretty sure that afterwards he would meet up with the men, so I didn't expect him home till the wee hours.

But one night, as I lay on the bed watching TV, a feeling of impending danger came over me. I had no idea why, but I knew that this was a warning from God. I quickly turned off the TV and began to pray. 'Lord be with me tonight. Send your angels down to cover me with your protection.' Then I added, 'I praise you Lord for also protecting Varun wherever he is. Fill him with your peace and joy. Guide him with your love.' Then I opened up my Bible to Psalms and as I began to read, I felt comforted and protected.

About half an hour later, I was startled by a loud banging on the door and Varun's voice yelling, 'Open up, dammit!' As I jumped up and opened the door, Varun came rushing in and slammed it shut. He stood before me with a crazed look in his eyes, his hands clenched into fists and his breathing labored. His shirt and his arms were splattered with blood. I knew immediately that the man who stood before me was not my husband...this was someone else. I backed away slowly.

'What happened?' I asked cautiously. 'Honey, are you hurt?'

'What? Me hurt?' he sneered, 'I'm the king of Purulia and no one hurts me. I hurt them!'

I stood there silent, staring in disbelief. What had happened to my husband? Who was this man standing in front of me? Then I saw it. An almost imperceptible red glow in his eyes and I knew what I was dealing with—a demon. Without doubt or hesitation I began reciting the Lord's Prayer loudly. 'Stop that nonsense!' he yelled, his hands clenched in rage. I kept reciting. Varun shoved me against the wall and clenched his hands around my throat. 'I could kill you right now. Do you know that?' he spat out with his face barely an inch from mine. His face contorted and twisted. 'You think you are so holy? Chosen by God?' he shouted.

'Varun,' I whispered, 'It's me, Janice, your wife. I love you!' I saw confusion in his eyes. His grip loosened around my neck slightly. 'I love you,' I repeated softly. A look of horror came across his face as it twitched and jerked, his mouth twisting in a snarl. His hand dropped to his side and he backed away from me. His entire body began to shake, then, with a huge sigh, he collapsed onto the bed, sobbing. I stayed against the wall, rubbing my neck.

'What just happened?' he asked me, looking up with eyes filled with tears. 'God! Did I hurt you?'

'I am fine, thanks only to God,' I told him, still trembling. 'You were taken over by a demon, a very powerful one, maybe the devil himself,' I said as I sat down beside him. 'I know that sounds crazy, but it's the truth. Now you have to tell me who's blood is all over you.'

I feared the worst, but hoped and prayed it wasn't as bad as it looked.

Varun slowly told me what happened.

He had finished his night computer class and had locked up and gone across the street to a tea shop to have a cup of tea. A young man who was obviously drunk, began exploding firecrackers near the tea shop. The owner of the tea shop asked him to leave, but the drunkard was obnoxious and just kept laughing and lighting the firecrackers. Varun said that suddenly he felt a cold chill run through him and the sound of the firecrackers drove him crazy. He got up and told the young man to do as the shop owner had asked and leave, but the drunkard cursed at him and lit another firecracker right in front of him. When it exploded, so did Varun...into a rage. 'I don't remember much,' he told me, 'except that I started hitting him and I was like in a nightmare...I couldn't stop! Blood was everywhere and I didn't care. These men came and pulled me away. Some other men picked the man up and put him in the back of a car. He-he wasn't moving... blood everywhere...Oh my God! Did I kill him?' he asked me.

'I-I don't know,' I said, looking directly into his eyes. 'But I do know that you must find out and find out now!'

'I can't do it!' he said desperately. I took a deep breath. 'Varun, call Peter and Arun and ask them to come here now. Tell them what happened and the three of you can go together. First go to that tea shop and ask. I am sure someone will know where this young man is and if he is alive.' As I said the words, I swallowed hard. My head was swimming with the terrible possibilities of what would happen, if what Varun feared became a reality. I also knew that we could not go on another hour without knowing the truth.

Peter and Arun came immediately when Varun told them briefly on the phone what had happened. Varun changed his shirt and the three of them left together out into the night.

After I closed the door, all of my strength left me and I began to cry out to God. 'Please Lord, let this young man be all right! Please don't let him be dead.'

Then, as my thoughts went back over what had just happened, I asked God. 'Please guide me. Tell me what to do? Forgive my doubts Lord, but am I supposed to be here? I don't know what to do!' In the silence of the hotel room I bowed my head. Then, the voice I had come to know so well, said, 'Just love him.'

∽

The owner of the tea shop told the men that the young man had been taken to the government hospital. They all rushed to the hospital immediately. There they found him, alive, but, of course, badly injured.

Miraculously, the family forgave Varun and the young man apologized for setting off the firecrackers and causing so much trouble. Varun visited him several times at the hospital. He swore that he would never lift a hand in anger at anyone again. As for me, I kept a close eye on any signs of demons coming back into our lives.

This incident also convinced Varun that I was right about wanting him to take medication for his ADD. Within a few days he started taking it and it made a huge difference in his behavior. He was calmer and more focused.

But there was something in my heart that began bothering me after that incident. Though I knew God had put us together for His purpose, I was not as sure that He meant for us to be married. I began doubting our marriage and indeed, if it was a legitimate marriage at all that had been performed that previous year. I had nothing to show for it, no marriage certificate or even pictures. I was told that the person who took our pictures had destroyed them for fear of reprisal if anyone discovered them.

More importantly, as the days and weeks went by, and I found myself alone most of the time, I felt abandoned and unwanted, by Varun and his friends. I prayed constantly about this, wanting to know what God was showing me. The previous year, the men surrounded us and we were like a family. This year I was in the hotel room, working out at the hotel gym and wandering the marketplace. I rarely saw anyone except the hotel owners and their family.

It was obvious that they only saw me as a source of money. The owner constantly wanted to share his desire to build a resort and the family kept bringing me gifts and inviting me to their home on the top floor of the hotel. Their children were spoiled rotten and extremely precocious.

Inside me I just wanted to get out and do God's work. The weekly Bible studies were not enough and I needed financial support to finish building the church.

One day, after doing my usual marketing, I decided to take the rickshaw to Varun's village. I discovered Varun standing around with all the men, laughing and joking. He was supposed to be at work. When he saw me, his face flushed with guilt.

'What are you doing here?' he asked aggressively, to hide his embarrassment.

'I was tired of being alone, so I thought I would come and visit with the guys.'

'You shouldn't be here,' he barked. 'Go back to the hotel and I will come later.'

'I will go where I please,' I snapped back. 'Since you don't seem to want to be with me, I will go where I am wanted.'

I told the rickshaw puller to take me to the Akash hotel, where I could sit and read the paper and eat. At least there I was always welcome and treated with respect.

Varun showed up half an hour later while I was sipping on a fresh lemon soda.

'What are you doing here?' he asked me as he sat down.

'I am enjoying myself,' I said abruptly. Silence. Shifting awkwardly in his seat, he said, 'I got off work early.'

'That's nice,' I smiled. 'Glad you were enjoying yourself.' More silence. He ordered a lemon soda for himself.

'Are we really married?' I blurted out. 'And if so, is this the way a wife is treated here, because if it is, I want no part of it or the marriage. I thought you, me and God were our family and that I took priority in your life. But I can see that you are too busy with the guys to even think about me. Nothing has changed from last time I was here. You still leave me alone...you *choose* to leave me alone!' I was growing angrier as I spoke. Varun just looked down. Then he sighed and said, 'Let's go back to our hotel and talk about this. I have something to tell you.'

I reluctantly agreed, still seething inside. But it was getting dark and time to head back to the hotel.

Once we were in our room Varun began, 'I love you very much. But there are things you don't understand about my culture.'

'Then tell me and teach me so I can understand,' I said.

'Men here don't spend time at home. It isn't natural for a man to spend too much time with his wife and family.'

'So you are worried that people will think you are strange because you spend time with me?' I asked. 'You weren't worried about what people thought when you married me,' I went on. 'Besides, staying at home for an Indian wife is fine because she speaks the language and has a home to take care of and friends to share her life with. All I do is sit around here alone day after day and I have no one but you. Surely you can understand how difficult this is for me?'

'I know…but what can I do? I don't want to raise suspicions about us.'

I boiled inside. 'If you are so afraid of people finding out then why did you marry me? How long do we have to live like this? When can we be honest and start telling people?'

'I will do it when the time is right, but not now. First we have to make our marriage legal here in India. Once that happens, then no one can deny that we are married.'

I thought about this…did I really want this marriage? Was this really God's will for us? I loved Varun very much, but I was beginning to feel more like his teacher and companion than a wife. I could see how our age difference was a huge hurdle, not only within his culture, but between us personally. In many ways he was like an unruly child to me…but other times he was very mature for his years. My heart loved him as a wife, but my mind told me that something was not right here. Doubts loomed heavily in my mind.

One of the things that was beginning to irritate me was that Varun rode around on his motorbike, often with two of the guys riding pillion, but he refused to allow me to ride with him. There were always excuses, but I knew the real reason was that he didn't want to be seen with me…not that close. Worrying about what people would think seemed to me to be the strongest concern of the society here. If I was not accepted as his wife, what did it matter? I had spent most of my adult life married and marriage was not a good experience for me, for the most part. But more than this, I knew that Varun was not ready for this kind of commitment.

∼

In spite of all my doubts, one thing was very clear; God wanted me to be here. There was the church building that we had started and the Bible studies that were so encouraging to me. I could not weaken. I had to follow the path that God was showing me. There was one other factor that kept haunting me. I had made a promise to Varun's parents that I would get him to America. We had already tried the tourist visa and failed. I knew that the only way I could get him to America was through our marriage.

∼

A new character had entered into our lives, an old friend of Varun's, Pranab. I quickly came to learn that he was completely different from the rest of our group and disliked by most of them. Though he had been raised in the same village, he was shunned because he was Brahmin and he didn't drink or smoke. In addition he had a real job of teaching history in a nearby college.

Pranab was a talkative fellow, but the problem was that his English was bad. This didn't stop him from talking rapidly to me. I tried hard to concentrate on his speech patterns, so I could understand him but this gave me a headache after just a few minutes. Often he would drift back into Bengali without realizing it, leaving me totally at sea. I had to make him slow down because his mind was going faster than his mouth!

He was doing research on religion for a thesis, so when he found out that I was a Christian, healed by God, he began calling me a guru. He asked me to teach him about Christianity. His enthusiasm was child-like and when I did read to him and talk to him about Christ, his eyes opened wide and he was full of questions.

Pranab, like so many I met, wanted to go to America. But unlike the rest, he was obsessed with America and its history. He was like a cartoon character, always dressed in brightly coloured shirts and tight pants, his hair styled in a sort of Elvis impersonation. He definitely was an absent-minded professor, in a likeable, but challenging sort of way.

He and Varun seemed to have something that connected them together that the rest of the group didn't understand and they teased Pranab relentlessly. Because of this, it didn't take long before Pranab dropped out of our Bible studies and began coming over on his own to learn. Though he had a few college degrees, his social ineptitude left him without many friends. He had learned to fit in into the academic world, but the rest of the world was a puzzle to him.

He was sincere about his spiritual journey and had a hunger to know anything that would lead him to know God. Pranab was the only person who understood my need to meditate and pray and often joined me in this. He often asked me to read the Bible to him. It may have been odd for a Hindu Brahmin and a Christian to pray together, but I knew that he believed in Jesus and was beginning to understand what Christianity meant.

The following year I brought him a 'red letter' Bible so he could easily read 'the Jesus parts' that he liked the most, but told him that the other parts were just as important and read them to him often.

It was Pranab who decided that we should get our marriage registered. He said he knew someone in that department who could help. He and Varun set to task to do whatever it took to make our marriage legal.

I was still plagued with doubts and discouragement. I found myself thinking of returning to the US. Loneliness filled my days and nights. What was I accomplishing by remaining? Varun had the best of both worlds. He could be with his friends and family and enjoy the life of living in a hotel with money in his pocket and his secret American wife. I didn't feel loved anymore, I felt used. What was I doing here?

I thought of all the other missionaries in the past who had spent years living here. They endured hardships that I could only now begin to imagine. Could I give up so easily after only the second trip here? I tried to draw strength from the day that I was healed and the command from God to go out and tell the world.

'But,' I asked God, 'am I supposed to do this as Varun's wife, or his mentor?' The answer came quickly. 'The two of you are now one.'

Somehow I felt that God was telling me that it was not His choice, but ours. Of our own free will we had chosen this path and He had blessed it, and would continue to bless it.

The next day Varun and Pranab came with papers for me to sign for the legal registration of our marriage. We had to pay the official in the registry office extra money to make sure that the recording wasn't published in the paper. I read the papers carefully in silence. I knew that this was a very important decision in our lives, one of those moments that would be reflected upon many times in the future. I wanted to express what was in my heart.

'Varun, I think we made a mistake by getting married,'

I said to him. 'I think that God wanted us to be together to do his work, but I don't think He meant for us to fall in love and get married. We did that on our own.'

'What are you saying?' Varun asked anxiously.

Pranab began speaking rapidly in his poor English. 'No, no, God wants you to be married and Varun is very brave man to marry you!'

'What is so brave about marrying me?' I asked.

'Oh, you don't know our culture,' Pranab said.

'Yes, I know,' I said, 'but the way I have been living is not the way I want to be married. This secret life is too lonely for me. I am always alone and have no one to talk to. This is not the way a marriage is supposed to be at all.'

Both the men stared at me nervously. I continued. 'But we are married in the eyes of God and we have been chosen to do His work here. There is still so much work for us to do.'

I could see relief in their eyes as I spoke. 'I will sign this paper, but I expect things to change and for our marriage not to be a secret. I don't like living a lie like this and I don't think God wants us to live this lie either.'

Varun took my hand, 'Honey, I don't like it either and believe me, soon I will shout it out to all Purulia how much I love you and that you are my wife.' He handed me a pen. The papers were signed and I was left alone again.

To my surprise, Varun and Pranab showed up an hour later. Varun gave me a plastic bag when he walked into the room. It had an ice cream and two chocolate bars inside. He stood there smiling. 'Wow! Thank you!' I said, grinning at him. 'That's not all,' he smiled, 'I have ordered your favorite dish, tandoori chicken...and this!' He pulled a bottle of whiskey out from behind his back. 'We will have dinner and drinks together tonight.' I walked over and gave him a big hug. 'I could use a drink tonight, but mostly I could use you by my side,' I said.

We had a wonderful evening, the three of us. Pranab talked on and on, as usual. He told me that the papers were accepted and we would hear from the man in the registry office in the next few days. Varun toasted, 'To the soon to be legal, Mr and Mrs Kashyap!' Then they both surprised me with a trip the next day to Jamshedpur, where we visited a few of Pranab's colleagues, went to the zoo and the park. Varun made sure that I was by his side all the time. We decided to stay overnight and booked a room in a cheap but reasonably clean hotel. The following day we headed back to Purulia, but stopped at a beautiful resort for a long lunch. Varun held my hand under the table, a gesture that was rare in public. I fell into a contented sleep with my head on Varun's lap in the back seat of the car we had hired for the trip.

Varun and I had started a habit from the first year, of me reading the Bible to him every day. He would lie down in bed, while I sat up and read to him. I had chosen 'the Living Bible' because of its modern day simple English, but I also had a King James Bible for reference and to read the old English version. I found that the Living Bible was best for our Bible study, easier for everyone to understand.

It was a special time for us and one that bonded us together. We always talked about the miracle of our love and how God had chosen us for His purpose.

'I can't imagine God choosing me,' Varun would often say. 'I am the last person He would choose!'

'God has a habit of choosing the most unlikely people for His purposes. I mean, look at the ones he chose to be his disciples,' I countered. 'If God chose me and healed me, then He certainly has brought us together and has chosen you too.'

Varun would always smile. 'You are right. He chose us.' This affirmation was important as we went through the struggles in our lives and in the ministry.

21. Blood Sacrifices

Pujas were a part of life in Purulia. I gave up trying to keep track of them the first year I spent there. After a while, they seemed to blend in with the rhythm of our lives.

But it was important to know when a puja was going to take place because the market would be closed for one or two days or more. It was late in the afternoon one day when I was told that there would be a puja the following two days. The market was closing early, so I had to rush to buy what we needed. It was around 5 p.m. when I entered the marketplace. I had my list of items and was walking along reading it when suddenly I heard a whoosh and a plop. I felt moisture on my face. I looked down at my feet and there was a goat kicking and writhing, its throat slit and blood pouring out onto the street. It made a wheezing sound as it gasped its last breath. I looked up and realized that I was standing in front of the temple. There I saw families, including children, watching a priest at the altar, slitting the throats of goats and tossing them, one by one, out into the street.

It was a gruesome sight. When I looked down at my list, it was splattered with blood. I hurried away from the scene, completely shaken. My mind kept replaying the goat, the blood, the last gasp or gurgle from his throat. The only thing

I could think of was to go to my friend who owned the corner store. I staggered there with tears in my eyes.

He was busy as usual, but when he looked up at me, he stopped everything. 'What is wrong? What is all over your face?' he said, grabbing a paper napkin and handing it to me. 'I-I was walking and this goat suddenly landed in front of me,' I said, wiping my face with the napkin. It came away covered in blood. 'Here, use this,' the shopkeeper said, handing me a wet cloth. 'This is the special puja where families offer goats for sacrifice for their sins. That is why I am a vegetarian. I hate this treatment of the animals too.' With that, he handed me an ice cream and smiled.

My nerves began to settle as I nibbled slowly on the ice cream and watched the customers ordering their goods. 'That priest cuts and throws like a maniac,' he said, as he took my blood-stained list and began taking things off the shelf. 'I am surprised the goat didn't land on top of you!' I smiled weakly. He handed me my bag of groceries. 'The ice cream is free,' he said.

'Thanks, I needed that,' I said gratefully. I paid my bill and looked around for a rickshaw, making sure that I didn't go anywhere near the temple again.

The sun was setting as I rode back to the hotel. 'Sacrifice for their sins' played upon my mind. I remembered reading in the Old Testament about the sacrifices at the temple. Never did I think about the actual act of killing the animals, the sight of the blood pouring off the altar, the sounds of the animals bleating, the smell of fresh blood and incense. Poor desperate, innocent animals lined up for the slaughter. 'Thank you Jesus,' I whispered into the warm night air, 'for being the last lamb, the last sacrifice for our sins.'

~

The time was nearing for me to go home again. My six-month visa was expiring in a few months. Part of me was ready to go back to hamburgers and modern conveniences. But the bigger part of me wanted to stay and continue the work we had begun and to be with my husband. I dreaded the long separation.

Varun and I had many discussions about my return to the US. This time our marriage was legally registered. I could apply for a spousal visa and legally change my name to his. This time he could come and join me in the US!

We talked a lot about what we would do together in the States, meeting my family, traveling to see Disneyland and Las Vegas, but mostly we talked about the many job opportunities for him, and having our own home. We also talked about sharing our testimony in churches and raising money to finish the church in Jhalda and to reopen the Leprosy Mission hospital one day.

Varun always said, 'I never really wanted to go to America like most of my friends. My parents want it, I know. But if I never go there it is fine with me.' But when we talked about it, his eyes deceived him. I knew America fascinated him.

Of course Pranab wanted to go too. He gave me his resume and begged me to find him a job at a college.

'Do you think our age difference will be a problem?' Varun asked me one day.

'Not at all,' I told him. 'The last time I was in the States, Oprah Winfrey had a special show about older women and younger men. She interviewed the men and they talked about the advantages of being with older women. It seems to be a trend there now. As a matter of fact, when I told my friends about you they gave me a high five and said "Way to go girl!"

Don't worry about us being accepted in my culture!' I would learn to eat my words later.

∽

It was never easy to think about leaving. Varun had heard that there was an easy way to extend my visa for another six months. All I had to do was leave the country for a few hours and when I came back, they would automatically extend the visa. This seemed too easy to me, so I called the US embassy to verify if it was true. The man I spoke to said yes, and that many people he knew had done this with success. He said that they went to Bangladesh or Nepal, spent a few hours there shopping and having lunch, then flew back to India. This was so encouraging for us! We immediately began pricing flights to both countries. There was some trouble and riots in Bangladesh, so Nepal was a safer destination.

In addition, there was a Leprosy Mission hospital in Kathmandu. Varun's father could arrange for us to be picked up at the airport and we could stay in one of the guesthouses at the Anandaban hospital, for free.

Making our marriage 'official' started me thinking that it would be nice to have an official honeymoon too. But our marriage was still a secret and the hospital was in direct contact with Varun's father, so it wouldn't be possible to appear as husband and wife there. The hospital was a conservative Christian-based organization with definite Indian-based standards too.

Varun and I talked at length about the situation and decided to stay a few days at the hospital and then a few days in the city alone. At least in the city we could behave as husband and wife. Even if it might shock some of the locals, I felt confident that we would be accepted as a couple. If all went well, it would be the first time that we could live in the open as a married couple.

Though I had heard of Kathmandu, I had no idea what it would be like. I heard that there were lots of tourists, many hotels, and shopping. After living so isolatedly, this sounded like heaven to me. I had visions of a romantic few days together, introducing my husband to romance and a taste of foreign food and lifestyle.

We looked up hotels and their prices online. We decided on the Kathmandu Guesthouse, since it was well-known and centrally located in Thamel, the tourist area of Kathmandu. I could hardly wait to get there. In addition, Varun had never flown in a plane before. This would be a good first-time experience for him, a sort of run-up to his long flight to America one day.

All the arrangements were made. We scheduled our trip ten days before my Indian visa expired. We both felt confident that this was an answer to our prayers. I watched Varun closely as the plane taxied and lifted off in Kolkata. He did his best to hide any anxiety, but I knew he was both excited and a little scared. It was a direct flight lasting an hour and fifteen minutes. They served us lunch and by the time we finished eating, it was time to land. I felt good that Varun's maiden flight and our first flight together had gone so smoothly.

The plane landed on the tarmac. We had to walk some distance into the old terminal and I needed to get a visa. Varun, as an Indian national, didn't need one. There were forms to fill out, I needed a photo taken and they wouldn't accept Indian rupees for payment, so I had to find the money exchange booth to get some US dollars. An hour later, we finally made our way out of the terminal. We found a man standing there with a sign with Varun's name on it. He loaded our luggage in a large van with 'The Leprosy Mission Hospital' written on the side, and we set off.

As we rode through the city, I was a bit shocked at the pollution and the filth. Trucks and buses were spewing black smoke everywhere. Most of the vehicles were motorbikes and I felt sorry for the riders, some of them children, who were inhaling the black fumes directly. The roads were in terrible condition, with a lot of construction tearing up the highways and slowing down the traffic. I was also surprised at the height of the buildings. It seemed that the buildings were trying to rise above the noise and pollution below.

Then we turned off the crowded highway and began to ascend slowly up into the hills. What a different scenery we encountered then! Quaint Nepali villages nestled in the hills with small shops and people dressed in traditional clothing. Corn cobs hung on many roofs and doorways. Some homes had a thatched roof and some clay tiles.

There was a manmade pond at each village and the familiar Hindu temple nearby. I watched women bathing, children and dogs playing and in some shops, rugs being made with looms. They were much like the Indian villages in many ways, but there was one thing that was different. At first I couldn't put my finger on it. I watched more closely for several miles. Then suddenly I realized what it was…smiles! Not only smiles, but nods and winks and waves. The people were smiling and laughing and talking animatedly to each other. Not only that, but when we stopped in traffic, they were responding to my own smiles! I honestly didn't realize how much I had missed this small but significant part of my own life and my own people. I watched more intently. The dogs were a very different sort of breed from the Indian ones, some short-legged and some big, black, long-haired and majestic. Some wore collars and were playing happily with the children. Some were in a very sorry state, but not at all in the numbers I'd seen everywhere in India. It was obvious that this was a very different people and a very different culture. I wanted, no, hungered to know more.

We kept climbing. The paved road ended and a rough dirt road began. The air was thick with the smell of the pine trees that now shadowed the road and filled the landscape around us. Majestic views of sunlit valleys peppered with villages and rice paddy fields spread out below like a fairytale painting.

Local villagers were hiking along the road with baskets on their backs held with straps around their heads. It seemed like we had driven through a time warp into the eighteenth century.

The Leprosy Mission hospital finally came into view above us, sitting on the top of a mountain. The landscape and the buildings reminded me of my childhood summer camps, but the atmosphere reflected the serious work and history of Anandaban hospital.

The van came to a stop and we were escorted down a path to a group of guesthouses. It was set up like a hotel with a common living room and kitchen area. We went up a flight of stairs to a section of rooms. Our escort designated a room for Varun and another one for me. My heart sank. But I knew that this was how it must be. The room chosen for me had twin beds. I looked at Varun expectantly. To my surprise, he went to the man and began to speak to him in Hindi. There was irritation in their voices with lots of hand gestures. I busied myself with my suitcase, trying to appear nonchalant. Varun returned smiling. 'We are staying together in this room,' he declared. 'There is no way I am going to sleep without you.'

'What will they think?' I asked apprehensively. 'Won't they report to your family that we shared the same room?' Varun shrugged. 'I don't care what they report. You are my wife and it is about time they accept it.' I couldn't believe what I was hearing, and my heart burst with happiness. He closed the door and gave me a long embrace. 'This is just the beginning,' he whispered.

We were told that we would be called for supper in a few hours and that there were several foreign doctors and volunteers staying with us. We had some free time to wander around the grounds. We both wanted to have a cigarette and we knew that no one here smoked, or approved of it, so we wandered into a patch of trees and lit up. I was beginning to feel like a fugitive, staying in the same room together, smoking and plotting for our first chance to escape to the city to have our honeymoon.

But at the same time, I wanted to know more about the hospital, about leprosy and to meet the people who worked directly with the patients. I asked Varun why the hospital was so high up and almost inaccessible to the patients. He explained that when the organization first came to Nepal, the king was in power. The king believed that leprosy was a curse and though he wanted to help those afflicted, he was worried that his kingdom would be cursed. So he donated this land, high upon the mountains, for this purpose.

I marveled at the dedication of those who first came and struggled to create the hospital in such isolated conditions. Beautiful though it was, it was also rugged. I had so many questions in my mind, like how did they get electricity here, not to mention building materials and medical equipment? Yet the hospital was here, a reflection of years of missionaries' and volunteers' determination and fortitude...and the work of God. Tonight we would meet the doctors and volunteers who carried on the work of those early missionaries. I was looking forward to the evening.

We all ate at a dining table next to the kitchen. There was an elderly British gentleman who told us that he had been coming to the hospital for years, as a volunteer. He was a devout Christian with a strong belief in traditional Christian practices, and spoke all evening about his contempt for some of the newfangled forms that had come up. I nodded politely, but was more interested in the doctors and their families who lived there.

After dinner we all moved into the living room. The children played as the adults had tea, coffee and conversation. The lead topic of conversation was about them all having to leave Nepal. It seemed that the government would not renew their long-term visas as they had in the past. After several years of living and serving at the hospital, they were being forced to leave. They lamented that when the king was still in control, this problem never existed for medical volunteers, but since the new Maoist regime, they were demanding more money from foreigners and creating more obstacles to get a visa.

I thought it strange that a country in such great need of medical services would create obstacles for doctors who wanted to work there. It would make more sense to welcome them into the country for free! But I knew my knowledge of the situation was limited, so I listened in silence.

When we all said our goodnights, we discovered that the British gentleman who had chatted with us earlier had a room across the hall from ours and we shared the same bathroom. When he saw that Varun and I were sharing a room, his eyebrows rose in surprise, then he turned and went quickly into his room and shut the door, mumbling something under his breath. Varun and I smiled at each other and shut the door.

~

The next day we were up bright and early for breakfast and were told that the director wanted to meet us. He had known Varun's father for a long time and hadn't seen Varun since he was a boy.

After breakfast we hiked up the steep hill to the director's office. My legs felt like lead weights as I climbed up the hill, huffing and puffing.

The director was very courteous and was gracious enough to give us a history and tour of the hospital. He explained the medicines used to fight leprosy and pointed quite a way down the hill to the buildings where the surgeries were performed and where the rehabilitation center was. We both declined to take the trip down there.

We were impatient to get back to the city to be alone together. Fortunately there was a van leaving to drop the children to their schools in the outskirts of the city. It was a great opportunity to see the sights along the way and locate the hotel where we intended to stay our last few nights in Kathmandu.

The van lumbered down the hill full of children, stopping several times to drop them off at their various schools. I watched Varun interact with them so naturally. He seemed to be in a different world when surrounded by kids. This was a part of him I had not seen before and it made me happy.

After the children were all dropped off, the driver asked us where we wanted to be taken. We had no clue, but mentioned the Kathmandu Guesthouse in Thamel. He knew where it was, but suggested that he drop us off at Durbar Square. So we got off at Durbar Square and the driver set a time to pick us up in a few hours.

We were instructed to go to a small booth and pay for my entrance into Durbar Square. Varun, as an Indian, didn't have to pay.

As we walked into the square, I was mesmerized by the ancient buildings and the architecture. We were told it was a national holiday that was celebrated in the square and that we should be careful as there had been bomb threats. As we walked, I noticed armed men posted on the rooftops. They seemed so out of place with the serenity of the temples and the many tourists and locals strolling around. One part of the square was lined with stalls selling trinkets and carvings. We wandered through it, looking at all the handcrafted items and discovered the Tibetan 'singing bowls'. These were made of brass and had a tool that, when rubbed around the edge of the bowl, would make a sound. It reminded me of when I was a child, and we would wet the edge of a wine glass and rub it around with our fingers to emit a very similar sound.

We were getting hungry and looked for a place to eat. I spotted colorful umbrellas on a rooftop where people were looking out over the square. It took us a few minutes to locate the small entrance to the restaurant and then several minutes to climb the many stories to the rooftop.

We were seated under one of the umbrellas with a perfect view of not only the square, but the snow-covered peaks of the Himalayas. The sky was dotted with billowy white clouds that floated over the surrounding hills and valleys. In the distance was one hill that stood out with a huge Buddhist temple perched on the top.

We ordered a bottle of the house wine and a wild boar lunch for each of us. The moment was magical, romantic and what I knew in my heart would be a memory that would never leave us. I was suddenly struck by the reality that I was actually there, gazing out over ancient history, the Himalayas, and sitting on the rooftop in the country of Nepal! Never in my wildest imagination did I think that I would one day be doing this. 'If only my family could see me now,' I said out loud. 'They wouldn't believe it.' Varun smiled. 'I know, it is amazing isn't it?' We were both lost in the moment, enjoying each other and the wine and lunch. Time seemed to slow down as our minds mellowed with the effects of the wine and the ambience.

Suddenly we realized that we were almost alone on the rooftop except for one man in military camouflage, carrying a rifle, standing at the corner. I glanced around and noticed that the rooftop across from us also had two armed men seemingly on alert for trouble.

'I guess we had better go,' Varun said. 'I want to buy a few things before we head back up the mountain.' The magical moment was gone as we paid the bill and climbed slowly back down the winding stairs and out into the square.

We made our way back outside the square and into the busy shopping area where we were first dropped off. Varun walked purposefully along the many shops until we finally went inside one. He purchased a small bottle of whiskey and winked at me. 'For tonight, when we are alone.' Still feeling a little mellow from the wine, I smiled and winked back. Something to look forward to on the mountain top. Was this the beginning of the honeymoon I so wanted us to experience?

The trip back up the mountain was the same as the one down, except in reverse. We stopped at the many schools and picked up the children. Again, Varun seemed to be in his element around them and the children liked him too.

My mind was envisioning the romantic possibilities of the evening ahead, as well as the next few days at the Kathmandu Guesthouse alone together. I wanted to show Varun what a real honeymoon was like and today was just a taste of it all.

Our dinner and conversation that evening lasted longer than either of us had planned on, and it was late by the time we made our way into the room. There were some comments about us sharing the same room, but Varun cleverly explained that I sometimes walked in my sleep and he was there to protect me from hurting myself. I almost laughed out loud because he was the one who often walked in his sleep!

But the reality of our age difference was always there, haunting us. Once again I wondered why it was so easy to accept an older man and younger woman together, but not the reverse? Weren't we allowed to be in love too? And I was so much in love with him.

∼

The following morning we said goodbye to the people and the staff at the leprosy hospital and headed back down the mountain. This time it was a school holiday, so we were the only passengers in the van. We were able to enjoy the scenery and take some pictures. But we were both anxious to get to the hotel and freedom from judgemental eyes. We would be alone and in a place where, hopefully, our relationship would be accepted. After all, with so many foreigners, the hotel staff shouldn't be so surprised to see us as a married couple.

When we reached the Kathmandu Guesthouse and alighted from the van, someone from the hotel immediately came and took our luggage to the front desk. We walked past a restaurant as we entered the hotel lobby. There was no trouble registering, though we had two different surnames in our passports. I told the check-in clerk that we were on our honeymoon. This seemed to embarrass Varun a lot, which upset me. When we got to our room, I was still upset but decided to let it go for the evening and see if I couldn't get a better room in the morning. Varun felt it was fine, but I was determined to have the perfect room with a view of the garden.

I was in my element among the other foreign guests in the hotel. I didn't realize how intimidating it all was to Varun. In addition, this was the first time we were 'coming out of the closet' as husband and wife. While I knew it would be a little awkward at first, I also knew it wouldn't be the huge deal that it was back in Purulia. It was important to me that he realized this and hopefully relaxed in our new 'openness'.

We spent a few hours alone, enjoying our privacy in the room, then showered and dressed for dinner.

We went directly to the restaurant at the hotel. We chose a table off to the side and next to the bar. The prices were a bit shocking, but we had already agreed that this was a very special moment for us. We ordered a drink and watched the many other white people coming in and seating themselves at the tables. Varun still seemed a little awkward. I tried to reassure him that he was doing just fine and to relax. We finally ordered our dinner and another drink. It was a quiet and beautiful evening. The drinks were beginning to mellow us and we settled into the comfortable atmosphere.

We were enjoying a conversation with a couple nearby when our food order arrived. Or I should say, we heard it coming before it arrived. Varun had ordered the sizzler chicken, and it sizzled all across the dining room making people turn their heads and watch as, much to Varun's surprise, it was set in front of him. His eyes widened as they set the plate and the accompanying utensils in front of him. My order was a much quieter one of fish and chips.

Everyone was smiling as the plate continued to sizzle in front of us. Varun sat there frozen and pale. This was just too much attention and too much for him to take in. He refused to eat.

I felt very badly. This was his first experience eating a dish he had never had, in a setting surrounded by white people, and not knowing how to eat it. I gently tried to reassure him and help him as discreetly as possible. He ate the vegetables, but wouldn't touch the chicken. He ordered another drink. I ate quickly and in silence. It suddenly dawned on me that in India, Varun always had a habit of closing doors and curtains before eating. I thought this was a strange quirk, but at this moment, it became glaringly obvious that he didn't like to eat in front of people. He always preferred to order food and bring it home rather than eat at the local restaurants.

How insensitive of me not to understand the position he was in now. It was the same feeling that I had when I had to eat with my hands in India. Though Varun knew how to use a fork and spoon, he was more comfortable eating the way he was raised. This sizzler chicken was like nothing he had seen before. I called the waiter over and told him to pack the chicken, and then I ordered a side of French fries for a snack. Varun never ordered sizzler chicken or anything sizzler again in all the years ahead. That night we enjoyed the French fries and he ate the chicken later in our room.

The next day we woke up ready to explore Kathmandu, or at least this part called Thamel. I was able to change our room to one that overlooked the garden. I was also pleased that everyone at the hotel greeted us as Mr and Mrs Kashyap without hesitation or adverse reactions, just smiles. We were tourists like all the other tourists wandering the streets. We walked along buying things, a few shirts for Varun and a Nepali purse for me. We had pizza and beer at the Roadhouse Café and spent the early evening out in the garden at the hotel, taking pictures. Our hearts were full of love and optimism. We were excited about my visa being renewed for another six months and talked about the things we wanted to do in the ministry when we got back to India.

Our flight back was in the morning, so we wanted to enjoy every moment together while we could. We stayed out in the garden and ate a steak dinner, which didn't sizzle. The evening sky sparkled with the promises of a bright future ahead.

The next morning, as we were checking out of the hotel, the staff informed us that a strike and protest rally had been called. All traffic had been halted. Our flight was leaving at eleven. We had to get to the airport somehow.

After a lot of searching and running around, we were able to find a taxi driver willing to get us to the airport.

We had barely left the hotel when the traffic was stopped by two truckloads of angry protesters, shouting slogans and waving flags, loudspeakers blaring. We could see that the police had gotten into an encounter with the protestors and watched in alarm as it began to escalate into violence.

Our taxi driver shouted something at the car behind us, which slowly backed up a few feet. Suddenly our taxi turned down a narrow alley full of small shops and carts selling goods. We held on for dear life as our driver twisted and turned down many alleyways and back streets for what seemed like an eternity, until we finally broke out onto an open road. I was impressed with the courage and the skills of the driver as he sped along the almost empty road dodging barricades and more protesters. However, when we got to the airport, we discovered that it had been forced to close. There would be no more flights that day.

What could we do? We were stuck another night in Kathmandu, and we had already checked out of the hotel. The driver suggested a hotel near the airport that was known as an 'Indian' hotel. We knew he didn't want to take the risk of going back in the direction we had come from, and frankly, neither did we. So we reluctantly decided to take a look at this other hotel.

From the minute we walked in, I could smell Indian oils and spices and everyone in the restaurant and lobby was dressed in Indian attire.

Varun spoke to the man at the front desk in Hindi and we were taken up several flights of stairs to see the room. I was not impressed with the condition of the room and even less impressed with the open doors we passed which gave us glimpses of families sitting on the floor, eating. The food smells seemed to permeate through the walls.

I looked at Varun pleadingly and shook my head. We politely said no thanks and went out to the waiting taxi. 'Let's just go back to the Kathmandu Guesthouse,' I said. 'I know it will be difficult to get back there, but it will be the best and safest place for us to be.'

'You're right, but I don't think this driver is willing to take us back there after what we just went through. He wants to show us some other hotel possibilities,' Varun said. Five hotels later, each one more dismal than the last, I insisted that we return to Thamel. When Varun told the driver, he mumbled under his breath but to our relief, turned and headed back to Thamel. Fortunately the protestors had moved on and we were able to reach the guesthouse without incident. We were so relieved! The driver was paid an exorbitant amount without argument and we wheeled our luggage back to the lobby.

The travel agency outside the hotel told us that there were only three flights per week leaving for Kolkata. Our next flight was two days later. My Nepal visa had expired and I would have to pay, not only for another visa, but penalties for overstaying. All of this was an unexpected expense but fortunately I had my credit cards set aside for emergencies. This was definitely an emergency situation. But there was little cash left for eating and other expenses for two more days.

In addition, my Indian visa would expire in four days, which meant I had to re-enter India and get it renewed.

We checked back into the hotel, able to get our old room overlooking the garden, but our spirits were down. This new turn of events left us in a totally different situation.

We sat despondently in our room. Trying to sound upbeat, I said, 'We can go to the market and get food to eat in our room or sit in the garden and have a picnic.' Varun took a minute to respond. Finally he said, 'Honey, everything is closed for the strike. We have no choice but to eat at the hotel and their prices are outrageous.' I thought for a minute. 'Okay,' I said. 'I have this one credit card I haven't used for a while, but I need to call them to make sure it is still active. If it is, it will get us through the next few days.'

Fortunately, the card was active and I informed them that we were in Nepal and would be using the card here and in India. We assured each other that this was all worth it for getting my new Indian visa.

The Leprosy Mission hospital director called to check on us. They had heard of some bombings near Thamel and warned us not to leave the area. They figured that we had missed our flight and offered us any assistance we might need.

We knew there was nothing they could do from up on that mountain, but were grateful for their concern and their offer.

The following day everything was back to normal. The streets were busy again and everyone was in the 'business as usual' mode.

Varun and I decided to walk back to Durbar Square and enjoy another meal on the rooftop. I was glad we did. The weather had warmed up and the walk was longer than we expected, but it was interesting to see how the local people spent their lives. Once again, I felt happy to see the smiles and children playing and the sheer friendliness of the people. I was also happy to be able to walk down the street without eyes staring at me, and to be able to sit somewhere without a crowd gathering around me. These people were used to foreigners. I loved that I blended in with all the others.

I hadn't realized how much this had affected my life in India until now. I had been carrying the tension of constantly being watched as an outsider and a sort of unwanted celebrity status simply because of my skin color and the fact that I came from America. Here there were many white people from all over the world. I was not alone…I liked that very much!

We ate at the same rooftop restaurant and ordered the same wine and wild boar. But this time the mood was different. That sudden strike had hit us so unexpectedly. But there was something else I was feeling. A change had happened in the direction of our lives. It wasn't just the strike. I tried to shake off the sense of foreboding I felt.

We continued to talk of future plans and make light of it all, but the wine that tasted so good a few days before, now seemed tart. The wild boar was overcooked and chewy. Yes, things had changed direction.

I silently prayed for God to show me what was happening.

Though this trip had broken my normal routine of praying and scripture reading, I felt sure that God understood and was with us throughout our days there. As we left the restaurant and were walking along the square, I felt as if someone was calling me. My mood had changed to one of wonder and peace, as I smiled at those passing by. I heard the beckoning again, inside me, and looked around, for what, I don't know. Suddenly I caught a glimpse of an old sadhu sitting on the steps of a temple. Our eyes locked and we recognized each other as if we were old friends. He smiled knowingly and nodded, nothing more, just a few seconds and a glance. I smiled back and silently said, 'Thank you.' He waved his hand and shook his head as if to say, 'It is nothing.' It was strange that I didn't feel the least bit surprised or amazed at this brief encounter. I felt peaceful and somehow reassured as Varun and I walked on. No one else witnessed this, but the wonder of that moment stayed with me over the years. Who was that? What exactly happened? As I write this, I want to go back to that place in time and experience it again, a truly mysterious moment in my life.

Our last day in Kathmandu passed slowly, but finally the time came for us to catch the flight back to India. At the airport there were additional taxes to pay and forms to fill out as we went through customs. Then there were security checks both at the airport and before boarding the plane. All of this made me anxious and I could tell Varun was tense too. They served us lunch on the flight and just before landing, gave us forms to fill out. 'Now when you go through immigration, just act normal and be yourself,' Varun instructed. 'I am sure they will stamp your passport and extend your visa automatically, so you don't have to say a thing, okay?' I nodded.

This whole trip, the extra expenses, all of it, had been

done for this visa extension. My heart beat faster as we left the plane and walked towards the door marked immigration.

The line was long and full of foreigners. I watched as the immigration officers, typically unsmiling and business-like, slowly looked over each person's passport and stamped it, and waved them on. Some took longer than others. Finally it was my turn. I watched, smiling, as the man leafed through my passport and looked at my Indian visa. 'Your visa will expire in three days,' he said.

'Yes, that is why I have taken this trip, to extend my visa,' I replied. He looked up at me sternly. 'Read what it says here on your visa, madam. A tourist visa cannot be extended.' He pointed out the small print and I read it. 'But I was told by the US embassy that it could be,' I objected.

'Well, they were mistaken,' he said. 'You have only three days left in India.' With that, he stamped my passport, handed it to me and called the next person.

I stood in shock for a minute, before I was waved to move on towards the exit. Varun was waiting for me on the other side. One look at me and his smile disappeared. I went to him with tears flooding my eyes. 'He said a tourist visa cannot be extended,' I said simply and began to weep.

'Oh my God!' he said, trying to take in the situation. 'That man at the embassy lied to us.' I nodded, searching for a tissue to blow my nose. 'I can't believe that we went through all that money and time for nothing!' I sobbed, 'All our plans gone and now so little time to pack and leave.'

Our plane arrived after three in the afternoon. It was too late to catch the train to Purulia, so we had to stay the night in a hotel in Kolkata. Another expense we could barely afford. When we finally did get back to Purulia, we were broke and very despondent.

---

22. Leaving Again

There was little time to say goodbye. The news spread amongst the men and the community that I had to leave in two days. I packed my bags in a daze.

We had another goodbye party and this time Pranab was invited too. The following morning Varun, Pranab and four of the guys came with us on the train to Kolkata. My flight was the following evening, so we had to find a place to stay the night. Usually the Leprosy Mission had a guestroom available, but they were booked up. They sent us to another Christian organization, but when we arrived, they told us that we couldn't stay together. Men and women had separate quarters. That didn't suit us at all. These were my men, we were a family and we had decided that we would have a small party on my last night in India.

We found an old church in the middle of Kolkata that had spare quarters for anyone who wanted to stay. The watchman took us to the rooms. The building was ancient and the rooms smelled of insecticide. Rusted metal beds were lined up along one wall of the large room. The watchman explained that these rooms hadn't been used in a few years and that the mattresses were stored away. If we were interested in staying, he would bring the mattresses to us.

I wasn't comfortable with the idea of drinking and partying in a church. Varun reminded me that we didn't have enough money to stay in a hotel and this was our only option. 'Okay,' I relented, 'but no drinking tonight. We will just treat ourselves to a good take-out dinner and go to bed.'

When the watchman returned, Varun asked him for a separate room for the two of us. He looked at me, and then looked at Varun. We knew this look very well. I was older and he was younger and the idea that we were actually married would never cross his mind. 'I have another room for madam,' he said curtly. We followed him to the front of the rectory. Just before the entrance to the pastor's home, there was another door to the right. He unlocked it and let us inside. It was much like the other room, only smaller, with two of the same rusty beds inside, nothing else. Again there was an odor of disinfectant or insecticide that pierced my nostrils and made me sneeze.

I looked at Varun pleadingly. 'Not here, so close to the pastor's home,' I whispered. 'I'd rather stay out in the other building with the guys.' Varun spoke to the watchman in Hindi and he left us alone. 'Honey, I know this is bad, but it is only for one night.' He gave me a quick hug. 'C'mon! Your tough! We can handle this. I will sneak in after dark and they won't even know.' I gave in. 'I guess we have no choice.'

Soon the mattresses were delivered. They were typical handmade cotton mattresses that were well-worn and thin. But worst of all, they smelled strongly of the same insecticide. We were told that they were sprayed with this to prevent bed lice or ticks. Great, I thought to myself, we may not have lice or ticks, but we will die from the strong chemicals saturated in these mattresses! This was not the way I wanted to spend my last night with my husband.

Then things got worse. The pastor of the church paid us a visit. He was a stern, unsmiling man. It was obvious that he didn't think too highly of the men and gave them a list of rules to abide by. We were told that the gates closed at 9 p.m. sharp and he expected lights out by ten. Varun just smiled and nodded as the pastor went on like a drill sergeant.

When he finally left us alone, Varun and the men gathered

together to count all the money we had and left to go and buy dinner. I was left alone in the room.

Suddenly the pastor showed up at the door. His manner had completely changed. He smiled sweetly and told me that he would be up late working and I was welcome to join him later 'for a bit of wine.' I thanked him, but politely refused his invitation, telling him that I had to catch a plane in the morning.

When Varun and the men returned, Varun popped his head in the window and told me to come to the other room for dinner. When I arrived I saw one of the beds set up like a table, with my favorite food, tandoori chicken and butter naan. For themselves, the men had got rice, curry and meat, and as they ate, they chattered away in the Bengali I was now so used to hearing.

Then Arun stood up with a guilty smile and took some plastic cups out of his pocket, reached under the bed and pulled out a bottle of whiskey.

'We agreed to no drinking here,' I said sternly. 'What if we get caught? What kind of an example would we set?' Then I added, 'Where did we get the money for this anyway?'

'The guys all chipped in for it,' Varun said. 'They wanted this last party with you. Come on honey, we will be careful and quiet. It's hard on all of us to say goodbye.'

'I know,' I sighed, 'I did want a party too, like last year, but this is church grounds.'

'So we'll have a Bible study first and prayer…then drinking,' Varun grinned.

'That is not going to save us from trouble if we get caught,' I scolded half-heartedly.

So we had an impromptu Bible study and even sang some songs, loudly, for the benefit of ourselves and the night watchman walking by. Then we all sat on the floor and shared the whiskey. Between the six of us, I noted, with some satisfaction, it was exactly three small drinks each.

I talked to them again about continuing the work and the Bible studies while I was gone. 'I will be praying for all of you,' I said. 'Please remember me and remember that you have a job to do for God now. You are my disciples and chosen by God. I love all of you.' We exchanged hugs and I went back to my room.

As I reached the rectory, I noticed the pastor inside at his desk with a bottle of wine in front of him. I tiptoed quietly into the room and closed the door. The night watchman was just finishing his last rounds and locked the gate. A few minutes later Varun knocked on the open window and climbed in. We stood and held each other in a long embrace. The reality of it all coming to an end…again, filled my eyes with tears. 'I'm going to miss you so much,' I said through my tears. We sat down on the smelly bed. We talked about our plans and what I was to do when I arrived back in America. 'Remember to change your name to mine,' Varun said. 'You are a Kashyap now and you are part of a long line of warriors. Our caste is well known in India, so you should be proud to be part of our family.' He looked into my eyes, 'Honey, don't forget that God brought us together and He will not let go of us now. If we do get to America, we must still do our work here.'

Arun's face appeared in the window. 'Trouble,' he said, motioning for us to come out.

We followed him to the other room and found the pastor and the watchman standing there. The pastor looked surprised as Varun and I had obviously come out of the same room. 'I smelled smoke and came out to find these men smoking,' he thundered as the watchman looked on smugly. 'This is church property and I will not have these type of men here. You will all have to leave now.'

'Yes, I am aware of their smoking,' I said to him. 'Can we go to your house and discuss this? I understand your standards, but I would like a chance to explain, if you don't mind,' I said firmly. He looked at me and then at the guys and nodded. 'Okay, I will be in my office.'

'What are you going to tell him?' Varun asked. 'He knows my father and our church, so this will surely get back to them.'

'I'm not sure what I am going to say, but God be with me,' I said as I headed towards the rectory.

I found the pastor sitting at his desk. 'Please sit down,' he said, frowning. 'And explain to me what is going on.' I sat down and began. 'As you know, we are all from Purulia. Are you familiar with this village?'

'Yes, I have been there a few times for meetings,' he said curtly.

'Well then, you know what kind of a place it is and how desperate life is there,' I continued. 'I have been a missionary there for the past two years and I have been working with these young men. They are a bit rough around the edges, but they have shown great improvement as we have been holding Bible studies and building a church in the area. When I first came, two years ago, they were troublemakers and drunkards. Now they limit their drinking and smoking and work hard for God. I personally don't care that they smoke. What I do care about is their relationship with Jesus Christ and the changes I have seen in them.' The pastor listened quietly.

'Now tonight is our last night together. I am leaving for the US tomorrow. I have been living in Purulia for six months. These are my men and they are good men. I believe in them and what God has shown me. They wanted to be with me for this last night, but we didn't have enough funds for a hotel. You were kind enough to allow us to stay here. All I am asking of you is to understand how important it is for us to spend this last night together. We will be no further trouble and will be leaving in the morning,' I finished. There was an uncomfortable silence. Finally the pastor spoke. 'You have been living in Purulia?' he asked.

'Yes. This is my second six-month visit there,' I told him. 'It is where God has called me.'

'Not many older American women would be able to live there. It must be a calling!' He sat there studying me. 'I know Mr Kashyap's son and I know his reputation. I must say I am surprised at the change in him. You must be doing some wonderful work with these men.'

'Thank you,' I sighed, 'Lord willing there will be even more changes in them as we continue to work together. They are not perfect, but I believe they have good hearts that God is using.' The pastor stood up. 'I am honored to meet you and hear about your ministry. Of course you are all welcome to stay.' He smiled.

'Thank you very much,' I said and shook his hand. 'You are very kind.' As he walked me out of the rectory, he asked, 'What time is your flight tomorrow?'

'It is actually at one, but I need to be there by eleven,' I told him.

'Then please let me give you a tour of our church before you leave,' he offered. 'It has a good history that I think you will enjoy.' We shook hands again and I walked back to the room where the guys were sitting, waiting.

They looked at me expectantly. I smiled. 'Not only can we stay here, but he has invited us on a tour of the church tomorrow,' I grinned. 'I just told him what wonderful guys you were. 'Now behave yourselves!'

I turned to Varun and said in a low whisper. 'I'm going to the room. You can sneak in, in a few minutes.' I said goodnight to everyone and went back to my quarters quietly and changed into my nightclothes. I was grateful that at least this room had a modern bathroom attached.

About twenty minutes later, Varun climbed in through the window, almost knocking over a light. He came over and sat with me on the twin bed. 'Honey, I want to tell you something,' he said seriously. 'I feel terrible about what I put you through that night in the hotel room when I beat up that guy, and what my family put you through with the wife thing.' He took my hand. 'I know that I have been bad about praying, but I want to pray for us right now.'

I was surprised. One of the things we argued about was him not wanting to pray out loud with me. I was always the one to pray. I knew it was because he was nervous about it, but I hoped that he would at least try. He prayed well enough in our Bible studies, in his own language, but not when we were alone. I gripped his hands tightly as we bowed our heads. Varun's voice was low and reverent as he began. 'Lord I praise you so much for bringing Janice into our lives. I am truly blessed to have her as my wife. Lord protect us as we are separated again. Keep our love strong through this separation. Send your guardian angels to surround us and keep us from harm or evil. But more importantly, please bring us back together quickly so that we can continue doing your will.'

We were both very tired, but we had so much to say to each other on this last night, our last time alone together. Finally, our words ran out and our eyes grew heavy. We spent the night on the metal beds with the smell of insecticide filling our dreams.

Early the next morning, we did get a tour of the church and heard the history of its founders.

All too soon we were back at the airport, hugging each other and saying our goodbyes. Just as before, we both let the tears flow as I walked through the gate on my way back to America.

---

23. Back in the USA

There is nothing like a two-day journey, mostly in the air, to give one time to think, pray and prepare yourself for the country in which you are going to land. After my last return home and the disasters that awaited me, I wondered what new surprises I would discover. But more than this, I was changed by the events and experiences I had had in India.

I felt like my heart was dwelling in two continents, two cultures, and two time zones. My heart and my calling were in India, but my family and my people were in America. The longer I was away, the less there was to come home to. I had sold or packed away all of my personal belongings, so now I had the problem of where to live when I arrived.

Ah well, I said to myself, God will provide. I dozed off in my seat till I was awakened by the stewardess presenting me with dinner. It was an American meal, my first in six months, which also signaled to me that we were flying over the US and on our way to Phoenix. My mind drifted again to what was ahead. E-mails back and forth and quick phone calls had given me a few details of what was going on in my family's lives, but much more would be revealed over the next few days when we met again.

Dad had always loved the Spanish language and culture, so after my mother's death, I suggested that he go on a trip to Spain and learn the language better. I showed him a few websites in Mexico and Guatemala. Surprisingly he sent me an e-mail a few months after I had returned to India, saying that he was going on a two-month trip to Guatemala to live with a family there. Dad was eighty years old, but still mentally alert and healthy for his age. It turned out to be the best thing for him, in spite of my sister's objections. When he returned, he was more upbeat and independent. Slowly he let my sister know that he didn't need her constant attention anymore. This did not sit well with her.

When I called to let dad know that I was coming, he said it would be best if I didn't stay with him for fear of conflicts developing between me and my sister. My sister's jealousy of me, and of Dad's and my close relationship, hadn't grown less even while I was away in India. Dad wanted to keep the peace, so he suggested I use his old motor home, and he would park it at my old house where my ex-husband now lived. I wasn't happy with this arrangement, but I didn't have a choice as I couldn't afford a hotel. Dad had reserved a shuttle to pick me up at the airport and take me on the two-hour drive up to Prescott Valley. Summer was over and signs of fall were all around. The sun was beginning to set and I was glad that the shuttle was heated. What few clothes I had, were meant for the heat of India, certainly not adequate for the cold winter approaching.

The shuttle dropped me off in front of a Safeway's grocery store where my son was to pick me up. He was late arriving, so I sat shivering in the wind waiting for him. Eventually, his car pulled up and Kevin jumped out to greet me. A long warm hug followed. It was so good to see him again and to be back in familiar surroundings.

Jet lag and time change has a strange effect on a body. I went through the next few days in a haze. I remember seeing my dad that night and being driven to my old house, meeting my ex-husband and moving my suitcases into the motor home outside. It was cold, but I was so exhausted, I fell asleep as soon as I had snuggled under the blankets.

Over the next few weeks the temperatures dropped dramatically. It was evident that winter had arrived in full swing as snow fell and ice began to form on the pipes and hoses that brought water to the motor home. Everything froze...including me. The heater in the motor home required propane and the propane I had was a small tank that didn't last through the night.

Kevin took me to a local department store and bought me an electric blanket. I found a larger propane tank at my dad's house and had it filled. But the snow kept falling and there was no relief inside the thin walls of the motor home. Then the skylight over the hallway cracked from the weight of the snow. I woke up to find snow powder all over the small kitchen and a huge draft blowing right through. I climbed up on the roof and duct-taped the skylight shut, but the pipes had frozen and without running water, it was impossible to live there.

I had no choice but to move inside Rod's house and sleep on the couch. Though Rod and I now shared an amicable relationship, it was still an awkward situation. Besides, housekeeping was not one of Rod's strong points, and he had let the two dogs sleep on the couch. It was covered in dog hair and dirt. I spread a sheet over it and bundled up under heavy quilts.

I got up each morning and walked the two blocks to my dad's house to have breakfast. I wanted to understand why he wouldn't let me sleep in his spare room. I wondered what kind of fear, or hold, my sister had on him. But I didn't say a word to him about it. Instead I just spent more time with him at the house sharing my life in India and talking about his trip to Guatemala.

There were two things I needed to accomplish as soon as possible; I needed to apply for a spousal visa for Varun and I needed to change my name to Kashyap. To do this, I needed a car and I needed someone to help me with filling out all the documents. Dad and I had always worked well together as a team, and he was more than willing to give me a hand. I had brought our original Indian marriage document with me so that I could use this for the proof of marriage. But, when I went to the Social Security office to change my name, they wouldn't accept the Indian document as it didn't show my previous last name. The only way that I could get my name changed was to file a petition in the local court. After a few weeks and an appearance in court, my name was officially changed to Kashyap. The next step was to change it on my passport and driver's license.

So dad and I spent the day together, doing all the paperwork and I spent my nights on the couch at my ex-husband's. I went into the motor home to change my clothes and when it was warm enough, to spend time on my laptop talking to Varun. The motor home had a foot peddle on the toilet. Sometimes it would get stuck in the flush position and it had to be pulled back up else the water would keep flowing. But since the water had been frozen for days, there was no water coming into the motor home at all and I didn't notice that it was in the down position.

But one day, while I was out with dad, the sun finally broke through the clouds and the hose to the motor home thawed, causing water to rush through the toilet and overflow out onto the floor. By the time I returned, the water had been flowing for several hours and the place was flooded. I was devastated! I had destroyed dad's motor home. I called dad immediately to break the bad news. He drove over and assessed the damage.

He stood outside in the snow and mud, scratching his chin, looking at me with one eyebrow raised. I knew this look from my childhood. I was in big trouble. I had really messed up! I stood there silently waiting for his rebuke. His hands dropped to his side, his shoulders slumped and his face softened. 'I'm sorry,' he said to me. I looked at him puzzled. 'No dad, I am sorry.' He ignored me and went on, 'No. I am sorry that I have made you use this motor home. Pack up your things and move over to the house!'

'Are you sure dad?' I asked. 'I don't want to cause any problems.'

'You aren't the problem,' he said firmly. 'Now let's get the things you need tonight and tomorrow we'll get you moved in with me.' My heart leapt with joy! I would be in a warm, clean environment without the tension I felt sleeping on the couch where my ex-husband lived. I was so glad to move in with my dad.

So from that day, dad and I were roommates, a team of sorts. We took care of each other. The only thing that came between us was God. Dad never missed an opportunity to criticize God and make wisecracks about my beliefs. When I read the Bible in the morning, dad would say, 'That book is full of lies.' When I left for church or came back, he would make some remark like, 'Well, did you get to see God today?' I tried to ignore it for as long as I could, until finally something snapped. I looked him in the eye and said, 'Dad, let's you and

I make a deal. I promise you that I will not try to convert you or convince you about my faith, if you promise to stop trying to convert me to your way of thinking. I will respect your beliefs if you will respect mine...deal?' He looked at me surprised for a minute, then said with a grin, 'Okay, deal.' We shook hands on it. Always a man of his word, I never had a problem with him afterwards. But I prayed for him all the time.

My application for the spousal visa came back approved. I was so excited! Varun would have to go through an interview at the American Consulate in Mumbai before the visa was granted. I didn't think that would be a problem. Varun and I chatted endlessly on the Net, making plans for him to come to America. We were sure that it wouldn't be long before we were together again.

Then we began to get requests from Mumbai for various documents, some of which we had already sent to the USCIS (the United States Citizenship and Immigration Services) in the States. But we complied and sent whatever they asked for.

Each time they sent a visa denial letter, with a note that they needed such and such document. This was a big problem because with each denial, Varun had to make the nearly seven-hour train journey to Kolkata and appear at the visa office. In addition, I had to send many of the documents they asked for to Mumbai via Federal Express. This proved to be quite expensive. But we persevered, and finally we got a letter that an interview was scheduled in Mumbai. This was a very good sign, we thought. We had heard that the interview was the final step, so we felt we were near the end.

Mumbai was many miles away from Purulia. It would

take nearly two days by train to reach there. We had to make sure it was well planned so he could be fresh and ready for his interview. Pranab accompanied him to make sure all went well. The interview lasted fifteen minutes. Varun had brought along all the documents they had asked for, but there was one missing—his police clearance, which was still in process. Varun showed them the receipt for it, but until they had the clearance, nothing could be done. He would have to come back for another interview. The visa officials told him they would notify him when it was scheduled.

Instead they asked for more documents, affidavits from friends and family about our marital relationship, copies of e-mails we had sent to each other proving we were in contact, photos of us together...the list went on. But again we complied and I FedExed all the papers to them.

Varun had to quit his job because of the many trips he had to make to Kolkata and the time he had to spend on all the paperwork. This went on for ten very long months. We missed each other so much, and Varun began to get discouraged and depressed. To make things worse, a few men from his village who had applied for a US visa, had got it and left.

Our entire life, our marriage, was on hold for a decision that never seemed to come. I felt something was definitely wrong, but I couldn't get to the bottom of it. My e-mails to the embassy in Mumbai went unanswered.

During this ten-month wait, I had managed to change my name on all the legal documents to Kashyap. I had joined a gym, gotten a physical and began attending church regularly.

To say simply that I joined a gym, would be an understatement. I became obsessed with getting physically fit. Throughout my life I had fought a battle with my weight. I had been on one diet or another since I was thirteen years old. Diet pills were the craze then and I tried these as well. I passed out in the courtyard one day, either from lack of food or a reaction to the pills.

Over the years I had lost weight and gained it so often that I had two sets of clothes, the skinny ones and the fat ones. My body and I were always at war with each other.

But this time I wanted to work out to live longer and be healthy. I decided to compromise with my body and said to it, 'Okay, so you want to be fat, I get that. But I want to be healthy too. I promise I will not starve you, if you promise to help me lose inches and get fit. Deal?'

This seemed to work well. I went at least once a day to the gym. I walked five miles on the treadmill. I used every weight-lifting and pulling machine in the building. I worked on the inner thigh machine as if it were life-supporting. I got advice from the experts to see which machines would get rid of my fat butt and the flabby wings under my arms and which ones would firm up my bosom. I desperately wanted to be in the best shape I could be when Varun came to America. The measuring tape was my friend as the inches came off.

I had given up on scales and mirrors years ago. I don't remember if it was when I was on the grapefruit diet, the cabbage diet or the long year on Weight Watchers, that I began to have nightmares about the scales ridiculing me and the mirrors chasing me. I avoided both with a passion. No full-length mirrors were allowed in my house and I never tried on clothes at the stores. Being inside those cramped dressing rooms, under surgical lights, surrounded by mirrors, horrified me. Every time I had done this, I was plummeted into despair and ate chocolate ice cream by the gallon for days thereafter. Avoiding the mirrors inside the gym had become an art form.

As for scales, even my doctor knew that, if weighing me

was necessary, it must be done with my back to the scales and to never say out loud, not even in a whisper, what the scales said.

I preferred to see myself in my inner beauty. The scales and the mirrors did not reflect who I truly was. They were an outward manifestation of worldly values. That was my story and I was sticking to it…while I pumped the iron in the gym.

The old church, the very first one my neighbours had taken me to, before my healing, and which I had left because I didn't agree with the pastor's behavior, had changed. The old pastor had left and the new pastor was someone I liked very much. I discovered old familiar faces that had known me in the wheelchair. The church was in a new large building on the outskirts of the valley, but it felt good to be with them again. They listened with interest as I told them the story about my life in India, and they even held a special Indian dinner where they surprised me with a check that paid for the roof of the church in Jhalda.

I immediately sent the money to India for the new roof. Varun and the guys sent me pictures of the whole process of getting materials and putting the trusses up on top of a bus to have them shipped the 50 km to the village. I shared the pictures with my church family. Things were looking up at last, I thought.

But the visa process was very discouraging. I grew increasingly worried about Varun. He seemed to have extreme mood swings, accusing me of not trying hard enough. I knew something was very wrong.

I decided to take matters into my own hands and called the Arizona state senator's office of John Kyle. I got in touch with the immigration specialist there. He promised to look into our case and get back to me. 'This is fairly typical,' he said a few weeks later. 'They get so many applications for these visas that are false, so they use delay tactics to weed them out. Either the applicants give up because they lose interest, or they run out of money or patience over time.'

'So that is why they are sending us repeated requests for the same documents?' I asked.

'Yes, they are hoping you will either give up, or fail to send the documents so they can close the file,' Kyle said. His words made my blood boil. All the money and time we had put into fulfilling their requests and it was just a game they were playing with our lives! 'Okay,' I continued, 'were you able to talk to anyone in Mumbai?'

'Yes, our office has sent a formal request for them to make a decision. I think you will be hearing from them soon.' I left his office with a flicker of hope in my heart.

Rod had remained supportive of my calling and my marriage to Varun and one morning he invited dad and I for a cup of coffee. When we arrived he had hot coffee waiting for us and we all sat around his desk in the living room. Rod was in a rare good mood, telling jokes and smoking cigarettes one after another.

'My tenants have told me that they are moving out next weekend,' he announced. 'I need to rent out the place again. I don't care about the money so much as I want someone in there who will take care of it, someone I can trust.' Dad nodded in agreement.

'The yard is big and it requires regular maintenance, plus there is some trash that needs to be hauled off.' He puffed away and looked at me quizzically. 'I thought I'd offer it to Janice and Varun as a sort of welcome to America gift.' I sat there stunned. 'Don't get me wrong,' he countered, 'I need some work done on it and in exchange I won't charge any rent for as long as the work continues.'

Dad looked at me with a smile. 'I'd say that is a pretty good offer!'

I thought of a prayer I had said daily for the past few weeks, 'Lord, help me to find a place for Varun and I to live together alone.' I knew this was the answer.

'If Varun gets the visa, which I don't see any reason why he shouldn't, you two can live there at $300 a month when the work is finished,' Rod went on. 'You can fix it up the way you want and just give me the receipts for the expenses in exchange for the rent amount.'

'Are you sure?' I asked him. 'I could really fix that place up nicely.'

'Of course I'm sure,' he said indignantly, 'You know me. I calculate the costs and benefits before getting into anything. I've been thinking about this for a few days. It will benefit me tax-wise and give you a leg up too. So do you accept my offer?'

'Yes,' I said, beaming, 'I accept. How soon can I begin work?' Rod grinned at me, 'As soon as the tenants move out, you can move in.'

When we left Rod's house, we drove by the rental house just to see what condition it was in. There was no doubt that there was a lot of work to be done. It was actually an old, sunbleached single wide trailer sitting on a huge lot. The whole place needed painting, including the rickety fence in front. Rather than being discouraged, however, I was excited at the challenge. Dad and I talked it over at breakfast. Though

I was moving out, we were within walking distance of each other. I still didn't have a vehicle, so dad offered his car anytime I needed it.

The following week I began working on the house. The inside needed a lot of repairs and I had no furniture, so I worked all day at the house and slept at dad's for a few weeks. I laid new flooring, repaired the doors and had lots of junk that was piled up in the yard hauled away.

One day Rod showed up at the house to see my progress. 'It's really looking good,' he said. 'Why don't you take a break?'

'Okay,' I said, 'What's on your mind?'

'I want to show you something. Can you come down to my house?' he asked, puffing on his cigarette.

'Sure, but I need to lock up first. I'll meet you down there,' I said.

When I drove down the street and pulled into his driveway, I saw a big blue truck with a camper shell parked in the yard. I thought Rod probably had visitors. He came out to greet me. 'What do you think of my new truck?' he asked.

'Nice!' I said, 'Very nice.'

'Why don't you take it for a ride and let me know how it drives,' Rod said. 'You know more about these things than I do. Take it out on the highway and let me know.' He handed me the keys.

'Okay, but it's been a long time since I drove a vehicle with a clutch. I'll need some practice.' I did drive the truck out on the highway. It didn't take long for me to get familiar with the gears and the clutch was smooth.

When I came back to Rod's house and went inside to give him the keys, he was on the phone to my dad. He hung up. 'How did it drive?' he asked.

'Pretty good actually,' I smiled, 'I got it up to 80 km on the highway with no trouble at all.' I tossed the keys onto the desk. Rod waved at the keys. 'You take them, I have my own set,' he said nonchalantly. 'The truck is yours until you can get yourself a car.' I stared in disbelief. 'Of course you will have to let me have it when I buy building materials for the remodel of this house, but otherwise, you need it to haul things while you are working on my rental,' he said.

'Rod, this is just too much,' I said. 'I can't accept this.'

'Why not? It is just a loan until you and Varun can get a car of your own. I've already added you on the insurance. I don't want your dad being without a car at his age.'

I had to admit that I didn't like using dad's car all the time either. 'Okay,' I relented. 'But you know a truck is not my style.' Over the twenty-two years that Rod and I had known each other, I always managed to buy old convertibles. I loved the feel of the sun and wind in my face.

'Yes, I know but a sports car wouldn't be practical now,' Rod grinned.

With the help of friends and the church, I was able to move into the house quickly. Over the next few months, I frequented the local used furniture stores. My interior decorator mind decided on an African theme, with bright colors, masks and lots of plants. I took pictures of the progress and sent them to Varun. We chatted every day, but it didn't help the loneliness we both felt. It seemed our conversations were always about the visa and the paperwork involved. We were both tense now. It had been a year since we had seen each other.

I continued to call the representative at the senator's office. I began to realize, through our conversations, that since the 9/11 disaster and the forming of Homeland Security, my country had basically closed its doors to immigrant applications from Asia unless they were from students or very rich people. Varun came from an ordinary middle-class background.

One night I had another dream like the one I'd had years ago, when I saw myself in India. This time, I saw myself walking through an Indian village with the typical mud houses and narrow dirt roads. People were standing at the side of the road looking at me. At the end of the road stood a man, waving. Then the scene changed and I was sitting surrounded by children. I had a little crippled girl on my lap. We were posing for a picture. A voice spoke to me in my dream, saying, 'Take care of the children.'

I woke up, knowing that this was a vision from God. It disturbed me because He was showing me in India. This was not our plan at all!

I rationalized that perhaps God was showing me returning to India after Varun and I had lived in America for a few years, but I knew in my heart that this wasn't true. God was telling me that our human plans would fail, that Varun would not get the visa. My heart sank. How could I let Varun know about this vision? All of the planning, the work and the decorating of our home were in vain. I prayed fervently for the next few days, begging God to at least let Varun come and meet my family, to spend some time in America, but all I heard was a continuing echo in my ears, 'Take care of the children.' The same vision came again and again over the passing weeks. The vision became clearer, more detailed each time I saw it. I woke up and immediately got down on my knees by the bed. 'All right Lord,' I prayed, 'I want your will, not mine. I will return to India if that is where you want me.'

After this, I tried hard to convince Varun to give up on

the whole visa process. But he refused, he said he wanted to see it finished. 'We've worked too hard for this and they have taken our lives and played with them,' he said angrily, 'I will not give up now!'

As for me, I stopped working on the house and began preparing myself mentally and emotionally for returning to India. I dropped hints to my father and to my friends that I might have to go back.

∽

Once again winter had set in. Thanksgiving came and went. Christmas was fast approaching. I silently and slowly began packing my things, but kept praying that God would intervene and see the benefit of Varun and I being together in the US, at least for some time, before we resumed our work in India.

Finally we got a notice from the Mumbai embassy. They had scheduled another interview on December 15th.

My first hopeful thought was perhaps God had changed his mind; maybe He was testing my faith like He tested Abraham with Isaac? Our entire lives had been uprooted and we had sacrificed so much time and money for this visa.

Maybe, just maybe, this interview would be successful. I promised God that we would never give up on our works in India or the church.

Again we made arrangements for the long train ride to Mumbai. Again, Pranab went with Varun. I had sent a large photo album of our lives together, as well as my divorce papers, which had already been sent three times. The police clearance was done and sent long ago. I couldn't think of any reason why they should deny Varun the visa.

I knew that Varun had a 10 a.m. appointment for his interview. That would be 9 p.m. in the US. He called me just before going in, so I paced back and forth waiting to hear from him. His first interview had only lasted fifteen minutes, so I figured it wouldn't be long before I heard from him. But two hours went by without a word. At midnight, I was exhausted and went to bed.

At about 2 a.m. my phone rang but it was dad. 'I just got the strangest phone call,' he said. 'This guy named Mike said he was calling from Texas and looking for you. I asked him why he was calling in the middle of the night. He apologized and said he needed to talk to you now. I told him that you were at your house and he said, oh okay, and hung up.'

'That is so weird,' I said sleepily, 'I think it was probably the guy interviewing Varun in Mumbai. I'm so sorry he woke you up dad.'

'No problem,' he said, 'I just don't understand why he had to lie about it. I offered to give him your number, but he said he had it.'

'Good. Then I will wait for his phone call. You go back to sleep and we will talk in the morning.' We hung up and I went to the kitchen to make myself a cup of tea.

A few minutes later, the phone rang again. But it wasn't Varun, it was Rod. 'I just got a phone call,' he said, 'some man named Mike wanted to talk to you. I told him you weren't here, that you were at your house.' He continued, 'He asked if I was sure you weren't there and I told him, of course I am sure, she is at her own house sleeping...Didn't you give them your new number?'

'Yes, of course I did. I sent it via e-mail and a hard copy. But you know how messed up they are down there and the right hand doesn't know what the left hand is doing. So this Mike didn't believe you, huh? Did you give him my phone number?' I asked.

'Tried to, but he didn't want it. He just hung up.'

I sighed loudly, 'Okay, I guess we will find out tomorrow what this is all about. I'll let you know what I hear from Varun.'

I sat on the couch sipping my tea in the dim light of a lamp. I had prayed for the interview to be a success, but my heart already knew that it wouldn't be. I was frantic with worry about what was happening on the other side of the world, in Mumbai. I hoped that Varun would just walk away confident that he had done all he could and not do anything drastic.

I fell asleep curled up on the couch by the phone. At 6 a.m., as the sun was just beginning to light up the sky, the phone call came. Varun was very upset. He was cursing and crying and almost incoherent. 'Honey,' I said, rubbing my eyes, 'slow down, take a deep breath and tell me what happened. This phone call is costing you big money, so let me call you back in a little while, okay? I'll fix myself some hot tea and call you back.'

'Okay, but I will fix myself a drink and wait for your call,' he growled.

'That's a good idea honey,' I said gently, 'You go get your drink and I will call in half an hour.' We hung up.

When we finally did talk, I was shocked and dismayed at the story that unfolded. Varun walked up to the interview window with the photo album and documents in hand. First a woman spoke to him. She asked when we were married. He began by telling her the date of our marriage and the date when we got it officially recorded. She interrupted him, saying, 'So you don't know when you were married?' Varun tried to explain that though we had got married on the first date he had mentioned, our marriage was legally recorded the following year, but he was interrupted again. 'So you expect me to believe you are legally married to a woman who is almost the same age as your mother?' Varun said, 'I hope you believe it, because it is true.'

'Are you trying to be smart with me?' the woman yelled, and then called a man to the window.

What took place was a six and a half hour grilling by a man named Mike. Varun couldn't get a word in. Accusations were flying. They threatened to have him arrested. At which point, Varun gathered his things together and stood up. 'What are you doing?' Mike asked him.

'Well if you are going to arrest me then I am getting ready to be arrested,' Varun said, staring him directly in the eye.

'Sit down,' Mike ordered. 'I want to know who your agent is.'

'I don't know what you are talking about. I have no agent,' Varun replied.

'Did you know this woman you claim to be your wife is not divorced?'

'That's a lie,' Varun said. 'We sent you her divorce papers three times, but evidently you can't keep track of the documents we have sent you. Otherwise, why would we have to keep sending them to you?' Mike was not amused and said, 'Wait here and I will prove to you that she is living with her husband.'

Mike left and made the two phone calls to my father and my ex-husband. When he came back, he told Varun that he had talked to my father and then called my ex-husband, who denied that I was there, but he heard me in the background. 'Your so-called wife is living with her other husband!' he declared.

'I don't believe you!' Varun yelled. 'I know her very well

and we love each other. She is living in a different house, I have pictures right here.' He attempted to give them the photo album.

'I don't need to see those pictures,' Mike said. 'I know this application is a fraud and both of you will be tried in court for submitting fraudulent documents. Your visa is denied.'

Varun stood up. 'Fine,' he said. 'Then I want our original documents returned to us, our marriage certificate and birth certificates.'

'They will be sent back to the USCIS in about a year and you can get them then,' Mike said curtly.

'I need them now!' Varun shouted. At this point Mike sent for the security guards. He was escorted out of the building. But he stood his ground and refused to leave without our documents. Again they threatened to arrest him and the situation became ugly. Pranab watched the scene in horror and rushed over to Varun. He was able to calm him down and get him to leave.

That was it. Not only was the visa denied, but it was declared fraudulent. God didn't just close this door, he slammed it shut!

I was furious at the way Varun was treated, at their false accusations and lies that 'Mike' told Varun. I didn't fault Varun for losing his temper. They had grilled him for six hours; I knew I wouldn't have lasted six minutes with their attitude and lies. They had no intention of granting the visa, they only wanted to harass and interrogate him. I vowed to talk to this Mike myself and let him know what I thought of him. I could accept being denied, but it was the cruel treatment that should never be allowed in a US embassy, that enraged me.

I called the Senator's office later that morning and

reported what had happened. I was told that there was nothing that could be done about it. The new Homeland Security laws gave embassy officials full power to do as they wished. Their decisions were final and not to be questioned. It was shocking to me that there was no accountability for their behavior. I could file an objection to their decision, but again, I was told that at this point, it was just a formality, mostly ineffective. After fourteen months of dealing with the immigration department, I wanted nothing more to do with them or their forms. But I was also sad for my country. Something had changed dramatically since the 9/11 attacks, something sinister within the high walls of the government. The words written on the Statue of Liberty, 'Give me your tired, your poor, your huddled masses yearning to be free,' had become simply a chapter in history. America was different now. When they told me that my husband's tourist visa was denied because 'he might become an immigrant,' I wondered, when did this become a bad thing?

But more disturbing to me was this terrible feeling deep within my soul that America had changed spiritually. The evidence was on TV, the news and in encounters I had with people every day. With deep sadness I realized that I didn't belong here anymore. How blessed I was to have been born in America. But now, not only had I changed fundamentally in a deeper spiritual sense, but my America had also changed. I could see clearly that it was moving into a path of spiritual and moral self-destruction of Biblical proportions. I vowed to pray for America, my people, and my family wherever I might go.

God was leading me away for His purposes. When He does this, He also prepares the heart for the journey ahead. My heart now longed to return.

I just wanted to be with my husband and begin our life together once more. I knew now that this life would have to be in India where God had started our mission and our marriage. It was time to move on.

∼

It was difficult breaking the news to family, friends and my church. The friends at my church were very supportive and encouraging. I was so happy to have had this time of worshipping and sharing fellowship together.

The pastor and his wife took me to lunch one day after church. I talked about life in India and how different it was from America. The pastor shook his head and asked, 'How can you go back there knowing the kind of life you must face?' I looked at him seriously and said, 'How can I not go? It is a small price to pay for a God that has healed me and made me walk again. As long as He will use me in India, I will remain there.'

'You are truly anointed by God,' he said. 'It is not everyone who would follow God as you are doing.'

'I don't know about being anointed,' I said, 'but I am greatly blessed. I mean, here I am at this stage of my life and God has chosen me to do His will in India. I consider this such a privilege.'

I had very little time to make all the preparations for my return, and so much to do. I needed money to pay for my plane ticket and hopefully, to raise more money to finish the church in Jhalda.

I worried constantly about how long it was taking to finish the church. I always thought of those families without a church or a pastor. How did they bury their dead or have baptisms or marriages? I thought that perhaps I could at least be their pastor once in a while. But I wasn't a pastor, I was a missionary.

So I took a fast track course online to get a pastor's 'Certificate of Ordination.' I was assured that this would be valid and recognized throughout the world. But to me, it was only to be used if the need arose. I thought of all the pastors who had studied for years to obtain their certificates and vowed to one day do the same. But for now, I wanted to help those Christian families in Jhalda.

In India I was asked many times to attend funerals and to pray over people. I considered it an honor to be counted as one of the pastors in the community. The words used by so many in reference to me, was 'anointed by God.' This phrase always made me uncomfortable. Does being healed by God and called into the missionary field also mean being anointed? Perhaps...but I felt being anointed was a very holy thing, something I felt unworthy to be called.

The other reference was comparing me to Mother Teresa. How absurd! Mother Teresa was born a saint and raised to serve God. I was called by God to serve Him after a life of many mistakes and sins. To me there was no comparison except that I was in India, in West Bengal where Mother Teresa did her wonderful lifetime of work. She was an inspiration to me, a testimony to what one woman could do. I could only pray that God would use me to make a difference in India as well.

---

24. After the Doors Were Closed

The trauma of our experience with the immigration department left a bitter taste in the mouth for both of us, but for Varun, it was so much more. It was a failure, not only in his eyes, but in the eyes of the village, his friends and family. They didn't know that we were married and that it was a spousal visa we had applied for, not a simple tourist visa. They only knew that he was denied a visa when others had succeeded. Questions arose that he was unable to answer and the gossip and jibes added to his humiliation. I knew from our online conversations that I needed to get to him quickly, to support him through this.

This time around, I had applied for a ten-year visa and miraculously, it was approved.

In an effort to raise money, I announced a yard sale and asked for donations from the church and friends. The response was overwhelming as people came to deliver clothing, furniture and appliances for my cause. Volunteers from my church came to help me during the three-day event. I had placed an ad in the local newspaper and my phone never stopped ringing. Kevin came to help lift the heavy items into vans and trucks. At the end of the last day I had raised enough money for my plane ticket and another 1,000 dollars for the church building. We all danced for joy in the driveway!

I booked my ticket for December 29th, to arrive in Kolkata on the 30th, so that Varun and I could celebrate the New Year together.

In Purulia, Varun and his friends began the search for a new home for us. We couldn't afford to live in a hotel this time round, so we had to find a place to rent. It was difficult to find one in such a short time, but they eventually found a house on the opposite side of town from the village of Bhat Bandh. The owner of the house was a colleague of Pranab's in the college where he taught. I was told that it was near two colleges. I hoped that this would help me find a teacher to teach me Bengali. This would open doors for me to share my testimony in many other places, not to mention allowing me to be a part of the daily conversations I had been left out of in the past.

India was to be my country now. I would no longer be a visitor for six months at a time. I was even more determined to honor our marriage vows and remain with Varun. One night when we were chatting online, Varun said to me, 'You don't have to come back here and live in this terrible place.'

'God has brought us together for His purpose,' I told him. 'God wants us to be together in India, not America. I am sure He has a good plan for us.' Then I sent him the scripture from the Book of Ruth 1:16-17:

'Don't make me leave you, for I want to go wherever you go, and to live wherever you live; your people shall be my people and your God shall be my God. I want to die where you die and be buried there. May the Lord do terrible things to me if I allow anything but death to separate us.'

Varun wrote back, 'You have brought tears to my eyes. I love you so much! I could not ask you to stay with me here, knowing the hardships we will face, but you have proven to all of us that God is leading you here. Who am I to question God? You have made such a big difference in our lives, in my life. I cannot imagine going on without you now. Come, Mrs Kashyap. Hurry home. This is where you belong.'

How can I explain the tremendous difference it made in my heart and mind, to know that going to India this time was a permanent situation? Though I had been preparing myself for this for weeks now, saying goodbye this time was hard. The fourteen months that I had been home, re-established connections with family and friends that had been broken by my earlier trips to India. I had settled back into my old lifestyle with ease.

Dad had begun teaching English to Mexican immigrants and developing his own circle of friends. Never one to sit still for long, he also joined a senior gym and went there every day. The two of us had got into a routine of taking morning walks at the local mall and having breakfast together. We had grown much closer in the last few months.

It was at one of these breakfasts that we discussed the possibility of this being our last goodbye. 'I am not getting any younger,' dad said. 'I am going to miss you very much, but I am proud of you for following your convictions.' He looked me in the eye. 'I want you to go and do whatever you feel you need to do. Don't worry about me, or feel guilty about going back to India. Whatever happens is part of life.' I took his hand, tears forming in my eyes. 'Thank you dad, for believing in me, for supporting me in this and encouraging me all through my life. I love you very much and I am also proud of you. I consider myself blessed to have you as my father. But,' I went on, 'I am going to establish a rule that cannot be broken. The rule is this, no one is allowed to die while I am gone!' Dad smiled as I continued. 'You are still healthy and active. I hope to come home for visits every few years and take walks with you again. So stay in shape and be ready.'

My ex-husband had his own way of saying goodbye. 'I don't support losers, so I expect you to go there and become known as the next Mother Teresa,' he declared. 'I also expect you to write a book about it so I can tell everyone that my ex-wife did this. I expect nothing but success and commitment from you. Never start something you can't finish.' Then he added, 'I'm glad you are finally going so you don't take up my time anymore. Now get outta here!' That was Rod's style.

Packing for the trip was grueling. How does one pack for a lifetime? Each item had to be carefully considered because the airlines had changed their rules regarding baggage allowance—you were only allowed two pieces of luggage, not more than 50 lbs each, and every extra piece had to be paid for.

As I had done before, I had gathered medical stuff, blood pressure cuffs, blood sugar testing machines and their needles, ointments and salves. I put a big label on the suitcase, 'Medical Supplies, Purulia, India' in the hope that the airlines might waive the charges for it.

My own personal items took me three days to pack. This time I wanted to take some family pictures and ministry materials. Each item of clothing had to be selected according to what was appropriate for the heat and the culture of India. After I finished, I took the luggage over to my dad's to be weighed on his scale. My large suitcase weighed 56 lbs. Dad and I went through it together to decide what could be left behind. It was a wrench to part with some things, but we finally got the weight down.

I ended up with two suitcases of personal items, one for medical supplies, my laptop and a carry-on. I had learned to carry a change of clothes in my carry-on, along with my toiletries and hairbrush. Dad drove me to Phoenix and helped me check in my luggage. The airlines did take pity on me and charged me less for the medical baggage, but it still cost me

75 dollars. Dad pulled out his credit card and said, 'It's on me.' I felt a surge of gratitude and love for him. It was so difficult to say goodbye.

25. Picking Up the Threads

My flight was from Phoenix to Los Angeles, then to Bangkok, and from there to New Delhi, then a layover for three hours in New Delhi, and finally to Kolkata. That was the plan...but it didn't turn out that way at all.

The plane was late taking off from Phoenix. By the time I landed in Los Angeles, I had thirty minutes to catch my next flight. Unfortunately the airline was on the other side of the huge airport. It was late at night and the buses were running only every half hour. I couldn't wait, I had to run like hell with my laptop and carry-on. I arrived just as they were boarding the plane, but I didn't get a boarding pass and they wouldn't let me on. Winded and cold, I sat down and watched as my plane took off. I was stuck there for the night.

When the counter finally opened at 7 a.m., I was first in line. They rescheduled another itinerary so I could reach New Delhi on time. This new itinerary put me on the next flight to Chicago, then to New York where I could connect with the Air India flight to New Delhi. Evidently my luggage was sitting in Thailand. I was assured that it would be waiting for me in New Delhi.

I had never been to New York and hoped the plane would fly over the Statue of Liberty, but I never got to see it.

When I landed, I was told to go to a terminal on the other side of the airport. I was impressed with the sky tram that whizzed me to my destination. It was the largest terminal I had been in. It took me a while to find Air India. But as I walked towards the counter in the distance, I saw many people, mostly in Indian attire, standing in groups in front of the counter. My instincts told me something was not right. After a great deal of being pushed from one line to another, I was told that Air India had declared a strike and all flights had been cancelled. My heart sank below my knees. I was tired in spite of the naps I had taken. I was aching all over from carrying my heavy laptop and pulling my carry-on. I was told to go stand in a line and they would re-route me eventually. Hours went by and my legs were about to give out on me. A kind-looking Indian woman told me to go sit in one of the vacant chairs near the counter, and she would push my suitcase along the line. I accepted her offer gratefully. I needed a bathroom break as well.

Finally my turn came at the counter. I was told the only flight available to connect me to New Delhi was via Amman, Jordan. We were guided by a cheerful young man to our waiting area.

I can't remember any details of the flight, except for looking out of the window before landing in Jordan. It was nothing but brown landscape. Not a tree or bush in sight. To me it looked like no man's land.

My fellow lost flyers, like me, were exhausted. We were all bound together by the unfortunate circumstances in which we found ourselves, strangers in a strange land. Slowly we began to get to know each other and share our stories, dividing into little groups. My group consisted of two Indian women, both married. One was returning from New York after a visit with her husband. She was hoping for a visa to the US. I shared my tragic visa story with her. The other woman was in her forties and was an interior decorator in New Delhi. I told them about my own marriage, and our missionary work in West Bengal. It was either my age or my story, but the two of them became very protective of me and took me under their wing as we were being shuffled from one room to the other. Staying together gave us strength.

By now it was clear that no one knew quite what to do with us. Because of the Air India strike, we had been shoved in their laps like wayward orphans. We were told that it would be a few hours before we could get any flights, so it was best to go get some food and relax. I couldn't relax. Varun was waiting at the airport in Kolkata and I had to contact him somehow. We had both agreed that if anything happened, we should send an e-mail or try to call. I couldn't reach Varun by phone, but I was able to call my dad at JFK airport and tell him about the strike. I had no idea if he had been able to inform Varun. Even if he had, he wouldn't know where I was or when I was to arrive in Kolkata. I had no cellphone and my attempts to use the airport phones met with disaster.

We were all sitting at a table at a small restaurant inside the terminal. My laptop was new and I didn't yet have the Wi-fi connection. I saw a large man with long hair and a beard typing away on his laptop. Bravely I approached him and asked if he had internet connection. He smiled and said yes. I explained my problem to him and asked if I could just use his computer to send a mail. He recognized my American accent. He was American too and introduced himself as Jimmy. 'Go ahead,' he said with a smile. Quickly I sent a mail to both dad and Varun. Dad replied almost immediately that he had talked to Varun and would let him know where I was. I was greatly relieved. I chatted a bit with Jimmy and learned that he worked on a ship and had traveled the world. I felt a momentary pang of envy for his carefree life on the open sea.

After many hours, we were all called to board a plane to New Delhi. By now it had been forty-eight hours since I left Phoenix. To say I was exhausted, would be an understatement. I settled in my seat and dozed off and on throughout the long flight. When the captain announced that we were landing in Delhi, those of us who had been through the ordeal together, cheered and clapped loudly. The rest of the passengers must have thought we were crazy!

Our celebrations were premature. It appeared again that no one seemed to know what to do with us. We went through security check—for me this was the sixth time—and were told to wait. After several more hours we were told that we had to go to the Air India office and talk to them. We all shuffled along, tired and grumbling, onto buses outside. We were dropped off in front of a large building. There was a small window that said 'Air India' but no one was there.

Finally a woman came to the window and said nothing could be done because of the strike and closed the window. There was a collective groan throughout the group. One man began shouting and then others joined in. Enough was enough! Soon the police were called and there was more shouting. Things were getting very heated up. I, being the only foreigner, stood away from the group. Two policemen approached me. 'What is going on?' one of them asked. 'Are you with this group?'

'Yes,' I said, 'We have been traveling for three days without any sleep and we want to get home. This has been a nightmare for all of us.' I looked at them sternly. 'I want to talk to the American embassy right now!' I sounded much more aggressive than I felt. The truth was, I was feeling faint and my legs wouldn't hold up much longer. But there were others who had little children who had been through it all too. I decided to use what little American influence I might have to save us all. The policemen I spoke to left immediately while other police tried to calm our group down.

Within half an hour a executive from Air India came and told us that he would get us all to our destinations. Slowly each of us were processed and sent by bus back to the large terminal. Those of us that were going to Kolkata were booked on a flight that left in three hours.

Once inside the large modern terminal, I headed for the bathroom to freshen up. I stopped for a snack at one of the food counters, then I went to the gate where my flight was to arrive. What I didn't know was that my flight arrived very early. What I didn't hear was the announcement of my flight taking off...I had missed it.

I fell apart. I went to a phone and called Varun to let him know. I stood at the phone crying in the middle of the terminal. Varun was also exhausted and angry. 'How could you miss it?' he shouted. 'When is the next flight?'

'At 5:30 a.m.,' I said tearfully. 'I don't know how it happened. I couldn't hear the announcement and I was just getting something to eat.'

'Well, there is nothing we can do but wait then,' he said more calmly. 'I have booked a hotel room near the airport. As soon as you get here we will go and get some rest.'

I waited at the gate, afraid of missing another flight, afraid of falling asleep, afraid my legs would give out on me if I tried to walk anymore. I felt old and depressed. The lack of sleep was taking its effect on my body and mind. When my plane began to board, I could barely walk. An airline attendant grabbed my computer case and carry-on for me as I shuffled onto the plane. Once in my seat, I told the hostess not to disturb me for meals or anything, then I fell asleep.

Of course it wasn't a long flight to Kolkata, but it was just enough time for me to rejuvenate my mind and body.

Fourteen months was a long time to be away from each other. But by the time Varun and I came face to face, we were both too tired to be excited. He had been waiting at the airport for the same three days that I had been through the nightmare in the air. The airport security had begun to eye him suspiciously and Varun was in no mood to be confronted by authority. Fortunately I arrived just in time, as Varun quickly grabbed my luggage and whisked me out of the building.

Once inside the hotel room, Varun ordered some food and a small bottle of whiskey. When the food arrived, I took Varun's hand and said a prayer of gratitude. We were together again!

It was only late morning, but we were both beyond knowing or caring what time of day it was. The whiskey was just what was needed to help us gently float into a deep sleep wrapped in each other's arms.

The next day we booked the afternoon train to Purulia. We arrived at 11:30 at night on December 29th. I was still exhausted. It was a relief to find a few of our friends waiting for us. We all piled into three rickshaws and sped through the nearly abandoned, dark alleys and streets for what seemed like an hour before we arrived at our destination. I was surprised to find a chill in the air and shivered in my light cotton clothes.

The house we had rented was locked, but a few loud knocks finally awakened the man sleeping inside. I didn't know who he was, and at that point, I didn't care. Varun and the men lit some candles and carried in my baggage. This, at least, was one thing that hadn't changed in the months I had been away—the electric supply was as erratic as before. Small wooden cots consisting of roughly hewn wooden frames and slats were arranged in typical dorm style in one of the rooms. Thin cotton mattresses were pulled down from a high shelf, dusted off and thrown on the beds. A few blankets were located as well, along with pillows stuffed with hard cotton and smelling of insecticide, but I chose to use my own clothes wrapped up in a bundle instead and quickly drifted off to sleep. I was too tired to care about the house or the arrangements. I just wanted to sleep for days.

Morning came too early with a visit from our landlord. I greeted him with a 'Namaskar' without getting out of bed and fell back to sleep.

When I finally woke up, it was to the harsh reality of being back in India and to the joy of knowing that my husband and I were together again. His dark face shone down on me with a broad grin as he said, 'Honey, time to wake up. The guys are here to see you.' And there was 'the God Squad', the motely group who had become our family.

After the guys and I had greeted each other with big hugs, we all walked through the house inspecting its possibilities. I felt a chill pass through me as we walked down the hallway, a feeling I had experienced a few times in the past. I shook it off, but made a mental note of it for later.

We all agreed that one of the rooms at the back would become the kitchen. I smiled as I watched the familiar scene of Varun giving instructions to get the things needed to make the kitchen functional. By the end of the day, we had a table to set the stove on, a gas cylinder, some basic utensils, cups and plates, and a large table for eating and preparing the food.

The entire day was spent in a happy reunion as we shared stories and caught up on the news and events of the people in

Purulia. It was New Year's Eve, so a celebration was in order. We had a wonderful evening together, but we sent everyone away early so we could get some rest.

Before going to bed, I lit a candle, sat on the floor and prayed. I thanked God for bringing me through the trip safely and for all He had done in our lives. Then, as was our old custom, Varun lay on the bed and I read the Bible to him. Afterwards, we held hands and I prayed again. 'Lord you have brought us together for Your purpose, please show us Your will as we go forth in faith. Increase our love, give us strength for whatever lies ahead.'

Varun's family had planned a New Year's day picnic and I was invited to join them. Early the next morning a car arrived to take us to Varun's parents' house. I knew they were not a communicative family and Varun shared few details of his life with them but I did wonder if by now they knew or suspected anything about us.

It was a bright and beautiful day as we all piled into a big car, loaded with food and supplies for the picnic. We drove some distance outside of Purulia, arriving at a dam with a large lake. We all got out of the car and the women began setting up the food and equipment for the picnic. I attempted to help, but I was their guest and they would not let me lift a finger. Varun's dad, the driver and another man who had come with us, set up a separate area for themselves and spread a blanket on the ground to sit on.

Varun and I longed to sit near each other and be together openly, but instead, we had to pretend to be just friends, ministry partners. We walked together to the water's edge. 'Don't you think now would be a good time to tell your family about our marriage?' I asked him. 'I really don't want to continue to live a lie here. They have a right to know.'

Varun stared out at the water. When he finally spoke, it was his standard reply. 'You don't understand, Janice. Trust me, I will tell them soon, but not now. You've just arrived here. Give them time to accept that first.'

I wanted to protest. I wanted to boldly announce our love for each other and just get it over with. Varun continued, looking into my eyes, 'Please trust me, honey, just a little while longer.' I shrugged. 'I guess I have to trust you, don't I?' I replied as we began to walk back to the picnic area.

When we arrived, Varun and his mom began talking in Bengali. Varun turned to me and said, 'Dad wants you to come and join the men for a drink.'

'Aren't you coming too?' I asked. 'No, dad would never allow me to drink with him. He wants you. It is a very rare thing and an honor that he has invited you. So please just go and have a drink with them.' Puzzled and a bit apprehensive, I walked over to where the men were sitting down. They were all smiling and indicated a place for me to sit. A round of drinks was poured. Varun's dad, Tapan, lifted his glass and said, 'Welcome back to India!' We all clinked our glasses together and took a sip. 'Thank you for inviting me to join you,' I smiled. 'I feel very honored.' Tapan was the only one who knew any English, so he translated as the other two men toasted me and welcomed me as well.

I kept looking over at Varun who was awkwardly standing with the women.

'Please forgive me for asking,' I said to Tapan, 'but in my country, we all drink together. I was just wondering why you haven't invited Varun to join us too?' Tapan looked at his drink for a minute, and replied. 'In our culture, a father never drinks with his son.' Then he added, 'Varun does enough drinking without my approval.'

'Actually, I think he is doing much better than he used to,' I observed.

'If this is so, then I credit your influence on him and we are very grateful for that,' he said as he poured another round for all of us. Then he did an amazing thing. He lit a cigarette and passed it around to the two men, then he took it and offered it to me. I declined. All eyes were upon me. 'We know you smoke and it makes no difference to us. We see the good work you have done and we want you to know that you are accepted. Please feel free.' It was a great relief and a huge compliment to me. I took the cigarette and puffed on it. They were all smiles, and so was I.

I looked over at Varun's mother, who was watching us intently from a distance. She nodded at me and smiled too. This was the first gesture of acceptance from them, the first sign that my presence over the past years was seen and recognized. I know many religious people who would scoff at this, but for me, it was definitely a sign from God. God was using me in spite of the smoking, in fact, He was using it to bridge a gap between me and this culture. 'In America,' Tapan said, 'you sip your drinks slowly and enjoy the flavor of the alcohol. But here, we drink only to get drunk and fall asleep.' He smiled. 'I like the American way better.'

'Yes, I do too,' I replied. 'Because it is more about socializing and spending time together.'

I was glad when the women called us all to eat and I was able to join them and Varun again. We all ate heartily as the afternoon sun shone on the water and moved the shade of the trees away from us. When we finished our meal, we shifted the blankets and things back under the shade and settled down again on the ground. Tapan sent his driver into a nearby village to get more whiskey and soon another bottle was opened and I was being waved over to join them again. I agreed to have just one more drink and then returned to where the women were sitting, but Tapan and his friends carried on drinking till the bottle was finished.

When the time came to pack up and leave, the driver and Tapan were obviously inebriated. I wondered how we were going to get home safely. Tapan insisted on driving, stating that the driver was much drunker than he was.

We all got into the car and started across the dirt field towards the road. Tapan was having great difficulty shifting the gears and we were all jolted around as the gears ground relentlessly. The driver kept insisting that he drive. We all fervently wished that he would. Finally Tapan gave up and the two men traded seats.

Surprisingly we all made it home safely before the sun set and Varun and I said our goodbyes to the family and headed to our own home across town.

It was our first night alone and we spent the evening talking and sharing our lives together, before drifting into a peaceful slumber.

The following morning I had one project I vowed that I would do—call the US embassy in Mumbai and talk to this 'Mike' who had interrogated Varun and accused us of lying. Though I knew in my heart that I could not change what had happened, I wanted to make sure that Mike remembered us. After being transferred to various people, I finally got Mike on the line.

'Mike,' I began, 'this is Janice Kashyap. You interrogated

my husband, Varun Kashyap, on December 15th, I'm sure you remember him and our file.'

'Yes,' he said, 'I remember.'

'Good,' I said, 'because I want you to know that because of you and your decision to mark our file fraudulent, I am now with my husband here in India. I also want you to know that in spite of our age difference, we love each other and our marriage is legitimate. Your decision has changed our lives dramatically. The way you treated my husband was abusive and insulting. As you probably know, I have reported all of it to my state senator's office.' I paused. 'I don't know how or when, but I do know that you will hear from us again one day. This is not the end of our story.'

Mike muttered something about having our file looked at again. I knew it was just to placate me and get off the phone. 'That would be nice, Mike,' I replied, 'But I am sure that the many copies of our records that we sent to you, have been lost in other departments and our file would be incomplete anyway. My husband brought in a photo album of our life together over the past two years and you didn't even bother to look at it, so I know you have already made your decision no matter what we say or do…goodbye.'

Ten days later, we received a notice that our file remained stamped 'fraudulent' and was scheduled to be returned to the US.

---

26. Deshbundho Road—Where Heaven and Hell Met

The house we had rented used to be a dorm for college students. It had one small 'English' toilet inside and two Indian toilets outside. It was nothing more than a hallway with two bedrooms on each side and a stairway up to the roof where there was a water storage tank and a tap for washing clothes. The paint and plaster on the walls was falling away, leaving large gaps of concrete exposed. But we were not alone, physically or spiritually.

The man who had been sleeping in the house the night we arrived, was, it turned out, our co-tenant, who had rented one of the rooms. He was a doctor of natural medicine. We were told he would leave in a few months, but as the months went by, he seemed to be an immovable fixture in the house

The house was situated in a part of Purulia that was predominantly Hindu. It was also on the other side of town from the Christian village where Varun was raised and his parents lived. It was a strange mixture of modern houses and old, traditional mud huts. Directly behind our house was a government apartment complex that rose six stories high and was surrounded by an open field. The field was occupied by a few cows and goats, undoubtedly belonging to the families that lived in the apartments.

News spread fast that a white American woman had moved into the neighborhood.

On the third morning I got up, fixed a cup of tea and decided to go up to the terrace on the roof to enjoy my usual prayer time. With my Bible in one hand and tea in the other, I climbed the stairs and managed to open the metal door. I sat my tea and Bible on the wide wall of the terrace and went back down to get a plastic chair. Just as I got settled into the chair and began looking at my new surroundings, people began coming out of their houses onto their rooftops. I had learned to not acknowledge them, so I opened my Bible and took a sip of tea. After reading perhaps four verses, I heard a voice yelling 'Madam!' I looked in the direction of the voice and spotted a small girl up in a tree, clinging to the tree with one hand and waving frantically with the other. 'Madam!' she repeated over and over. What could I do, but smile and wave back, hoping that this would satisfy her. All was quiet for a few minutes as I went back to the Bible and sipped at my tea.

But suddenly several little voices were yelling, 'Madam! Madam!' I tried to ignore them, but they just got louder and more insistent. I gave up trying to read my Bible and stood up, expecting to find a few children near the same tree that the girl had climbed up. What I discovered was, not only about twenty children jumping and waving on the ground below, but every rooftop in the neighborhood full of people looking at me. 'Good morning, madam!' one young boy said, grinning from ear to ear.

'Good morning,' I said. Then, feeling like I *had* to do something, I waved all around me and shouted, 'Good morning!' It seemed like the entire area echoed 'Good morning, madam!' back at me. I felt like I was on display and completely vulnerable. I picked up my tea and Bible and headed quickly downstairs where I found Varun just waking up. 'What's all that shouting?' he asked.

'The entire neighborhood wishing me good morning,' I replied.

'Honey, didn't I tell you not to encourage them?' he yawned. I stood in the doorway with my hands on my hips, giving him my most exasperated look. 'I was just trying to have my tea and prayer time when they started yelling and waving. What am I supposed to do?'

Varun just smiled and said, 'Welcome back to Purulia!'

'Gee, thanks,' I grinned. 'I guess I will move to the backyard if you want to join me.'

But before I could even settle down in a corner of the backyard, several children climbed up on the fence. Within minutes the entire fence was filled with smiling, waving children. I was not amused. I marched back into the house and summoned Varun. 'Come and look at this,' I snapped.

He reluctantly followed me out the back door. Just as we arrived, all the children began to sing 'A, B, C, D, E, F, G.' My heart melted. 'They are singing the only real English song they know,' Varun said, and began singing along with them. As always, he was in his element with the kids. I listened politely and smiled. When they were finished, Varun spoke to them all in Bengali and one by one, they disappeared.

He put his arm around me. 'Just give it some time, honey. The newness of you being here will eventually rub off and you can have some peace and quiet.'

'I know, hon,' I sighed, 'I guess I just forgot what it was like here. You know how I hate being treated like a monkey in a cage.'

'Yes, and I don't blame you. These kids are from a low caste and are not taught any manners. If they give us too much trouble, I will talk to the parents.'

I never liked the 'caste system' or putting people into boxes in any way. 'No, no, that's okay. I will just learn to deal with it myself,' I insisted. 'We will get used to each other.'

Over the next few weeks there were a lot of adjustments to make. At first, Varun and I fell into a sort of honeymoon mode. It was reassuring and I felt much better with my new, firmer, healthy body. I had not lost a lot of weight, but I was much healthier and confident of myself.

This was the first time that we had moved into an all-Hindu area. There were two temples within half a mile of our house. One was quite large and the other, small, but made up for its size with large bells and a loudspeaker. I became keenly aware again of the daily worship and pujas that took place all year round.

Our front door and windows faced a small alley. It was just wide enough for a rickshaw to pass through, but it was a popular footpath for the locals. Whenever I opened the windows, the children would immediately appear, peeking in and looking around with curious eyes, so I learned to keep them closed. Sometimes I would find a merchant knocking on the window trying to sell me fish, bangles or rugs.

One window was situated at the end of our hallway. To my dismay, I couldn't wear shorts and sleeveless T-shirts, not only because of people peeking in through the window, but also because of our male roommate. Varun warned me to dress properly and according to custom, even in our own home. This was more than an inconvenience, this was an intrusion to me. I wanted privacy and the ability to be comfortable in the coming hot months. Varun assured me that the roommate would be leaving soon.

A new rickshaw puller was found so that I could go to the market or to have breakfast at my favourite hotel, and attend any meetings that came up. Hira was chosen because he lived close by and could come at a moment's notice. His wife, Minu, was hired to clean the house and wash our clothes. Both of them came from a farming village nearby. They and their families had created a mud hut village in the neighbourhood, just a short walk away from our house.

Hiring local people could be risky because gossip spread fast in the community. Varun made sure that they knew that what went on in our house was a private matter and if any rumors were discovered, they would be fired immediately. This was very important because we were Christians. My own daily prayer and worship was crucial to me. Our Bible studies were very important too, but could be dangerous in this area.

In addition, we ate beef once a week, usually on Sunday afternoon.

Though many of our Hindu neighbours did eat chicken and fish, beef was considered sacrilegious.

Often Varun's mom would cook the beef at her house and Varun would bring it in the afternoon. But sometimes, we would cook it under the strictest of conditions, closing all windows and doors and masking the smell with incense. If any surprise guests arrived, we had to hide the beef in a cupboard. This was truly out of respect for our Hindu friends. While I was admittedly totally ignorant of their faith, I respected them and their beliefs.

We would buy the beef early in the morning from a shop in a Muslim area. Sometimes a Muslim friend would come and take our order for the following Sunday and discreetly deliver it to our home. The beef was usually chopped into small chunks and pressure cooked. Sometimes I would ask for finely chopped meat, to make hamburgers, when I craved a real American dish. But the meat was hand-chopped on a tree stump, so often I would have to pick out bits of wood before cooking. We always joked about getting the 'extra fiber' in our hamburgers. Finding the right bread for our burgers was also very difficult, so often we would just use the white bread that was available. No dill pickles anywhere and the rare mayonnaise we found was often outdated and stale. But we piled on tomatoes and onions and enjoyed every bite. In all the houses around us, the fuel commonly used for cooking was dried cow dung. The smoke from the fires seemed to fill the air with a pungent cloud so thick that we would have to close the windows until all the fires were burning well. Nine p.m. was the common dinner time, and the pressure cookers would start hissing shortly before that. Often I would sit on the roof and listen to the hissing noises that echoed across the rooftops. It was the one time I could sit on the roof, unnoticed as I watched the fireflies dance, the small bats flutter and the giant white owls swooping across the dark sky.

The vision I had in the US and the voice telling me to 'Take care of the children,' haunted me. Who were these children and where was this place that God had shown me? Months came and went without an answer.

As I settled into a daily routine of going to the hotel for breakfast and then to the market, Hira became familiar with my habits and the routes to the places I usually went.

The route to the market took us through another small village area, past mud huts and a pond in the center. A strange thing began to happen around the third week I was there. As soon as we entered this village, children would come out of their huts and run towards me. The older ones would lift the younger ones up to me. They simply wanted to touch me, all of them smiling and reaching for my hands, or to touch my feet or dress. I was puzzled by this behavior, but delighted with the children. Hira though was upset at this new phenomena. Concerned about my safety, he would stop only briefly and shout threateningly at the children to get out of the way, unless they wanted to be run over by the rickshaw.

I told Varun about this but he just smiled and brushed it aside.

∼

The truth was, Varun was growing increasingly distant and preoccupied when he was home. He had quit his job when the demands of the visa kept calling him out of town. He had been without work for over six months now and it had changed him. I understood the pressures he was facing and his feelings of failure and despair. I tried to encourage him, to love him enough that those feelings would disappear.

But when I arrived, the pressures mounted. I had returned fully expecting Varun to let everyone know that we were married now. I didn't think this was an unreasonable demand after what we had both been through. But as the days turned into weeks, I realized this was not going to happen any time soon.

I had begun the Bible studies again with Arun and the guys. But because we lived on the other side of town, the men had to travel in pairs on motorcycles or bicycles to get to our house. Often Varun would go out to round them all up and give them a ride on his motorcycle.

I had arrived with lots of ideas for community work for the team. I even designed a logo for T-shirts and hats with 'God Squad' written on them. My ambition was to increase our membership and include women in our Bible studies, to show our love to as many people as possible.

Slowly, I began to realize what an uphill task this was going to be. It seemed that Satan had taken possession of Varun and the guys. Though we continued to take trips to Jhalda to finish the church, things were not the same. I felt a dark cloud of oppression surrounding us. It seemed that all my attempts to get them involved in community work were blocked. Worse still, I was spending more and more time alone. Varun stayed away most of the time.

Drinking was their favorite pastime, as usual, and it took over our lives.

One afternoon Varun was pensive and pacing the floor. Arun and Peter showed up and Varun jumped up to meet them outside. I saw Arun pull out a small bundle of newspaper from his pocket and hand it to Varun. Varun opened up the newspaper and inside was something in a plastic bag. He took a pinch of what looked to me like chewed grass and put it in his mouth. I was used to seeing packets of tobacco and betel leaves that the men chewed. The entire area was filled with tiny shops displaying these packets. There were even natural herb shops that sold all sorts of leaves to cure ailments. I wondered what this new stuff was.

Arun looked up and saw me watching. Varun turned to look at me. 'Stomach medicine,' he said, 'I asked Arun to stop and get me something for my stomach.'

'You should have told me, honey,' I replied, 'I brought Zantac from the US for stomach problems.'

'Well, I have been using this medicine for a few months now and it seems to work well,' he said, 'I'll try your medicine next time.'

I really didn't think anything of it, that first time, but then I began to find small bundles of newspapers hidden away in the top shelves of the closet and wondered why he didn't just throw them away in the trash. I also noticed he was behaving strangely, erratic and completely unfocused. He was constantly fidgeting, and his eyes darted back and forth when I spoke to him. It appeared to me like he was drowning in anger and self-pity. I tried desperately to reach him, to get back the man I fell in love with, but the harder I tried, the further away he became. I was deeply perturbed and it did cross my mind that he may be on drugs, but whenever I tried to confront him about it, he said he was just taking some stuff that helped him to think straight and keep calm. I asked him to stop taking it and I would find better medicine for his ADD, but he refused. Varun's routine was the same each day. He would wake up, shower, get dressed and leave. He would return in the afternoon for lunch and a siesta. When he awoke, he would leave again, usually for the rest of the evening. On the nights that he stayed at home all the guys showed up. They would drink till late in the night, talking, playing music and cards. I could not understand what they were saying so I sat and listened, and watched carefully.

One night I saw them all crowding around Arun's cellphone, staring into it. When I tried to see what they were looking at, they kept hiding it from me. It became a game for them as I kept moving in to see it. When I did get a glimpse of what they were looking at, I saw that it was pornography.

I knew that Arun was into such things and I had deliberately chosen scripture in our Bible studies that would send a message to him. What I had realized long ago was that I was like a mother to them, the only woman trying to teach this group of single young men. But unlike their mothers, they felt they could behave naturally in front of me, knowing that I would not freak out or condemn them.

They also knew that I would not tolerate certain behavior, like drunkenness or fighting, but like children, they often tested me, like this business with the cellphone.

In my heart I was discouraged but determined to step up my prayer time for each of the young men. My husband was their leader...and their leader was not in good shape at all. My gut was telling me that there was something else going on, something that made my stomach knot and turn. I used to feel so close to all of them. But now I felt isolated.

Before, Varun tried to set a good example and spent all the time he could with me. Now it seemed he didn't care anymore. I had given up so much, my family, my country, to be with him, to follow God's plan for our lives, believing that I would return to a loving husband and a ministry that was alive and well. What was happening? Varun's behavior and attitude were so different. Our relationship seemed to have changed dramatically, and I was scared and worried. For the first time distrust and suspicion entered my mind.

My self-doubts emerged in the long hours alone. Was Varun only interested in me because he thought he could get a visa? Was he so distant with me now because that plan had failed? After fourteen months, I had come back here to be with him, yet he didn't want to be with me, that was obvious. Anger rose inside me. I had to shake off all of these thoughts and remember that I had promised to serve God here. It was not a conditional promise. I didn't say, 'As long as Varun and I are together, I will serve you.' But the thought of being alone in this country without him terrified me. Was my faith strong enough to endure this alone?

I tried to get a grip on myself and my thoughts. What was I thinking? If anything were to be done here, it would not be because of me and my own strength, but with God. I just needed to pray more, study more and allow God to work through me. I had not learned yet to simply let go and let God do His work; that was something I needed to do.

∽

As in those first few years in Purulia, all my physical needs were taken care of. Water, food and a new comfortable mattress were provided. Luckily, I was now familiar with the area and the culture, as well as the marketplace. I had Hira to transport me around, and Minu to do the housework. Hira and Minu were the only ones, apart from the guys, who knew that we were living as husband and wife.

I spent most of my time praying and reading scripture. When it came time for me to pray, I told Minu to leave me alone. But I am quite sure she peeked in on me as I was in deep prayer. At first, she kept a respectful distance from me, but after a month, she began to smile and try to communicate with me through sign language. When Varun was around, she would cover her head with her dupatta and never lifted her eyes to him. Varun would joke, 'See how she shows respect for me? You should be doing the same!' I would just raise an eyebrow and give him my look of disapproval.

To pass time, I kept a journal and drew pictures. There was no TV or refrigerator. We only had my laptop for entertainment and the old ice chest I had purchased the first year. I spent many hours playing games on the computer and talking to God, out loud.

The old adage, 'An idle mind is the devil's workshop,' came to me often.

One afternoon I began to weep. 'Lord, I know you've got this whole situation under control, but I am going crazy here! Do you really want me to just sit here day after day in this heat, alone, when I could be out in the villages praying or in the churches sharing my testimony? I mean, I get it that I had to learn patience and all, but I need some real work to do,' I cried out in frustration, then I added, 'Something has happened to Varun and he is scaring me with his behavior. Please tell me what to do.' I was pacing the floor back and forth, gesturing to the heavens. 'Oh! By the way, it would be really great if you could tell me who are these children that you keep telling me to take care of? Is it the children that are chasing me in the rickshaw? If so, could you please give me a little hint as to what I am supposed to do?' I collapsed on the bed, burying my face in the pillow.

A few minutes later, Minu came in to sweep the room, and I tried to pull myself together. She could see that I had been crying and asked, 'Theek hai?' meaning, are you okay?

'Yes,' I nodded, blowing my nose. 'Theek hai.' I quickly went into the bathroom to wash my face.

Eventually we got an internet connection so I was able to send and receive mail too. I also began doing some Bible study online. I hungered to know more about the lives and times of that period.

Varun was spending lots of time on the internet too, either at home, or at the internet cafés in town. One day, while marketing, I passed by the internet café and saw Varun's motorcycle parked in front. There he was, chatting on Yahoo. As soon as he saw me, he logged off before I could see the page he was on.

I had hoped that, now we were married, he would stop his online chatting and visiting the cyber cafe—where we ourselves had first met, in the Christian chatroom. We got into an argument about this one day. He said that he was only keeping in touch with his friends and not chatting with any women. I told him he could do this at home, now that we had the internet connection, and stop wasting money that we could ill afford. But, when we got the first internet bill, it was based on usage and was a very big amount.

Alarms went off in my head. It was a USB modem

connection and I knew I didn't use it that much. I also knew that he often took the modem with him when he went out. I put a stop to that and insisted on keeping the modem with me. I hated that I had to 'police' the usage, but we couldn't afford another huge bill.

Varun seemed to be addicted to the internet. I knew that he had an addictive personality, but I had never encountered this type of addiction before. He was a downloading maniac. He kept downloading music, videos, free software and only God knew what else, until my desktop was covered with icons and the laptop became slower and slower.

I knew Varun had too much free time on his hands. Now that I had returned to Purulia, and the ministry was still not flourishing, I felt it was time for him to try to find a job. We certainly could use the extra income. But how could I bring the subject up without upsetting him? It was a touchy subject and one that had to be discussed at the right moment and in the right way. When I did bring it up, he became defensive and angry. He said that his parents were taking up so much of his time now and with taking care of my needs, where was there any time for a job? It was true that his family had become more demanding of him lately. I decided to let it go for now though I knew I should get to the bottom of it—but in the face of his anger, I didn't have the courage.

∼

The winter months disappeared too quickly and summer heat arrived with a fury. The local wells and ponds dried up and the mosquitoes were relentless.

All was tolerable when there was electricity. But more and more often the electricity would go off.

We paid an additional monthly fee for a back-up

generator service. But this service was only available from 11a.m to 11p.m. The ceiling fan was our only source of relief from the humidity and heat. Often the electricity would go off shortly after eleven at night. Then the bugs and mosquitoes would invade us through the open windows. There was no relief, except to light mosquito coils that filled the room with pungent smoke. This was the season of katydids, or long green-winged insects that arrived in swarms, only to shed their wings and die. There were also tiny cricket-like creatures with black spots on their bodies that hopped around in clusters. Neither of these were biting insects, but both were attracted to light and the open windows. I could not sleep as my body was drenched in sweat and the bugs crawled across my face. I often poured water on myself, clothes and all, to get relief or I would soak the sheet and wrap it around me. I wanted to strip down naked under the wet sheet, but we still had the roommate living in the house with us, so this was not possible.

Varun did not like mosquito nets. He told me that as a child they frightened him, so we had nothing to keep the bugs off us. I tried to ignore the bugs crawling across my body, but I just couldn't stop swatting them. Varun would say, 'Just lay still and breathe deep. All that thrashing around will just make you hotter. When the electricity comes back on, the fan will make them go away.' Soon he was snoring away. I guess the drink helped.

I lay wide awake, brushing the bugs and sweat off me in a sort of mental terror, thinking of the many night insects that could invade us while we slept. Then I remembered the people I saw in the town, including children, who slept outside every night. How could they do this? I concluded that it was just a matter of mental control. I strived to keep my mind busy with prayer and pleasant thoughts. I pretended

I was lying on the beach with cool breezes drifting gently across my body. Slowly this began to work in a kind of deep meditation and then gradually I was able to lift myself out of my surroundings and actually feel the soft sand and cool breezes of my childhood days. I sort of floated in and out of that state, losing my concentration when a mosquito bit me.

All I really wanted was for that fan to blow away those insects and for my body to stop producing what seemed like volumes of sweat. I said a silent prayer of thanks when the electricity finally came on and I was able to drift off into a restless sleep. I woke up to insect bodies and wings all over the bed, the floor, and in my hair. All I could think about was taking a shower and the dreaded fact that this was going to happen every night. It was no wonder afternoon naps were a requirement here.

---

27. An Unexpected Visitor—and a Prophesy

A few days later, early in the morning, an unexpected visitor came to our house asking for me. This was surprising because we didn't make a habit of letting people know where I lived, not only for privacy, but to prevent unwanted visitors from coming to me for money. It was sad, but necessary because of the common belief that I, as an American woman, would have plenty of money. We had all learned in those first years how important it was to protect me from what I called, 'treasure seekers.' I learned to recognize 'the look' in the eyes of these people. It was a look that in my younger, thinner days, I got from men as they eyed me up and down and flirted with me. That seductive smile and predatory eyes were always a sign to me to put up my defenses and exit as quickly as possible.

The same rule applied in this world, but 'the look' was no longer a desire for intimate encounters, it was a lust for a quick ticket to money. In my early days in India, I would naively listen to anyone who came to me for help, and often become a victim of lies and deception and ulterior motives. As a result, I had become wary and cynical of anyone who desired to become my friend too quickly and Varun and the guys had become all the more protective of me.

It was not that I didn't understand the desire to make a quick buck with so much poverty all around. I admired their tenacity in maintaining hope in such a hopeless world. What these people didn't understand was that I was not a rich American, that I too was struggling on a pension and allocating what I could to help the most needy. Those first few years I tried to help all who asked because I knew that I was so blessed, but it became apparent that I had to draw some lines and create some boundaries for my own protection.

So when this stranger arrived, he came with Rajat. He stood outside as Rajat explained to us who he was and why he had come. He came from a village very near the town where we were building the church. His brother was a pastor and had an orphanage of over thirty children. They had lost their funding from a South Indian church and they desperately needed someone to help them.

As I listened to Rajat, the alarm bells went off in my head. Another 'treasure seeker,' I thought as I looked out the window and studied the man standing outside. He was handsome in a rugged sort of way. He looked like an Indian version of Charlton Heston when he played Moses. Except his dark beard was trimmed neatly and he was well-dressed, a sign that he came from a respectable family.

Varun listened intently as Rajat spoke. One of the things I liked about Varun was his empathy for the needs of others. He had compassion underneath that macho exterior. I knew he would want to listen to this man, and I was curious too, so we agreed to let Rajat bring him in.

Over the course of an hour, the man, David, told us his story. They lived in the village of Jargo, about 30 kilometers from Jhalda. His brother, Nathan, had been running the orphanage for three years but now both he and David felt that they needed someone else to take over. He said that it wasn't just about the money, it was about a prophesy Nathan had been told years ago. This prophet had told him that a woman with a great healing would come from America to his ministry and would be a great influence on it. David said that the minute Nathan heard about me coming to Jhalda and building the church, he remembered this prophesy. They had also heard that I was living in Purulia.

Rajat was their 'cousin brother' who also lived in Purulia, so they talked to him. They were pleasantly surprised to discover that Rajat was part of our ministry team. David caught the first bus the next morning to come and talk with Rajat and hopefully, with me.

As I was listening to his story, especially about the children and the prophesy, I remembered the voice telling me to 'take care of the children,' and the prayer I had recently spoken out loud for God to tell me who these children were. My mind was putting all of this together over and over again, as if to mentally pinch myself. The prophesy, the healing, the calling to India, the voice to 'take care of the children,' and building the church near their village. It was unbelievable. This could only be God at work!

Varun and David were talking in Bengali and I tugged at Varun's shirt sleeve. He turned to look at me. Seeing the expression on my face, he raised his eyebrows. 'What is it?' he asked.

'Remember I told you about the voice I heard in America that said to take care of the children?' I asked.

'Yes, of course I do,' he responded...then as his mind registered what I had said, his eyes grew as big as mine. We looked like two owls staring at each other. Varun translated what we were talking about for David. There was a long silence between us as we tried to grasp the reality of it all. Finally an almost inaudible whisper came from David. 'Praise God!' I nodded, still filled with the wonderment of it all. 'Yes,' I said. 'He planned this all along!'

We immediately set to task to make arrangements to go to the orphanage to meet the children and Nathan, confident that we were following God's path. We asked David to stay for lunch, eager to know more about the children and their situation. Rajat was sent out to bring back some food. He came back with a few samosas for me and fishhead soup for themselves. For me, this was difficult to watch as they chewed on the crisply fried fishhead, bone and all, sucking the eyeballs and brains with delight. I silently thanked God for the samosas.

David could speak a little English, but preferred to talk in his own language, so I could only follow a little of what they were talking about. He told us that there were thirty-two children at the orphanage, mostly boys. Most of these children were abandoned, either by their own mothers, or found in railway stations or wandering the streets. When I asked how a mother could abandon her own children, David explained. 'In this part of the country, if the father dies, or leaves a woman alone, she has no way of making money to support her children. Her only hope for survival is to remarry. But the new husband usually will not accept children from the previous husband, so the condition of the marriage is that she get rid of her children.'

There were all sorts of terrible ways to get rid of the children, David told me, but the kindest way was to give them to an orphanage, where they could at least have food, clothing and an education. Other children were not so lucky. They were sold as child labor in sweatshops or the girls were sold to the sex trade in Kolkata. I shuddered at the thought, I could not even fathom the lives of these unfortunate children. It seemed ludicrous to think of the children in the orphanage as 'the lucky ones,' but it was the reality of this world.

David said that they wanted us to take over the whole operation. He even wanted to put our names on the bank accounts and the registration for the non-profit status, which we were told was a seven-year process and very difficult to get—they were in their fifth year. He told us that they could pay someone what they call 'sweets' under the table to get the process done quickly, but as Christians, they didn't want to do this.

I personally wasn't very enthusiastic about taking over an entire orphanage and the responsibility of those tiny lives. After raising two children of my own and mostly as a single mother, I knew it was a huge responsibility. Varun, on the other hand, was visibly excited. After all, he had worked with children as a teacher and had often told me how he helped raise his nieces when they were young. I could see the light of happy possibilities in Varun's eyes for the first time since the trauma of the visa. I knew this was something he really wanted to do.

I had a flashback memory of my own ambitions, as a young girl. After seeing the movie *Cheaper by the Dozen*, I wanted to grow up and have twelve children too. I thought it was so wonderful how the family supported each other. The children not only got along, but really loved their brothers and sisters. This was a strange concept to me, since my sisters and I seemed to be aliens deposited into the same family from different planets.

A few years later I realized that this just wasn't practical if I was to become a famous singer or actor, which I had by then decided I wanted to be. If that didn't work out, I could always have the twelve children later. After all, anything was possible at the age of twelve!

But three and a half years later, when I was sixteen and the Vietnam War was in full swing, and for reasons I cannot understand today, I was married to a sailor. By the time I was eighteen, my son Kevin was born, and at twenty, my daughter Tracy. At the tender age of twenty-two, with the help of my parents and friends, I managed to escape the drunken abusiveness of my husband and file for a divorce. Life has a way of knocking dreams right out of you...for a while.

Years later, as a single mom, I seriously thought about owning an orphanage and actually looked into the possibilities. Not only could I be at home with my kids, but they would have many sisters and brothers too!

After months of poring over rules, regulations, requirements, and talking to a lawyer, I realized that it would take an enormous amount of effort and money to do this, exposing my children and me to major liabilities. Besides, the hard fact of life was that I was barely able to raise the two children I had, working two and three jobs at a time while trying to be a supportive mother. I was always filled with guilt at the little time I had with them.

The irony of it all was that this was the time of women's liberation when I was told that I could do it all…to quote a popular song at the time, I could 'bring home the bacon and fry it up in the pan and never let you forget that you are a man.' My lifestyle was considered to be the ideal—an independent working woman who was raising two children on her own.

In reality I would sit at a business lunch, gazing at the women eating at the table across the room with strollers, diaper bags and toddlers, envying their lives with a passion so deep that it almost brought me to tears. I wanted to just be a stay-at-home mom like them!

It was true that I could quit working and go on government welfare like so many of the single women I knew, and there were a few times I had no choice but to depend on the welfare system, but I wanted to set a better, more ambitious example. I didn't want to raise my children on charity. They had to know that they could rise above the ashes of poverty, bad decisions in life and despair!

I am still not quite sure how that worked out. I often said that my children raised me. They were my entire reason for living, for getting up in the morning, for going back to get my diploma, for remaining optimistic…and on some days, for simply breathing.

So I could empathize with the mothers who took their children to the orphanage. It was a better option than letting them starve or live on the streets. It was more than they, as single mothers, in a much crueler world, could give them. I decided that these mothers really loved their children. This was the very best they could offer them. Now I wanted to meet the children that I was supposed to take care of.

∼

That evening the entire God Squad came to our house. Varun told them the whole story. They all did the 'owl eyes' while their minds tried to grasp the story. A lot of discussion followed as we made our plans and worked out all the details.

The next morning I got up early. Varun always slept late, and I was grateful for this, because it was my private time with God. My heart danced inside me in excitement. This was the answer to so many questions that had plagued me for months. 'Show me what I am to do Lord,' I prayed, 'open my spiritual eyes so I can see. Reveal to me your will.'

It was the monsoon season. The sky was dark with the promise of rain. This didn't dampen our spirits as the men showed up. Arun was the first to arrive with bags of hot puri subji, a breakfast that I loved. It was the perfect dish for a rainy day. A young man I hadn't met before had accompanied Arun. He was a 'cousin brother' of Arun. His name was Jonas, a fine Christian name, I thought, as I introduced myself. Jonas came from a different part of India where they spoke Hindi. He didn't understand much Bengali, but most of them spoke Hindi, so it wasn't long before they were chattering away together.

Soon our car arrived. As was my custom, I gathered everyone around in a circle, holding hands, and prayed for God's presence that day and for the safety of the journey. We all piled into the large SUV and headed to Jargo. Varun had brought along his pen drive with music, so we all listened to songs for the 80-km journey.

It was a familiar road we had taken many times to work on the church, but this time we drove past that area and continued on the highway lined with palm trees, banana trees, ponds and with the familiar volcanic mountains jutting up across the horizon.

Finally the car slowed and we turned to the right onto a very narrow and muddy road flanked on both sides by mud huts. The car inched its way past goats, ducks, one stubborn cow, and children dashing in and out of the alleyways between the houses, until we came to a sharp turn in the road. The driver refused to go any further so we got out of the car and began walking. After getting directions, we continued along the path as people began to emerge from their homes. We walked past tiny shops, a small temple and a covered shed where goats were tied together eating contentedly.

The villagers came out of their homes to stare at us. It wasn't every day that a white foreign woman and seven Indian men came to their village. Not every day…my mind stopped right there, in pure revelation. I suddenly realized that I *had* walked here before, many times. I knew these faces and I knew exactly what was going to happen next…because this was one of the visions I had in America! Just as in the first year a vision I had had materialized into reality, it was happening all over again. My eyes began to tear up and my heart pounded, feeling the very presence of God in each step I took. 'Thank you Lord!' I whispered as a tear trickled down my cheek. 'Your promise has come true!' In my vision there was a figure at the end of the path, standing and waving at me. There stood David, waving at us and showing us where the orphanage was. I wiped my eyes as we approached David and entered into the gate of the orphanage.

---

28. Great Expectations

The compound consisted of two sections, the main house where Nathan lived with his wife, two children, mother and brother, and the orphans' quarters. Nathan's house was nicely furnished and very neat. It was obvious that they had all dressed in their best for our arrival. In the back of the house was an old mud hut that was used for the kitchen where two women were busy cooking in large pots. There were bags of rice and vegetables strewn on the floor. I wondered why this hot, dark room was used for cooking when there was an airy, modern kitchen inside the house, which we had just passed through.

We walked to the back of the house as Nathan pointed out the row of toilets that were built for the children and told me that one of them was a Western-style one. I was delighted to know this!

We walked past an open shady area where the day's wash was strung across on clotheslines. There was a huge well to the right of the steps leading up to the children's quarters. The older girls were carrying up buckets of water from the well and trying to get the younger children to wash themselves. Nathan pointed out the distance between the well and the toilets, explaining how difficult it was for the younger children to carry the buckets of water when they had to use the toilets. His plan, for the future, was to get a water pipe built, with a pump, to bring the water directly to the toilets.

A short flight of stairs led up into the orphanage building. The first door on the left led into the children's sleeping quarters. There were rows of metal bunk beds, arranged dormitory-style, some with mattresses, but many with only mats spread over the wooden crossboards. There were a few pillows, but certainly not enough for all the children. There were two children lying on a top bunk who were obviously sick with a cold. This didn't stop them from joining in the chorus of 'Good morning madam' that greeted me. In the hallway outside stood three young ladies who, we were told, were the teachers. Their room was directly across from the children's room. We were invited to see the room they shared. It was neat and clean, with pictures of Jesus on the walls. I tried to speak to them, to find out more about them and the orphanage, but they were guarded in their replies and kept glancing at Nathan for approval before answering. One woman in particular glared at Nathan for a brief moment. I made a mental note of this as we continued our tour of the classrooms and the chapel and meeting hall. On the other side of the orphanage was a large compound that must have served as a playground, though there were no swings, slides, or any signs of toys.

I know it sounds ridiculous for me to have noticed this, when there were so many obvious needs pointed out to us, like textbooks, notebooks, pens and pencils, Bibles, clothing... the list was endless; but it was the thought of no toys, no stuffed animals, no dolls, nothing for these children to play with, that really tugged at my heart.

At the end of our tour, the children, now all washed and dressed, had lined up outside the chapel. Nathan ushered us inside, explaining that the children wanted to sing for us. I was given a chair to sit on in front of the pulpit. When the children came marching in, lining up in rows in front of us, one little girl stood out. She had club feet and short arms but she didn't seem to notice that she was different. As a matter of fact, I was caught first by her beaming smile and the way she rushed excitedly into the room, before I noticed her deformities. She made me smile too.

For the next hour, with Nathan in the lead, the children said the Lord's Prayer in unison, sang many Christian songs in Bengali and some in English. They had been taught hand movements and little dances to some of the songs. It was very entertaining, charming...and a bit too staged. Nathan even pointed to different children asking them to recite certain scriptures. They obediently obliged us with faultless recitations. Then he told them it was time to pray. We all bowed our heads, but I could not resist watching the children in prayer.

The littlest ones were adorable, with their hands together and their eyes squeezed tightly shut. A few of the older ones were quite sincere, some with hands raised in the air. Then, within a few minutes, almost in unison, the children began, as Nathan did, praying in tongues. A minute more and they were waving their hands in the air, some screaming, some moaning. A few of the children began crying because of all the noise. The teachers ushered them out quickly.

I really wish I could say that I felt the Holy Spirit's movements in the room. But instead, I felt I was watching children who had been trained to imitate the behavior of the adults they must have observed in Pentecostal prayer. All of them kept glancing at Nathan for cues. As his prayers grew quieter, they followed suit. Finally it was over. The children stood up and finished with a short song. Nathan told us that the children who started crying had just arrived at the orphanage a few days before and had not yet been exposed to this kind of worship. Again I caught the looks of disapproval from the teachers as they filed the children outside.

Something was not right here. I tried to shake off my

misgivings by telling myself that I was reading more into the situation than there was, but my senses were on alert.

We had given Peter the task of taking pictures of our visit. I decided that we should get a group photo of the children with the teachers. I playfully gathered them together, grabbing the stragglers to get them all in the group. I waved to one of the boys to come and join the picture. Nathan, a hint of annoyance in his voice, said loudly, 'That is my son. He is not one of the orphans,' and told the boy to go stand with his mother.

I was taken aback by his tone. I apologized coldly for mistaking his son for one of 'those orphans', hoping he caught the sarcasm in my voice. He just nodded and told us that lunch was ready.

We had already agreed, on our trip there, that we would not eat lunch at the orphanage. After hearing about the struggles they had just to feed all the children, I didn't want to burden them further with feeding us. We did our best to refuse, but they would not hear of it.

A sumptuous meal of chicken curry, rice, dal, spiced vegetables and boiled greens was spread out on the dining table in Nathan's house. The guys, as usual, ate mountains of rice. I was expecting the children to eat with us, but was told that they ate their meals in the orphanage building.

I was becoming increasingly uncomfortable with the now obvious separation between the family and the orphans. Nearly all of my expectations and excitement of coming here had crumbled. I just wanted badly to leave.

After lunch, we all began to make our way to the car, but David and Nathan insisted that we have tea before leaving and talk about the future of the orphanage. We were ushered into the master bedroom which also served as the living room.

Varun and I sat on the bed and David and Nathan on chairs. There weren't enough chairs to go round, so Arun and Rajat joined us while the others went out to visit the children. Nathan told us his story of living in South India and preaching there. He also told us in more detail about the prophesy that he would meet an American woman who had received a healing from God and would be called to India. The prophet who told him this said that this woman would have a great influence on his ministry. 'I praise God so much for this prophesy coming true. When I heard about you, I told my wife, she is the one!'

Frankly I was puzzled and confused by everything that had happened. There was no doubt that this was where I was supposed to be, but I was very uncomfortable with Nathan and the way the children were being treated. I knew there were things yet undiscovered about the entire situation.

It ended up being a very long meeting. Nathan got out all the documents and he was honest about the debts he had accrued trying to keep the orphanage going. He had started taking in day scholars whose families paid monthly fees for their schooling. His wife's family had been helping with some financial support. His father-in-law was the pastor of a church in Jamshedpur—and he wanted me to come to his church and give my testimony. He told us that the orphanage building and funding first came from a church in South India. But the agreement between them was for a period of three years. That period ended nearly a year ago and they had been struggling to survive since then. Nathan told us how much they had fasted and prayed for help and a sign from God.

That was when I saw it, that look in his eyes that made me shiver. It was only for a few seconds and I could have been mistaken, but I was quite sure it was the 'treasure seeker' look.

I spoke up. 'I have no doubt that God has brought us together. The vision was very clear to me as we were walking through your village this morning,' I continued. 'But, as we explained to David, our own ministry is struggling to get funds to complete the church in Jhalda. We have had to cut back on the construction quite a bit. I have also been fasting and in much prayer for God to help us finish our project. I have been dedicating as much as I can from my meager monthly income towards this.'

Nathan nodded. 'Yes, David did tell us this and that is fine.' There was a long pause. 'But I am sure that if you take over the orphanage, you could get donations from the US. We are alone in this village in India with thirty-two children to feed. This is quite different than building a church.'

'Yes, it is quite different,' I said solemnly. 'Those children deserve to have a future with full stomachs, surrounded by people who love them unconditionally. To me, it is more essential that they feel the love of Christ than it is that they learn scripture.'

There was an awkward silence. I continued, 'I think we all need to pray about this now and in the next week. Varun and I will do some research online to find out if there are any organizations that can help us get funds. I will send out a newsletter to all of my own friends and family too.' I smiled, 'Let's see what God shows us and meet again next week.' There were smiles all around the room. We all stood up, held hands, and prayed together, first in Bengali, then in English. How I hoped that God would show us all what we were to do.

It was on the trip home that my worst suspicions were confirmed. The guys had done their job of observation and asking subtle questions. While we were sitting at that large dining table laden with food, the children and teachers, were given only small servings of rice, dal and bananas. The teachers confirmed that they were given barely enough food to fill their stomachs, while the family ate well. They also said that they had not been paid in three months. Two of them were leaving within a week.

Nathan had already told us about the teachers' salaries, so this did not surprise us, but my blood boiled at the differential treatment meted out to the children. I knew it was all about the caste system. David and Nathan were raised in an upper caste family. These children came from the poorest and lowest castes. To Nathan they were as different as night and day.

It wasn't that he didn't care about their welfare; he spent many sleepless nights taking care of them when they were sick, helped them with their studies and often took them to the local pond for swimming and bathing. But the conviction that they were of a lower breed, used to terrible living conditions, so it wouldn't be good to spoil them too much, never went away. This was the reality of the world that they would eventually return to.

It reminded me of when I was maybe eight years old. I had a wild bird that I nursed from babyhood. I was so proud that, with my love and care, it grew up and began flying around the room. Dad said that it was time to release it into the wild so it could live with other birds like him. Sadly, I let him go and watched him fly away. But every day I found it perched outside the door and it kept trying to get into the house by banging on the window, until one day it broke its neck. I wept bitterly, but I understood that my love was a selfish kind of love that eventually killed him—because he couldn't survive in the world to which he returned.

It was hard to reconcile this kind of thinking when it

came to children. I had raised my own children to be strong and independent. I had seen the results of spoiling children by giving them too much, and I didn't want this for my own kids. Varun had shown me how they made a newborn baby sleep on a hard bed and gave it the local water. It wasn't to be cruel; it was to make them tough. He had said, 'This is a hard world in India. A child must learn early about this hardness or it won't survive.'

I realized that Varun was right. My Western motherly instincts would have, if I had the money, provided those children with soft mattresses, lots of clothes, toys and stuffed animals, along with fans and coolers in the summer and heaters in the winter. None of this was wrong...if you were willing to raise them into adulthood and provide them with the education they would need to remove themselves from the prejudice of the caste system and the realities of their world. It would be a longterm, lifetime commitment, with huge financial and emotional obligations. I couldn't even think of raising a puppy right now.

Setting aside my own personal feelings about how the orphans should be treated, I knew that we had to do whatever we could to 'take care of the children.' Varun set to task to do online research to find a larger organization or group that could help us with donations, even if it was simply clothes, books, toys, or the much needed pipeline and pump to the toilets.

We had all noticed the sweltering heat in the children's bedroom. The monsoon season, while bringing in the rain, also brought suffocating humidity. Without air circulation, this turned the room full of children into a sauna at night, so two ceiling fans were a priority in my mind.

Some of the guys knew of a wholesaler who often supplied

rice, lentils and wheat, at a very low rate, to the needy. Their task was to talk to him and find out if we could get a steady supply at a good price. There was another thing that haunted all of us...that little smiling girl with the deformities. Sunita was her name. Nathan had told us that her parents were local farmers who were very poor. When she was born, they managed to take her to a few doctors to see if her twisted feet could be fixed. But the prognosis was not good and the surgeries required cost too much. Sunita also needed help to do daily tasks, such as using the toilet. Both parents had to work and as she got older, they knew there was nothing they could do but turn her over to the orphanage. My online research project was to find a medical team that would help little Sunita.

With her family's approval, we brought Sunita to Purulia and had her feet and body X-rayed. I sent the X-rays to my dad, asking him to contact the local hospital and see if there was anyone there that would take a look at them. Dad was eager to help. I sent out a newsletter to all of my friends telling them about the orphanage and little Sunita, asking for donations.

Then I focused on prayer. I knew that I had to go into deep prayer and meditation. I had learned that preparing my heart and mind for prayer was extremely important. To me, prayers meant talking to God. Meditation is listening. It is the listening, the dwelling in that place, that I loved the most. It is where indescribable peace dwells and love is felt so powerfully that it absorbs you, envelops you, becomes you... or you become it. You are one...and you never want to leave.

It is strange how our memories seem to return at the oddest times.

As I was preparing for prayer, getting a pillow to sit

on the floor, lighting the candle under the wooden cross, I remembered 'being' in that deep place of prayer as a child. How many times I had been there, I don't know, but I do know that it wasn't through my own effort so much as it was meant to be. It seemed to me that I had spent my entire life with one foot on earth and the other in a spiritual world.

∼

My two days of fasting and prayer strengthened me and gave me reassurance about the path we were on. Varun was very absorbed in the online research and, at times, it seemed like he was becoming more like his old self. He smiled more and was happy to be supervising the men for a cause he believed in.

A few nights later I was woken in the middle of the night with a voice telling me, 'Genesis 3:4'. At first I thought I had dreamed it but it came again. 'Genesis 3:4'. I jumped out of bed and picked up my Bible. I took it into the kitchen with a flashlight, so I wouldn't disturb Varun, and opened it up, searching for this scripture. It said: 'That's a lie!' the serpent hissed. 'You'll not die! God knows very well that the instant you eat it you will become like him, for your eyes will be opened—you will be able to distinguish good from evil!'

I read it over and over again, trying to figure out what the message was and why I had received it in the middle of the night. This was the first time I had been woken up from sleep like this and I didn't want to miss whatever it was I needed to know. Nothing came to me, so I went back to bed, deciding to wait until the morning.

When morning came, I quickly made tea and took my Bible back into the kitchen. I read the scripture again. I could think of many possibilities, the first one being that Varun had lied to me, so maybe that had settled into my mind and woken me. But that didn't make sense at all, because the scripture was specific and at a crucial point in our Biblical history, the day Eve ate the forbidden fruit. I knew that this was a warning...of a lie, but from whom? I decided that I needed some insight from someone else, someone who knew scripture and had some spiritual gift that might help me understand the meaning. I immediately thought of my son. So when Varun woke up, I told him I wanted to use his phone so I could call my son.

I took the phone into the bedroom while Varun went to the bathroom and called Kevin. It was 9:30 at night there, so I hoped I would catch him at a quiet moment. I told him what had happened, and the scripture. 'Let me get my Bible,' he said. In a short time he was back and read the King James version out loud. There was a long pause on the line.

'Mom,' he said seriously, 'God is warning you that someone is deceiving you, that maybe even Satan is deceiving you. Be very careful who you are associating with and keep your spiritual eyes open. That is all I can tell you.' I took a deep breath. He had confirmed what I was thinking.

'Okay, I agree with you,' I said. 'I just wish I knew who it was, because right now there are a few possibilities.' I told him about David and Nathan, and our trip to the orphanage.

'It sounds to me like you are in the middle of something very big,' he said. 'This could be a turning point in your life. Be very careful mom.'

'Thanks honey, I will be very careful,' I assured him. 'But I must get off the phone now because of the cost. I love you.'

'I love you too mom, and I will be praying more on this. If anything comes to my mind, I will call you right away.'

We said our goodbyes just as Varun was coming in with his morning cup of tea. 'What was that all about?' he asked.

'Nothing,' I lied, 'I guess I just missed him and wanted to hear his voice. He is doing well.' I wasn't ready to share this yet and I didn't want to worry Varun. 'That's good,' he said absently as I gave him his phone.

Over the next few days, Varun and I took turns using the computer. He was sending out requests for information from various charity organizations throughout the world, trying to find out their requirements for giving funds for the orphanage. I was doing the same except searching for charity medical organizations that would do surgeries in third world countries. Though we were both being educated on the difficulties of qualifying for aid, neither of us was getting positive feedback.

We had hired a carpenter to make the front door of the church. He said it would take him a few months to design it, so I diverted the money to the orphanage. We had decided not to give money directly to Nathan, but to purchase the items needed instead. We bought two ceiling fans and a large sack of rice and dal at less than wholesale prices.

Nathan was calling us almost daily, wanting us to raise money for a plumber and a pump to bring the water line to the toilets. This was an expensive project that would require donations from outside. I just didn't have that kind of money myself. We even cut back on our own expenses so we could purchase vegetables and fruit for the children.

All of us were excited about our success and of course everyone wanted to go on the trip to deliver the goods.

I was delighted when another young man joined our group. Ajit was eager to become a part of our Bible study group. His mother told him that she would buy him a motorcycle if he showed that he would attend regularly. I was so encouraged that our group was growing, that I made a list and began a daily prayer time for each of them. So now we had:

Arun—serious accountant and organizer.

Peter—ladies' man, cook, and Arun's sidekick.

Nitesh—Tall, with a good sense of humor who taught children's Sunday School.

Bharat—our Hindu guitarist and dear friend—he took the Bible studies seriously.

Rajat—loved to laugh, but angered easily, serious about politics and life in general.

Jonas—ambitious, hard-working and innocent.

Ajit—stuttered, handsome, dressed well, had some compulsive behaviors, and of course: Varun. I had seven men, plus Varun—the leader, my secret husband.

Seven is a good number, I told myself. It was a number used often in the Bible. I had visions of multiplying this number hundredfold, but for now, it was a good start! Everything seemed to be falling into place, except that we still hadn't been able to get any donations for the orphanage.

We were all excited on the day we took the supplies to the orphanage. Somehow, all ten of us, including the driver, managed to fit into the car. The rack on the roof was loaded up with the food supplies and two ceiling fans. We stopped at a roadside fruit stand and bought an entire stem full of bananas. We were a happy group as we listened to music and sang along. I told the guys how proud I was of all of them working together as a team.

When we arrived, the gates were open and we drove into the compound near the family house. There was an immediate stirring of activity as the men unloaded the rack on top of the car. They carried the supplies into the kitchen and Rajat presented the bananas to Nathan.

Once everything was unloaded, we all stood together, beaming, looking at Nathan, his wife and David. They looked back at us silently and somberly. It didn't take long for it to register that they were not happy.

We were politely invited to a cup of tea.

The men, sensing that something was wrong, slowly wandered off as Varun and I went inside. We were directed once again into the bedroom by Nathan and David. It had been two weeks since we had seen either of them, but I noticed that Nathan was thin and pale. He began by telling us that the teachers had left and he and David were trying to keep the school open, since this was their only income. 'We have been fasting for five days and praying for money to come from the US,' he said, looking directly at me. He took a deep breath, 'So tell me, have you been fasting and praying too?'

I didn't like his tone at all. 'Yes, of course,' I said indignantly, 'I fasted and prayed for two days right after we first met and have been praying every day for the orphanage.'

'And what has the Lord shown you?' he asked. I immediately thought of Genesis 3:4, but decided to keep that to myself.

'He has, as you can see, provided us with the means to supply the things we have brought today.' Nathan feigned a smile. David remained quiet. 'Have you heard from any of your people in the US?' Nathan asked.

I tried to keep my temper in check. 'We told you from the beginning that we were having trouble raising funds to finish the church,' I said, looking him directly in the eye. 'If I was able to raise funds so quickly and easily, don't you think the church would have been completed by now?'

Varun spoke up. 'We have been sending out requests to many organizations and researching others. But because we are not a legitimate non-profit, we don't qualify to receive funding.' He added, 'Janice did contact "Save the Children" and they sent us a questionnaire. They want to know more details about the children, their names and ages and circumstances. A few of her friends have shown an interest in donating monthly fees, but they would like to see pictures and know more about the children too.'

Nathan stared into space while David shifted nervously in his chair. The tea arrived just then and David commented, 'It's too bad you gave us such short notice of your arrival. Otherwise we could have prepared lunch.'

'Oh we all ate a huge breakfast on the way. None of us are hungry,' Varun said. He knew it was a sore subject with me and I was frankly appalled that they would even consider feeding all of us when they claimed to be struggling to keep the orphanage going.

We sipped our tea quietly when Nathan suddenly spoke up. 'A friend of mine has a bus we can buy.' Varun and I looked at each other, wondering where this was leading.

'It would be a perfect way to bring money into the orphanage and it would be steady income! We only need one lakh.' Nathan continued on about bus routes, then switched to buying land for a meeting center for Christian meetings. The thought crossed my mind that he was just throwing out ideas to try and get money out of us.

'I think I would like to go see the children,' I said, putting my cup down. I looked at Varun, 'Do you want to come?' Grateful for a way out of the situation, he quickly nodded and we both stood up and left.

We walked over to the orphanage building and found the guys playing with some of the children. I wandered around, finally ending up in the children's bedroom. There were a few children lying in their beds and some bouncing around like monkeys from one bed to the other. 'Namaskar,' I said as I sat down on a bed. They crowded around me, smiling.

Little Sunita, our crippled girl, was sitting up on a top bunk with a small boy who had almost no fingers on his right hand. He was also deformed. Despite this, the two of them seemed to have no trouble climbing down off the bunk bed.

I started tickling one little girl and that started a big tickling match that landed me on the floor, laughing. I drew Sunita onto my lap. Again, like a flash of lightning, I recalled another vision I had had. It was this exact same picture! I was surrounded by children with a crippled girl on my lap.

I don't think I could ever get used to that feeling of déjà vu and the realization that God had given me this vision more than six months before I returned to India. It was such a feeling of awe and wonderment each time a vision was realized. All I could think of was how very blessed I was.

Varun found me and the kids and broke out laughing. He began talking to them and soon I had ten little hands offering to help me get up off the floor.

'The guys want to go,' he said as I straightened myself up. 'They are all a little upset.' I nodded and followed Varun outside.

There were some awkward goodbyes as we got into the car. Nathan approached me one last time, reminding me that the plumbing for the toilets still needed to be done. All I could say was, 'I know, and we will keep trying. We all want God's will on this, don't we?' He had the grace to look shamefaced, and said, 'We will keep fasting and praying.'

Once we were on the road towards home, everyone began talking at once, expressing their disappointment and anger, in a mixture of broken English and Bengali. I didn't blame them. They had all put in such an effort to make this day happen. While they were expecting big smiles and gratitude, I would have been happy with a 'Praise the Lord!' from either David or Nathan. But there wasn't even a small thank you.

I reminded them all that we were doing it for the children and we should feel good that they would have enough food for at least a month. Arun mumbled something. Varun translated, 'That is unless Nathan sells the food to get cash.' Sadly, I knew that this was a possibility.

We stopped 30 km away in Jhalda. Varun wanted to check on the progress of the church door. It was important that we knew when the door would be finished, because we would have to pay the carpenter. The carpenter suddenly decided that he wanted a deposit before doing any more work. He had never mentioned this before and we had no money to give him. All of our money had been spent on the orphanage.

Varun called the church secretary and explained the problem. He told us not to worry, that the church had enough funds to pay the deposit. Within a few minutes, the secretary arrived and paid the carpenter. While we were all very grateful, this incident just added to our depression and we finished the journey in silence.

Samir, our driver, put on a CD with Hindi music to try to lighten our mood. A few kilometers down the road the driver shouted something over the music. I saw the guys' eyes light up. 'What did he say?' I asked Varun. He looked a little sheepish but replied with a mischievous grin, 'He said, he would put his own money on a bottle of rum, if the rest of us would chip in.' I rolled my eyes in exasperation. 'I should have known this would come up. What am I going to do with all of you?'

They all looked at me pleadingly. Finally I gave in, 'Okay,'

I said, 'We will have a party at our house when we get home. But only three drinks each.' They all broke into grins, and the dark mood lifted. I figured they had all earned a little merriment.

Another chicken lost his life that night to feed our stomachs. Rajat was our experienced chicken killer, while Peter was our designated cook. Bharat took joy in cutting vegetables creatively and arranging them artistically on the plate. The others were busy chopping onions and peeling garlic while Varun played music on the computer.

I always enjoyed these impromptu parties because it gave me the opportunity to observe and get to know them a little better. While everyone had fun, no one had too much to drink. Gathering for prayer before and after was a well-known requirement. The two new guys fell right into the activities as if they had been with us from the beginning. I was a happy mother hen.

29. The Next Chosen Wife

We were woken early the following morning by the phone ringing. It was Varun's father. This was becoming a regular routine, which I had grown to resent. It was apparent to me that 'Dad' wanted Varun to be at his beck and call night and day. Varun and his father were always tense around each other. Often Varun would come home gritting his teeth and angry.

This particular morning Varun said that his dad sounded very serious and told him that there was a family meeting and he needed to be there by 9 a.m.

We both looked at each other. 'Do you think they have found out that we are married?' I asked.

'Well...I don't think so,' he said, sounding uncertain. 'But this past week they have been acting sort of strange.'

'Great,' I sighed. 'This is the last thing we need right now.' Varun looked at me surprised. 'I thought you wanted them to know.'

'Oh I do! I hate living a lie and in secret,' I said. 'It's just that with the church and the orphanage problems...not to mention financial issues, I don't want another thing to think about.' Varun smiled at me, 'You need a cup of tea, because I am the one reminding you that God is in control!' I chuckled, 'Yeah, you are right. I will leave it all to God after my cup of tea.'

Late that afternoon Varun and Arun walked in, both of them looking very serious. I braced myself for bad news. When both of them came and sat beside me on the bed, I knew this was going to be a shocker.

There was a long silence; long enough for me to smell the liquor on their breaths. For them to be drinking this time of day, raised my anxiety level to an all-time high. 'We need to talk,' Varun finally said.

'Okay, just tell me,' I told him, 'I'm tough, I can take it.' I held his hand to reassure him.

'My family has set a wedding date for my marriage. Both families have agreed.' He got this out in one breath.

'Ooookaaay,' I drawled out, trying to absorb the whole thing. 'Who is the lucky girl this time?'

'My old girlfriend in Jamshedpur,' he almost whispered.

Varun had told me about her years ago when I was in the wheelchair. I knew they were 'an item' for a few years and Varun had broken it off with her. I had pictured a very beautiful Indian girl. He said she was very vain, spoiled and materialistic. But I also knew that he could have just told me this at the time, to make me feel better...maybe she was a very nice girl...maybe he would be better off marrying her...maybe I would be better off too.

'Well then,' I said, matter-of-factly, 'I think you should do as your family says and marry her.' I went on, 'I'm sure we could get our marriage annulled with a little baksheesh.'

With that, I got up, calmly walked into the bathroom and locked the door. I was shaking inside, not aware of exactly what I was feeling. Then I identified it clearly, I was livid with anger.

This family meeting was the perfect opportunity for Varun to speak up and tell them that we were married. Why didn't he take it? What a coward he was. I was screaming inside. For years I had put up with the secrecy, I had given up everything in my own country to be with him and this was my reward? Good riddance! Let him get married to her, I fumed. I paced up and down the toilet, wanting to hit something. 'Grrrrrrrrrr!' I finally let the anger come out of my throat. It felt good, so I growled loudly again. I felt strong and powerful with that last growl. Then the tears came. I could hear Varun calling me in a gentle, soothing voice, 'Honey, come on out of there. Everything will be okay.'

Then I got the hiccups. I hated the hiccups more than the tears. I held my breath really, really long and exhaled. Another loud hiccup came. 'Okay, okay, just calm down,' I told myself. 'Just breathe slowly.' I sat down on the toilet seat. Inhale, exhale, inhale, exhale...

Varun was getting frustrated. 'Honey, Arun and I have got it all figured out. Please come out and let's talk it over.' He tapped on the door.

'I will be out in a minute,' I said, gathering myself together. When I opened the door, Arun and Varun were standing right there.

'What?' I asked, as if nothing had happened. I straightened my shoulders and walked past them back into the bedroom as nonchalantly as I could.

Varun came over and wrapped his arms around me. 'Honey, I love you,' he said. 'I don't want to be married to anyone but you.' Not wanting to appear desperate, I said firmly, 'Then you need to fix this and tell your family. We cannot hide it any longer.' He ran his fingers through my hair, looking into my eyes. 'I know, and I will,' he whispered and pulled me close to him. That is when I let the tears fall freely. 'Please do it soon,' I wept. 'I don't think I can take much more of this.'

Arun, who had politely slipped out of the room, poked his head around the edge of the door. We both looked at him and laughed. We all sat down on the bed and I listened as they explained to me how Varun was going to get out of the marriage. It was actually Arun's idea.

It was the Indian custom that the oldest daughter married first, then the younger daughters. Most marriages were arranged before the woman was thirty, after which she was considered 'on the shelf' or off the marriage market.

The ex-girlfriend, the chosen bride, was fast approaching thirty. She also had two younger sisters, who, along with the parents, were anxiously waiting for her to be married. Varun didn't want to outright refuse to marry her, because this would be a major insult to her and her family's honor, especially after the two families had agreed.

So he would agree to marry her, but only on the condition that she wait five years while he helped me to build the church and the ministry. Of course she would reject his proposal out of pressure from her family. Her honor would be saved and she would be free to marry another chosen man.

'But what if she accepts your conditions?' I asked.

'That won't happen, I can guarantee it,' Varun said confidently.

'And what about your family? Won't they be very upset?'

Varun nodded, 'Yes they will be. And that is when I will tell them about our marriage.' I was so overjoyed to hear this that I broke into a dance.

And that's the way it happened...sort of.

∼

All hell broke loose after Varun made his proposal to the woman. I don't know exactly what happened, but I do know that, as expected, the woman's family rejected the five-year waiting period. There was a huge fight a few days later between Varun and his father. Varun simply told them that he wasn't ready to be married yet...but he said nothing about our marriage.

I was very disappointed and ready to walk out. But Varun kept saying he would tell them as soon as their tempers had cooled. After all these years, I was skeptical that he ever would. Our relationship was crumbling.

I cannot tell you how much I prayed to God at this time, how much I questioned myself and the ministry. But it is hard to put into words how much God kept reassuring me every step of the way.

In the meantime, the food we had delivered to the orphanage was running low and so far, no one had donated any money to help us feed the children.

Varun and I had exhausted every avenue we could think

of to get donations. One fifty-dollar donation finally did come in from a dear friend of mine. This allowed us to bring more rice and dal to the orphanage. Nathan was calling us nearly every day telling us what they needed as if ordering from a menu. No matter how often we told him that there was no money, his phone calls continued until we finally had to stop answering.

All I could think of was the children and how much I was letting God down by not 'taking care of the children.' In my prayers I kept crying out, 'Show me how! Bring someone to help us!' But nobody came.

I often wondered about Nathan. There was no doubt in my mind that the needs were real. My concern was his heart and his sincerity. Had I misjudged him? Soon we were going to visit the orphanage again, to report of our failure.

In the middle of the night I was woken again, with a scripture in my mind. I obediently stumbled out of bed, picked up my Bible and the flashlight and went into the kitchen. I opened the Bible to Jeremiah 7: 5+6:

'You may remain under these conditions only if you stop your wicked thoughts and deeds, and are fair to others, and stop exploiting orphans, widows and foreigners.'

This time I didn't need to figure out the meaning. I knew exactly what God was telling me. This scripture was for Nathan. It was confirmation that God himself stepped in and stopped our efforts. Nathan wasn't a bad person, just a desperate one in a very cruel world. Desperation can drive a person to do things that he would otherwise never do.

I thought of the 'prophesy' he had told us about. Was it real? Or was it just a ploy to get to me? It didn't matter, because God had shown me the village and the children. Only God knew the reasons why things happened as they did.

I underlined the scripture and dated it, a habit I had begun from my first year, and went back to bed.

∽

The church door was finished at last and ready to install. We scraped up enough money to make the final payment and for the trip to Jhalda.

Of course all the men came. I took lots of pictures and actually played a game of cricket with the local children while the door was being installed.

At one point, I sat down and looked at the unfinished church building. Nearly four years had passed since we first began construction. But rather than being discouraged, I was lifted up with amazement that we had accomplished so much.

I knew, from the very beginning that it wasn't really about the church, or even the Christian families that we were building the church for. It was about our continuing faith and effort over the years. It was about the memories and the relationships that had been built as we all joined together for one cause. In my mind, it was all one big miracle. God had used me to make a difference in people's lives here in India, I was sure of that. It wasn't out of a sense of pride that I thought this, but a sense of amazement. I was the most unlikely, unworthy person on this earth…yet He chose me to do His work.

I pictured the church when it was finished. I wondered, in the future, how many babies would be blessed, how many weddings performed, how many people would give their lives to Christ in this tiny remote area.

It was the missionaries who had come before me, the ones who had worked in the Leprosy Mission hospital, who had truly laid the foundation and planted the seeds. When they left, there was a void, unfinished business. This church was an answer to prayers sent up to heaven. The chain of events that led up to this point, was nothing less than tiny miracles. God had orchestrated all of us, connecting events and souls one by one, to accomplish His will. That realization made all our troubles seem worthwhile.

30. Trials and Tribulations

I will never forget the afternoon, when Varun came home and said that he had told his mother that we were married. It was a hot afternoon like any other and we sat on the bed playing rummy. He was winning as he usually did. Then he said casually, 'Mom and I had a talk this morning, and I told her that we were married.'

I was shuffling the cards at the time. I stopped breathing. I continued shuffling the cards. 'How did she take it?' I said when I could speak again.

'Actually pretty well,' he said, nodding his head.

'How do you mean well?' I finally asked.

'She was sort of shocked at first, which is to be expected...I told her that I loved you very much and I was happy,' he went on, 'I said that I was sorry for not being able to give her grandchildren, but this is what I wanted for my life.'

'But what did she say?' I persisted,

'That is what surprised me. She said that Juhi had already given them a grandson, and my other sister had given them two granddaughters, so it was just fine.' He was smiling at me.

'So you really did it,' I said, putting down the cards. Inside, my heart was leaping for joy. 'We don't have to live in secret anymore!'

Varun's face grew serious. 'Honey, you don't know this country or the customs...though you know them more than most foreigners, you don't have a clue what could happen next.' He looked me straight in the eye. 'Telling my mother was the easy part, the first step, but when this news gets out to the family, anything could happen.'

'I understand that it will take some time for them to accept me in the family,' I said. 'But they know me and have seen us working together for the church all these years. I know our age difference is a huge issue here, but...' Varun interrupted, 'It isn't just a huge issue, honey, our marriage, if it gets out into the community, will dishonor my family. They could lose everything if it isn't handled right.'

'Oh come on!' I said in disbelief. 'This is the twenty-first century and surely they will understand that they cannot remain with the old customs anymore. It is about time someone breaks the customs and opens up a door into the new ways of the world.'

Varun shook his head, 'Many have tried, and many have lost their lives because of it.'

I remembered reading the newspaper about this and the gruesome way the families handled a young couple's disrespect for the old customs, the honor system. I shuddered. I never imagined that we would be put in this situation.

'So do you think our lives will be in danger once the family hears about this?' I asked.

'Well, I don't think we have to worry about my immediate family. But this sort of thing affects the entire Kashyap clan, my uncles, aunts and cousin brothers, some of them live in parts of India where this sort of thing just isn't accepted.' He went on, 'But because you are a foreigner, probably nothing will happen to you.'

'What do you mean?' I asked in disbelief. 'Surely your family isn't that backward that they would kill you?'

'I just don't know honey, I would like to think that they wouldn't, but anything could happen.' Varun was staring into space. 'They could show up at our door and slit my throat.'

'Well, surely you wouldn't let that happen?' I asked, astounded.

'It would be a terrible dishonor to the family if I didn't,' he said, 'But I would, as a final request, ask them to send you back to America.'

'You mean to tell me that you would just stand there and let them slit your throat?' I asked, incredulously.

'Yes,' he said matter-of-factly, 'Because then I would die restoring honor back to the family. If I fought them, it would bring shame.'

'Please tell me you are joking,' I pleaded, 'This just can't be real!'

Varun just sat there silently. Chills ran up my spine. I was feeling a mixture of emotions from fear, to anger, to defiance and back to anger.

'Why didn't you tell me this before?' I asked, 'At least I would have understood why you weren't telling them all these years instead of doubting you. I didn't know that this would be life-threatening news.'

I suddenly understood why Pranab kept telling me what a brave man Varun was to marry me; that no other man would do what he had done. 'Is it just because I am an older woman, or because I am a foreigner?' I asked.

Varun took a deep breath. 'In our culture, older women don't marry younger men.' Then he added gently, 'And younger men don't fall in love with older women. It just isn't done. We both broke the rules here.'

'But surely they can see that God brought us together?'

He smiled. 'They know that, and that is what might save us, but I think that even if you were younger, the fact that I married a foreigner would cause some problems too.'

'But you knew this from the very beginning,' I said. 'Yet you married me anyway. Why?' I hesitated with my next question, 'Was it only to get the visa?'

'That is ridiculous,' he said angrily. 'I didn't and don't care about going to America! But I certainly didn't want us living here either. That is why I wanted to join you in America. Do you think I would ever deliberately put you in any kind of danger?

'I love you and I love the work we are doing for God. I hoped, and still hope that it will make a difference. That is why I finally told my mother. She said she will pray about it.' His face brightened. 'I almost forgot! She has invited you to a women's prayer meeting at the house on Friday.'

'Really?' I said. 'That is a very good sign.' Then I added, 'Are you sure it won't be a trap?'

'No, because mom is our biggest supporter. She really likes you. Plus she is very wise. Your attending that prayer meeting is very important,' Varun said comfortingly.

'Then I would attend ten prayer meetings if it helped your family accept us.' I cleared the cards off the bed. I was feeling more confident now. 'Nothing is going to happen for a while, so let's get some rest.'

We held each other close and drifted off to sleep soothed by the cool air wafting from the cooler and the ceiling fan.

∼

As a final attempt to save the children and the orphanage, we decided to get complete information and pictures of each of the children. If we could plaster their pictures and names across the internet, maybe someone or some organization would step in. We just had to keep trying. Even though God had shown me that he had closed this door, I felt that maybe He might change his mind? If I tried hard enough, prayed longer, was good enough?

So we took the long trip back to the orphanage and gathered the children together in the chapel. Varun put their information on the computer, while I called them one by one for a photograph with me. I had the best job, I thought, since I could cuddle each of them.

Learning the true story of each of the kids was sobering. There were several sets of brothers and sisters who had been abandoned when their mothers remarried. Many of the children, while not true orphans, came from families who were so poor that they couldn't feed them anymore. A few were found in railway or bus stations and turned over to the orphanage by the police. It was only by slowly getting information from the child, that their names were known. Many of them didn't know their ages.

Nathan did his best to provide us with as much information as he had.

There were a few times that I almost broke into tears as I could see the look in some of their eyes, that look that only a child can give, so young and confused and lost.

This was a very different picture of the children, than the one we got on our first trip here. These children were not singing or reciting. They were obedient, but looking around apprehensively, wondering what was going to happen to them next. It was very obvious that everyone in the orphanage, including Nathan and his family, had lost a great deal of weight. They were slowly starving to death. Since the teachers left, the school had closed down. Everything looked empty and abandoned.

It was extremely hot and humid. Nathan had installed the two ceiling fans in the chapel, instead of the children's bedroom. He told us that they moved the children into the chapel at night, where they slept on mats on the floor. I noticed many of the children were covered in mosquito bites. When we finished getting all the information we needed, I suggested that we all pray together.

The children sat on the floor, while all of us adults gathered across the front of the chapel. One by one we joined hands. I stood in the center. I asked for a few moments of silent prayer. I was fighting back tears as I looked at the children, gathering them into my memory bank, trying to find words to say.

The truth was, I had prayed for them so much that I just didn't have any more prayer left in me. Then, I knew.

I started, loudly and slowly: 'Our father, who art in heaven, hallowed be thy name.' Immediately the guys recognized this and began saying it in Bengali. Then the children recognized it and began reciting, quietly at first, then loudly and confidently. Jonas was saying it in Hindi. Three languages reciting the Lord's Prayer, yet all in unison. The air was filled with the electricity of emotion. Such a short prayer, yet so powerful!

There was a moment of silence, and then Nathan stepped forward and began to pray. He began in English...'Father in heaven look down upon us and hear our prayers' then he prayed in Bengali. Immediately the children began to pray, but quietly and reverently. Nathan finished and signaled to the children. They all stood up and began singing 'How great thou art' in Bengali.

That was the last time I saw them.

In spite of all our efforts to find funding, in spite of sending the children's pictures and information to every possible source we could find, no one responded. My heart was broken but all I could do was to fast and pray to God to save the children. I finally had to accept that that door was, indeed, closed.

The last time we heard, the children were gone. Some of them went back to their families or distant relatives; some were taken to other orphanages.

I don't know what happened to little Sunita. Dad had talked to many doctors about her, carrying the X-rays with him, but they couldn't, or wouldn't help.

We also heard another version, that the orphanage was still running—that Nathan's younger brother married a woman whose family funded the ministry. I never could find out what was the truth.

Each of us took this disappointment in our own way. All of us were in a sort of slump. I did my best to keep my own spirits up. I had to be the strong one.

I attended the women's prayer meeting at Varun's parents' home. I thought they were the strongest, most faithful women I had ever met. I studied their weathered faces and saw the years of wisdom in their eyes. They were very gracious to me. Varun's mother gave me a long lingering hug before I left, which meant so much to me. I didn't know that this would be the last time I saw her.

∽

Our Bible studies helped to encourage us and lift our spirits, but the bitter disappointment manifested itself in incidents of fighting and emotional, angry outbursts.

To lighten the mood and bring in some harmony, I planned a fishing trip with the guys. Before we left, I said our usual prayer and added. 'Today is strictly a fishing day, okay? It is not a party.' Everyone agreed.

We went to a pond in a village just 20 km away. It was owned by an old school buddy of Varun's. He guaranteed us that we could fish in privacy without any onlookers staring at me while I fished.

I had my trusty pocket fisherman and fishing supplies from the US. I considered myself an experienced fisherman, having fished for years in both California and Arizona. The men, however, weren't impressed with my pocket fisherman and laughed when I suggested that we get some worms for bait. 'Indian fish don't like worms,' Varun said.

They had already made some sort of bread and mud concoction that they guaranteed would catch some fish. Thinking that fishing in India might be different from what I was used to, I went along with the bait concoction. I had seen fish bite on the strangest things.

As there were a lot of pond lilies and weeds, I decided to use a plastic bobber and fish on top. The men had never seen a bobber before and shook their heads at me. I sat there watching the bobber, waiting for a bite. Suddenly the bobber went down and I pulled the line.

Before I knew it, everyone was yelling excitedly. Someone grabbed the pole out of my hand and, not knowing anything about a reel, began to wind it backwards and forwards, tangling up the entire works. Someone else grabbed the actual line trying to pull it in by hand. I tried to stop them, shouting, 'Don't do that, you'll break it. It doesn't work like that. Just give it to me!'

The fish got away. My entire line was in a tangled mess

and my bobber had disappeared in the murky depths. I stared at my pocket fisherman, which someone had finally given back to me.

'You should have jerked it faster,' Varun said.

I was livid, but tried to keep my temper in check. 'I tell you what,' I said very slowly, 'I would like it very much if all of you would leave me alone, right here, and go fish elsewhere.'

Varun looked at me, puzzled. 'Are you sure?' he asked.

'Yes honey, I am absolutely sure,' I said with a forced calmness. 'I will call you if I need anything.' He and the guys moved a few yards away, looking at me. Slowly they all found their own fishing spots and settled in, while I spent the next half hour trying to fix my line and pole.

When I was finally able to cast my line out into the water, the sun was hitting me directly in the face. I couldn't see the bobber, so after a few minutes, I decided to remove it and take the chance of bottom fishing with a small, wooden floater. I didn't trust the bait at all. What decent fish would bite on bread and mud balls? I kept my line a little tight, concentrating on any slight tug that might come. An hour went by but nothing happened.

Suddenly I heard a shout from the other end of the pond. It was Peter. I could see Rajat, Varun and Arun gather around him. 'Good,' I said to myself, 'at least we know there are fish in here.'

A few minutes later Peter showed up, beaming. He held up a huge fish. It must have been at least six or seven pounds. 'See? Bait works!' he said triumphantly.

'It sure does,' I laughed, 'that is very big fish!'

Peter studied me for a minute. 'You red,' he said, concerned. 'Come.'

He helped me move further up the slope under the shade of a tree.

'Where is Varun?' I asked when I had settled down. 'I need some water.' Peter pointed somewhere to the right where he had caught his fish. Deciding that I needed to take a walk, I handed my pole to Peter and started along the shore line.

There was a cluster of trees above the pond, ending at the main highway. I walked between the trees, trying to stay out of the sun. I spotted Varun with his old school buddy and a few other men. Varun was busy texting on his phone and didn't see me approach. 'What are you doing?' I asked. He immediately switched off the phone. 'Just playing a game,' he said quickly, and put the phone in his pocket. I had already seen that it wasn't a game, but the keyboard that he was on.

I pretended to accept his lie. 'I need some water,' I said. 'And I need to find a toilet.'

'Okay, I will send the driver for some water and let's go find you a place to go.'

A short distance from the pond was a bridge that crossed over a wide river. Varun and I walked to the other side of the bridge and down an embankment to the concrete footing. There was no one around, as far as we could see. Varun turned his back while I went as close to the concrete wall as I could and peed as quickly as possible. I always felt embarrassed doing this in public, especially in broad daylight.

We climbed back up the embankment and across the highway to the group of guys. That is when I noticed a bottle of whiskey, almost empty and plastic glasses sitting on the ground.

'You guys have been drinking?' I asked, incredulously. 'We all agreed on the way over here that we weren't going to drink today.' At this point the driver pulled up, got out of the car and presented two bottles of water and another smaller bottle of whiskey.

'Ahh come on honey,' Varun objected, 'I am with my old school buddy and we just decided to have a few drinks.' I was upset that they were drinking behind my back. Then there was that little lie about the phone. What in the hell was Varun doing? They had left me there baking in the sun while they sat in the shade having a party. Then I noticed our driver was staggering towards the pond.

'I just don't believe this!' I said, shaking my head. 'I need to be alone.' I stormed back up to the highway and began walking across the bridge towards home.

I knew Varun would send someone after me, so I quickly went down the embankment and hid under the other side of the bridge. I saw the car slowly cross over the bridge. As soon as it was out of sight, I climbed back up and continued down the road.

I knew that I was overreacting, which is why I needed to be alone. I was having a temper tantrum of the century! I thought it was best there were no witnesses.

As I walked I began talking to God. 'You see how useless I am here,' I said, 'All these years and nothing has changed in them. Instead, it is I who has changed.'

It seemed that with each step I was taking, I was falling apart more.

'I know I am supposed to "love the sinner and not the sin". I know I give in to temptation way too easily.' I began to sob. 'I am such a failure Lord, and I don't know what has come over me.'

A car passed by, and all its passengers craned their necks to stare at this strange white woman who was crying and talking to herself. This did not deter me.

'Don't get me wrong, Lord, I am so grateful for the healing and for your trust in me...but did you have to trust me this much?' I threw my hands up in the air. 'All I have here is a gang of drunkards and misfits in one of the hottest countries in the world.' I took a deep breath, 'Couldn't you have sent me to a cooler place, with an ocean, like Costa Rica?'

Once I had vented enough, my temper was replaced with resignation. 'I guess you are just going to have to find someone else for this job, because I give up. I am finished.' That was it. I had resigned. I was not a missionary anymore.

I felt a brief moment of relief. I could do as I pleased now. I didn't have to worry about Bible studies or the behavior of the guys. No more giving my testimony in churches or speaking at funerals. I could just be the rotten sinful person that I was!

A few minutes later, I saw the car coming towards me with Varun and the guys. 'Where in the hell did you go?' Varun shouted. 'We went at least five kilometers down the road looking for you.'

Peter opened the door to let me in, but I had a few words to say to them first.

'You all left me alone and started drinking, hiding it from me,' I said, my anger rising up again. 'Now I feel like I can't trust any of you. Damnit! We're supposed to be a family, we agreed not to do this today.'

'We sorry,' Peter said, 'Please get in.' He took my hand and I climbed into the car. Rajat held up a full glass of whiskey. 'Here, now you can join us,' he grinned.

Why not? I figured. I had already resigned; I might as well join them. I took the glass and drank it in a gulp. They were all shocked into silence.

We went back to the pond to pick up our things. Everyone was starving, including me, so it was agreed that we would stop at a nearby roadside hotel and get something to eat.

Any other time I was very strict about us, especially me, being seen in public smoking and drinking. But today I didn't care. We all sat in the back room of the hotel and ordered food and drink. The driver, much to his chagrin, was not allowed to drink, though I think he snuck a few sips when I wasn't looking. I didn't care anymore, I told myself.

Everyone was laughing and talking and I am sure we looked like a happy party. But not me. I was overwhelmed with guilt. The reality of what I had just done out on that road, hit me. I stuck to my three-drink limit and devoured the food as it came in front of me.

I tried to put on a show of small talk, but I felt as if eyes were watching me from above and shaking their heads in disapproval. This time I had really messed up. I wouldn't be surprised if a busload of Christians walked in, shaking their fingers at me and telling me I was going to 'burn in hell!'

One thing I knew for sure...Satan was having a field day that day!

When we got back on the highway, the driver was going full speed and weaving back and forth across the road. Nobody seemed to notice but me. But then again, they had all had quite a bit to drink. I felt completely sober.

Hindi music was blasting on the radio, with the driver singing and bouncing to the music. Arun was actually sleeping through it all. I wasn't worried. I figured a quick death was too good for me right now.

If anyone could die a slow, lingering death of overwhelming guilt, it would be me.

When we reached home, it was decided that Peter's giant fish would be a great appetizer and a nice ending to the day. I didn't care. I had no intentions of eating a pond fish, even if it were the best-looking fish I'd seen. The fish was scaled near the outdoor toilets as the sun was setting. The smell of fish drifted through the house, mixing with the heat and humidity. Not a pleasant aroma at all.

Everyone was sobering up and as I expected, wanted more to drink.

They all gathered together and pulled out all the money they had in their pockets as Varun added it all up on his phone calculator. Soon three of the men left with the money in hand.

Peter was busy in the kitchen preparing his prized catch. The fishy odor was replaced with the pleasant smell of onions frying with curry masala. I couldn't believe that I was getting hungry again.

Varun stayed in the room playing music on the computer while I went up on the roof. The sun had almost set, and the lingering light was filling the sky with pastel colors of yellow, red and blue. I always loved sunsets and this one was especially beautiful. My anger and guilt, though subdued, still lingered like mud in my veins. I watched the colors disappear in the sky and the dusk become night.

'I am sorry Lord,' I began, 'I guess this whole business with the orphans really made me feel helpless.' I began walking slowly across the terrace. 'But when you told me to take care of the children, I took it very seriously. I didn't want to let go of it, even though you showed me that I had to.' I went on, 'I admit that I am a control freak. I really panic when things start to happen that I can't stop from happening. And frankly I am scared. Varun's family is very upset and I have no idea what they are going to do about our marriage. Lord, I am trying to trust in you in everything, but sometimes I really blow it…like today. Please forgive me for my awful temper…and for resigning today…I guess you know I didn't mean it?'

Then I added, 'Thank you for your mercy and grace, which I really, really need right now!'

I sat down on the chair in the dark, hoping for a sign that my prayer was heard, that forgiveness was still an option for me. A mosquito landed on my cheek and bit me. I decided not to take this as a sign from God and went back downstairs.

When I walked into the bedroom, I caught Varun putting a piece of 'stomach medicine' in his mouth. When he saw me standing there, he looked a little sheepish, like a kid caught with his hand in the cookie jar. This was something that I really needed to talk to him about later, I thought, when the time was right. I had lectured him and begged him to stop taking that medicine, so many times. He promised me he had stopped. I wanted to believe him, but this incident proved me wrong and became just one more lie and deception in our relationship.

Peter walked in with a platter full of yellow, crispy fried fish. All the guys were sitting in a circle on the floor. There were glasses in front of each of them and the bottle of whiskey in front of Arun. He was always the designated bartender. Peter set the platter of fish in the middle of the circle and disappeared back into the kitchen. He returned with a bowl of one of my favorite dishes. It was a snack that they told me was Indian popcorn. It contained what we Americans know as 'puffed rice' mixed with chopped onion, tomato, cilantro and boiled eggs. A little oil and lemon was also blended in. Messy, but delicious, and just what I needed at that moment.

Drinks were poured all round and everyone started chattering and laughing.

I made sure that the Indian popcorn was close to me and helped myself to generous handfuls. Varun was sitting on the bed with the computer on his lap. He was the DJ in this mix and always selected the music. Peter brought him the fish head, which was the treasured piece, and very large.

∼

It had been a very long and eventful day. I was sunburned and exhausted emotionally. But Varun was energetic, vibrating, playing the music louder. He seemed to be in his own world, his eyes wide and glazed over. I tried to get him to turn the music down, pointing out that the party was over and the guys were cleaning up. He just smiled at me and nodded. Arun was watching him too, with a serious look. I signaled for Arun to follow me up on the roof.

When we got up there, I said, 'Arun, I know this stuff that Varun is taking is not stomach medicine. I want to know exactly what it is.'

Arun stood there quiet for a moment. 'Don't know,' he replied. 'But I took it one time and it is very strong drug.'

'I am worried about Varun,' I confided.

'I too worried,' he said, then turned and went down the stairs.

The house was cleaned up and the guys said their goodbyes and left. It was 9 o'clock, early for their usual evenings. They all noticed Varun's odd behavior, but pretended not to. He was mesmerized by something on the computer. I went over to him and touched his arm. He jumped, as if I had stung him and looked up at me wide-eyed. 'Honey,' I said gently, 'It is getting late and I am really tired.' He looked at me as if for the first time. 'Where did everyone go?' he asked.

'They all went home,' I replied.

He giggled, 'They all snuck out of here, did they?'

'Actually, they all told you goodbye, but you were busy on the computer.'

He looked a little puzzled. 'Oh yeah I remember. Arun took the guys home on my bike,' and he laughed. 'I was downloading some music.'

'Yes, that's right,' I agreed, stroking his hair.

Inside, I was petrified. He had mixed a lot of alcohol with an unknown drug, which was obviously powerful enough to worry Arun. More troubling was the fact that I discovered that he had been taking this drug for quite some time now. On top of that, I made sure, that he took the medicine for his ADD every day. It was no wonder he was so spaced out. Why didn't I address his behavior when I first noticed it? Why did I not question him more about this medicine? But more importantly, why was he turning to the drug for some sort of escape?

'I am going to get ready for bed,' I told him. 'Why don't you turn off the computer now?' But he was in his own world, staring at the computer like it was speaking to him.

It was nearly midnight before I was able to get him to fall asleep. I was completely exhausted, emotionally, physically and mentally. I said one quiet, short prayer before falling asleep. 'Lord, please help me.'

We both woke up late to the knocking on the front gate and Minu calling, 'Sir! Madam!' I went out to unlock the gate. A few minutes later, Arun arrived to return Varun's bike. I looked at the clock. It was 9:20. Arun and I watched Varun as he stumbled out of bed. I was just grateful that he was alive.

Within a half hour, Varun was showered and heading out the door with Arun. I was having my cup of tea and biscuits as I waved goodbye to them. Normally Varun would drop Arun off and go to his parents' house for breakfast. But Varun told me that he was staying away from his family home since he broke the news of our marriage to them. I didn't know where he went before he came home for the midday nap.

The other sign of trouble was that his dad had not called for several weeks. I wondered what else was going on that perhaps Varun had not told me, so I wouldn't worry. But I knew there were two things that I had to do today. The first one was to set things right with God. I picked up my Bible and prepared for a long session of prayer.

31. Then It All Fell Down

Varun came home early that day with Arun. Both of them had a serious look on their faces. Varun stretched out his arms and hugged me. 'Honey, I am so sorry about last night,' he said, 'And I will not take that stomach medicine again.'

We all sat down on the bed facing each other. Arun still had a stern look on his face. He said something to Varun, that sounded like an order. This was a side of their relationship I had never seen before.

Varun cleared his throat. 'All the guys surrounded me this morning and really ripped into me,' he said, his eyes cast down, 'They made me promise to stop the drugs and to take better care of you.' I was truly surprised and grateful. 'Then Arun took me aside and we had our own little talk. The truth is, honey, I haven't been honest with him or with you about what is going on. I thought I could handle it myself, but instead I screwed up. I shut everyone out.' He looked at me, then at Arun, who was giving him a look and nodding his head like, 'Go on.' Varun went on, 'A few days after I had told my mom about our marriage, she called my older sister, who called my younger sister. After this, someone told my dad. I showed up for breakfast and my mom told me to leave. When I asked why, she said...your dad wants to kill you.'

'Oh no!' I gasped, 'What happened next?'

'I just got out of there quickly. But for the next few days I kept calling my mom and she said she wasn't allowed to talk to me anymore, that dad said I was dead to them and ordered the whole family to never talk to me again.' Emotion was building up in his voice. 'After that, when I called, mom would just hang up.'

I knew that Varun was very close to his mother and she was always his biggest supporter. This must have hurt him severely.

'Honey, I started taking more and more of that drug and drinking and doing stupid things.' His voice was cracking, 'All the time when we went to the orphanage, I was so high, I don't know how I got through it. Here you were doing everything for God and trying to do right and I resented you for it.'

My eyes were stinging and my heart was beating fast as I listened.

'Then a few days ago Arun heard that there was a big family meeting at my house. My uncles and aunties were there. They came from all over India to discuss what they were going to do with us. Honey, they are still there and I think they are planning on killing me.'

Tears fell from his eyes and his bottom lip quivered. I looked over at Arun and he was fighting emotion too. I wiped my own eyes and took Varun's hand. I didn't know what to say. A thousand things came into my head, but I knew that they would sound contrite, or meaningless, so I just gripped his hand tighter.

'Mom called yesterday when we were fishing,' he went on. 'She told me that dad wanted the bike back and it wouldn't be safe for me to bring it. Get Arun or Peter to bring it, she said and hung up.' Varun was biting his lip. 'I knew mom was calling me to warn me, that it wasn't about the bike, but about trying to save my life.' He shook his head as if to clear the thought from his mind. 'So we sent Peter today to return the bike. He said that all my uncles were standing around and dad asked if I was still at Deshbundo Road. Peter told him he didn't know, that he hadn't seen me in a few days.'

I sighed with relief, 'That was very smart of Peter. Maybe they won't come looking for you here today.' Arun said something to Varun and he responded with a shake of his head.

'What did he say?' I asked.

'He said that all of the guys could stand guard for us.' He looked into my eyes. 'I don't want that, honey. The guys will wonder why this is all happening. They will have questions. I don't want them involved. This is a family matter and I am just going to have to face it on my own.'

'On your own?' I said almost angrily. 'Have you forgotten that we are a family? Remember you, me and God? I don't know about you, but I plan on fighting this all the way!'

'You don't know what you're saying,' Varun said. 'You can't fight this! If they come tonight, what are you going to do?'

'I don't know, but I do know this, I will not give in to fear. God brought us together to do His will, and as far as I know, that hasn't changed. Do you think that your father and uncles are more powerful than God? I don't think so. And if it is our time to die, then we will die, but not without putting up one hell of a fight.'

Both Varun and Arun were staring at me with wide eyes and grins. 'Okay, honey,' Varun said, 'We get it.'

'Good,' I said, 'So we can all just relax now, because I am hungry!'

∼

Long before I arrived in India, I knew that living there would place me in all kinds of situations that would threaten my health and challenge my Western way of thinking. I had no idea that there would be life-threatening situations, but it didn't matter. I had placed my trust in God to protect me. I knew I would be completely ineffective if I lived my life in fear.

I often reminded myself of the brave missionaries of history who had gone into jungles of Africa, South America, and other uncivilized countries where they faced greater dangers than I could ever imagine, so by comparison, India was a cakewalk. Most of the threats I faced were microscopic, bacteria, many forms of fungus that grew in humid climates, viruses, and the dreaded amoeba. There were also human parasites and the ever-present mosquitoes. Over the years I experienced most of these critters and not with a little suffering, but survived. I quickly learned to identify my symptoms and to find the local medicine to eliminate the problem. I am sure that my body now contains a bit of India floating through my blood stream and dwelling in dark corners of my intestines.

Also, to my amazement, the use of asbestos roofs was quite prevalent in the poorer areas, so my exposure to this, the fine dust that billowed everywhere, and mosquito coils challenged my lungs as much as my smoking did.

The fact that I am still alive is a testimony to the mercy of God!

Then there were the Maoists and Naxalites, especially in the Purulia district, who were ever present, both in the news and in our daily lives. During 2005-2008 there was an ongoing war between the Maoists, the local police and the government. I chose to remain mostly ignorant of it all, but the guys often talked about the recent activities in the area. I got bits and pieces of their conversations that Varun shared with me, but for the most part, I didn't allow any concern or fear to take hold. But there were a few occasions that we came face to face with their presence.

One such occasion happened when Ajit, our newer member, requested that I go to his village to pray with the Christian families there. At first, we were too busy with the orphanage to take the trip, but with Ajit's insistence, we finally scheduled the journey.

The village was about a three-hour drive from our home. Ajit arranged for us to do some fishing in the village pond while our meal was being prepared by his grandmother and aunts. So, early morning, we all piled into the car and set out for the village. I had brought my Bible, my prayer shawl and anointing oil for blessings.

About an hour and a half into our journey, I noticed men were standing along the roadside staring intently into the passing cars. We went through one small village, then another. The number of men on the roadside doubled. Varun and the men were talking in monotones, looking worried. Something was not right. Varun whispered to me, 'Did you bring prayer shawl?'

'Of course,' I said, wondering why he asked this.

'Wish you had a burkha,' he whispered again.

'Why? Is there a problem?' I asked.

'Yes, there are a lot of Maoists here. They hate Americans and white people. But they really hate Christian Americans,' he replied.

We were approaching another village. I could see that it was crowded with a gathering of men. 'Here,' Varun said, handing me a blanket. 'Cover your head with your shawl and your arms with the blanket. Don't show your white skin.' I quickly obeyed as my heart began to race. The car slowed down and then came to a stop as the men blocked the road.

Varun started yelling at them with authority. I have no idea what he said, but they slowly moved aside allowing us to pass through, staring into the car as if looking for a reason to stop us. We all held our breath until the car finally broke free and was able to accelerate. 'Wait,' Varun said, as I began to uncover myself, 'There might be another group ahead.' I sat there sweating under the blanket, trying to peek out at the road. My heart leapt to my throat as a group of men came running onto the road, waving the car down. 'Duck!' Varun shouted, pushing me down on the seat. He shouted something at the driver. The car began to pick up speed, heading right towards the men. I prayed for protection as I lay sprawled awkwardly across the lap of one of the guys and almost on the floor of the car. The car swayed violently twice, then sped at top speed. It seemed like an eternity before Varun told me it was safe to get up. When I removed my shawl and blanket, I was bathed in sweat. I tried to mop myself up with the shawl and inspect the white salwar I always wore for religious blessings. Varun had a wide grin on his face and all the men were smiling too. 'What's so funny?' I asked. 'What did you tell them that made them move out of the way?' Varun chuckled. 'I told them that you were a leper and we were taking you to a priest.' My mouth flew open. 'Oh, thanks a lot,' I grinned, 'That was quick thinking, my dear. So glad they didn't ask to see my leprosy.' Everyone laughed.

'And the driver almost ran over that roadblock of men too,' Varun added. 'It was fun to watch them scatter.'

'Thank God that no one was hurt,' I said.

'Oh, I would have had no problem killing them,' Varun said. 'Do you have any idea what they would have done to you if they saw you?'

'I don't want to know,' I said soberly. 'I am just grateful that no one was hurt.'

A little further down we stopped at a village where a market was in full swing. It was good to get out of the car and relax. We bought some water chestnuts to eat and I sat in the shade of a tree eating an ice cream. We all needed to recover from the drama of the Maoists and steady our nerves. Twenty minutes later we were back on the road.

As we approached another village, I saw people lined up on either side of the road. A rush of fear ran through me—was this another Maoist ambush? But then I realized that these were women, children and men watching us as our car drove along the road. It was Ajit who explained what was happening . 'They are the people from my village. They have been waiting to welcome you, Janice.'

I was stunned. It looked as if they were all waiting for a film star!

Ajit spoke again, 'We told everyone that this American Christian woman was coming to pray over our village.' He grinned. I couldn't believe my eyes as I looked out at the people lined up on both sides of the road, their hands folded in a 'Namaskar'. Some bowed. Children sat on the shoulders of their parents to get a peek into the car at me. I smiled and waved and bowed back. I felt so strange, like a celebrity undeserving of such honor, humbled beyond words.

Varun was not happy about all this attention because his security guard mind saw it as a danger, so he was on edge as we found the pond we were to fish at. None of us were really in the mood to fish, but we decided to make a show of it.

That was a day I shall never forget. Not only because of the Maoist encounters, but because I prayed over some wonderful people and felt greatly blessed by them. After all we had been through in Purulia, the Maoists paled before the peace I felt after praying with those people.

∾

Over the next few days, Varun explained to me that the family could choose any method to kill us, but more than likely it would be one of his uncles who would do it, because he didn't think his dad, despite his anger, could kill him. 'Or they could hire someone to kill us,' he said, making it sound like an everyday occurence. 'But it would be more honorable if they did it themselves.' When I asked what he thought they would do to me, he shook his head. 'I don't think they would hurt you, because it would become an international situation...but they could make it look like an accident.' That wasn't too reassuring.

We talked about leaving, and even looked into the possibilities, but the cost of it was prohibitive. It would take us months to save up for flights out of India.

For the next few weeks, we didn't leave the house. In spite of my Holy Spirit declaration that day, I began living as if waiting for our execution. Every strange noise or bump in the night had us holding our breath. The guys brought us whatever we needed because Varun didn't want me to step out at all.

We spent our time playing rummy, reading the Bible and praying together. It is strange how the mind goes through stages at a time like this. Varun and I went from fear to terror to a calm acceptance of our situation. My mind played out different scenarios of my own death and Varun's. No matter how hard I tried to shake it off, the feeling of doom lingered in the shadows of my mind.

I began using our Bible study room as my own prayer room. I needed the private time away from Varun to do my prayer and meditation. One day, while in prayer, a powerful thought came to me. 'Rejoice! Pray blessings over your enemies.' It was like a 'light bulb moment' for me. Of course! Didn't Jesus always say to love your enemies, to pray for them?

I knew I had to pray with complete sincerity and conviction. So I sat in silence until I began remembering the happy moments I had with Varun's family.

It was shortly after the New Year's picnic that we were invited to the family home in the evening. Much to my surprise, I was given gifts of a pair of real gold earrings and a beautiful blue shawl. They told me that these were my Christmas gifts from the whole family. The entire evening was full of happy memories and I cherished those gifts very much. Juhi was there with little Charlie, who was a chubby smiling little baby. It was the only time that I felt like a real member of the family.

Filled with these memories I was able to begin to pray for them all. The prayers came without effort and with sincere emotion, a desire for them to be blessed.

I had never met the rest of the family, especially the uncles that were supposed to kill us, but I could see the same blood running through their veins as my husband's. Therefore I prayed for them to be filled with love, so much love that their hearts would be changed forever. The more I prayed, the more my own heart was changed. I was no longer afraid of them or what they might do. And no matter what they did, I forgave them completely.

I now understood the verse that said, 'The peace that passes all understanding.' I was at peace in the purest sense of the word.

When I came out of the prayer room, I found Varun in his usual position, on the bed, with the computer on his lap. He looked up at me briefly, and then again, this time a long, lingering look. 'You look strange,' he said. 'You are all lit up and happy.' It was true. I had a grin on my face that I couldn't remove if I wanted to. I nodded at him, sat on the bed and began to tell him what happened. Varun closed the computer and listened intently, smiling himself.

'So you prayed a blessing over them?' he asked, a puzzled look on his face.

'Yes! Don't you see? This is our weapon. Turning them over to God to fill them with blessings.' Varun nodded, comprehension dawning.

'This is the way I see it, we have been giving in to the enemy, allowing him to make us live in fear. I refuse to live like this anymore. Like my dad always said, "you gotta die of something, so you might as well live while you can!"'

I was excited, happy and relieved. I went to the Bible and opened it at random. The page showed a verse that I had highlighted in yellow and dated in 2006: 'Not by might, nor by power, but by my spirit, says the Lord of hosts—you will succeed because of my spirit, though you are few and weak' (Zachariah 4:6).

I smiled at Varun. 'It is by His spirit that we will succeed,' I said, with determination. 'I don't know about you, but I think it is time we got on with our lives as usual. I am going to the market today.'

Varun was still trying to take it all in. 'Well, okay,' he said hesitantly, 'I'll call the rickshaw...maybe I will go see the guys too.' Then his eyes lit up. 'Ajit has got his new bike, so I'll call him to come and get me.' Ajit had not only gotten a new motorcycle, but showed up at our last Bible study proudly displaying a plaque on the front that said, 'The God Squad.' That really put a smile in my heart.

Getting out of the house without fear was a wonderful experience. I deliberately asked Hira to go through the village where the children always came running to me. It was just the medicine I needed. As they came out to greet me, I tried to touch all the little hands that were reaching out to me. How I loved these little children!

At the market I felt like walking through the entire shopping area. I hopped off the rickshaw, told Hira to wait, and went in and out of the small alleyways full of tiny shops, pretending that I had lots of money and 'window shopping' like I used to do back in the US. I bought myself a bracelet for a hundred rupees, just because I liked it. It was a rare thing for me to do. We had been living on such a tight budget so we could help the orphanage and finish the church, that there was no room for little trinkets like this. It felt good!

Then I went back to shop for the items needed at home and bought a Thums Up each for Hira and myself.

The sun was beginning to set as we reached our home, which I expected to be empty, but I heard music and voices inside. Then I remembered that it was Bible study night, and I hadn't prepared for it at all.

Everyone was in a cheerful mood, stretched out on the bed and the floor, talking. They all greeted us, with Peter following me into the kitchen looking to see if I'd bought new cookies. Of course I had. I gave the packet to him and

Arun, my other cookie monster. It was then that an idea came to me.

I walked into the room and stood there silent for a minute. Varun looked up at me and muted the music. I waited quietly until everyone was looking at me. Finally, I announced. 'Tonight I am asking for a volunteer to do the Bible study. I hope all of you have been reading your Bibles at home. Is there anyone who has a scripture that God has shown you this week?'

Varun translated to them. This was something I had never done before, so there was a long silence and odd looks as they all absorbed this new experience. I was relieved when Rajat volunteered.

It was one of the best Bible studies we had. Everyone was in high spirits as we sang and clapped and I used my plastic water bottle with sand and rocks to beat out the rhythm. The music books were laid out and there was debate over which song we would sing next.

Then Rajat opened up the Bible to the section he wanted to use. We all opened our Bibles to that page. I looked across the floor and counted the Bibles. There were ten; seven in Bengali, one in Hindi, and two in English.

All eyes were upon Rajat as he spoke. I didn't understand any of the words, but I understood what was happening in that room. I didn't need a translation as I read the scripture he had chosen: Revelation 3:20: 'Behold, I stand at the door, and knock; if any man hear my voice, and open the door, I will come in...'

When Rajat had finished speaking, I thanked him and asked if anyone had any prayer requests. Again I sat quietly as one by one the men shared their individual needs.

When it was time for the final prayer, in which everyone

took turns, the men pointed to Varun. They all knew he was nervous about praying out loud, so they really put him in a spot. I was surprised that he didn't try to get out of it. Instead, he cleared his throat and began.

I was expecting a quick prayer, but he prayed earnestly and long, addressing each of the prayer requests given. It was a solemn and precious moment in time for me. It was as if God was saying, 'See? You have made a difference in their lives, Ye of so little faith!'

They all lingered longer than usual after the Bible study, but eventually I hugged each of them and said goodbye.

I was used to being left alone afterwards with Varun taking a few of the guys home on the bike. But now that he didn't have his bike, I wondered what would happen next.

I had no illusions. I knew they would all gather to have drinks. Sure enough, Varun got on Ajit's bike and with Ajit sitting behind, he waved goodbye. The others had bicycles, while some walked, but eventually they would all meet on the other side of town.

I was bathed in an afterglow of the day's events, praising God for the things He had revealed to me today and for bringing peace back into my heart. When I went into the kitchen I found dinner, ordered from a fast food restaurant, waiting for me. Varun forgot a lot of things, but he never forgot to take care of my food, especially if he wanted the evening free of worry while he was 'out with the guys.'

---

32. The Betrayal

I ate my dinner and decided to get on the computer for a while to check my mail. But when I went to the bed, I noticed that Varun had left his phone behind. I thought, instead of sending an e-mail, I would call my dad. It would be so good to hear his voice.

So I settled myself comfortably on the bed and picked up the phone. Then I got into the phone list and hit 'D' for dad. Instead I got 'Debbie.'

Who is this Debbie? I wondered. I saw that there were a lot of messages for Debbie, so I went to 'messages'. My heart began to pound, as I realized that the number was a US one. When the messages opened up, I couldn't believe what I was reading! There were lots of messages that this Debbie and Varun had sent back and forth over the past week. As I read them, my heart pounded louder and my eyes filled with tears. The 'I love you's and 'I miss you's' were like knives going through my chest. I could hardly breathe, yet I read them all. She said, 'Why didn't you call me today darling?' Varun replied, 'I'm so sorry, but my boss kept me working late.' She said, 'Meet me on Yahoo so we can do it again. I miss you baby!' The messages went on and on like this. I couldn't read anymore. I dropped the phone on the bed.

I don't know how long I sat there in shock, but the electricity went out and I didn't bother to light a candle. I was numb, trying to get the reality of it all into my head. I didn't even know that I was sobbing loudly until our roommate came into the room and asked me if I was alright, shining his torch at my face. All I could think was, when did he come in, and why does he always show up at the damndest times!

I waved my hand and told him to go away, I was fine. He hesitated for a minute, then left. I heard his door close. I got up and lit a candle.

Everything I did was mechanical. Sweat began to pour off my face and the bugs came in with a fury. I swatted them away and wiped my face and my tears.

I don't know how long it took, but I began to gather my wits together, realizing that it was crucial for me to think straight. There was no room for doing something stupid that I would regret later.

I got down on my knees and prayed. 'Father, you know what has been going on. You know my heart and the pain I am feeling right now. Please guide my steps and show me what I must do.' Then I got up and paced the room, cursing under my breath, then saying 'Forgive me Lord', after each curse.

I remembered the fishing trip when I caught Varun texting...and the lie.

That night when he was drugged and mesmerized by the computer...was he talking to her while I was stroking his hair?

It was like pieces of a puzzle that had begun falling into place. All the time I thought he was downloading music or doing research on the computer, he was also having a love affair with Debbie.

The computer! I went over to it, opened it up, and turned it on. Varun was a computer teacher and knew how to hide anything. I only knew how to get into my own e-mail and send e-mails back. How could I possibly get into Varun's mail? Did I really even want to see his mails? Like someone stopping to see a gruesome accident on the highway, I realized, yes, I wanted to see everything. I reasoned that it was evidence I needed.

I don't know how it happened, but after one click and another, I was in Varun's Yahoo mail.

The bugs were landing all over the computer, attracted by the light. I was wiping sweat from my eyes as I read five e-mails to Debbie. I checked the times and the dates. They were sent only over the past four days.

I could also see that he was getting mail from a popular dating site.

I picked up the phone again and looked at the dates of the messages that were sent. They too were only sent within a four-day period. I thought, if this was happening in just four days, then he couldn't have been sending her messages on our fishing trip, or later that night, when he was so high on the drugs.

Somehow I felt a little relieved. But it didn't matter. After all we had been through, were going through, with the death threats and the financial and emotional struggles, this was the last thing I needed...adultery. And it was adultery. I don't care how much anyone might justify online affairs as harmless; it is adultery pure and simple. For me, it crossed a line in the sand, a big red line.

I sent an e-mail to this Debbie, as a reply to her last loving e-mail, simply telling her that I was Varun's wife and that he was lying to her. I gave her my e-mail address and told her if she had any questions, she could contact me. I clicked send. The wicked, revengeful side of me felt so much better.

I was on a roll now, there was no stopping me. I decided to try to get into his profile on the dating site. Again, it just opened up for me. There was Varun's picture. It was one I had taken of him on our trip to Kathmandu. I cursed at his face in the picture. Then I went into 'edit my profile' and wrote, 'I am a married man who lies and cheats on my wife. I don't have a job and what I do best is drink whiskey.' I was actually giggling to myself as I re-read it. 'Perfect!' I said with what I'm sure was an evil grin on my face. I hit 'finished editing' and waited for the new profile to appear. 'Yes!' I said triumphantly, and shut the computer down.

I was reasonably calm now and had gathered my evidence. I was prepared for the next step.

By now Varun would have realized that he had left his phone at home and I was surprised that he hadn't sent someone to get it. I knew one thing for sure and that was that I did not want Varun near me that night.

The electricity came back on and the fan began to whirr again. It also cleared my head. I picked up the phone and called Arun. When Arun answered, I asked to speak to Varun. When Varun came to the phone I said. 'Varun, I have just read all your phone messages to Debbie.' I paused to let this sink in. 'I am calling you to let you know that you had better not come home tonight. I am locking the door now. Goodnight.' And I hung up.

Within ten minutes, I heard the roar of a motorcycle and the voices of Varun, Arun and Peter. They always came together as a group whenever there was trouble. There was lots of knocking and pleading and yelling, but I didn't budge. Unfortunately, the roommate, obviously woken up from his sleep, went through the back door and opened up the front gate. 'Damnit!' I cursed, when I realized what had happened.

The three of them walked in, smiling. I could see they were all quite drunk. The minute I saw Varun, anger raged inside me. 'I told you not to come home tonight. And if you know what's good for you, you will turn around and leave me alone.'

'Awww, come on, honey,' Varun slurred, 'It's late and you just woke up our roommate and prob'ly the neighbors. Let's just make peace right now and we can talk about it in the morning.'

I gritted my teeth. 'Let me make this perfectly clear,' I said glaring at all of them. 'If any of you come near me, I will scream so loud that the entire neighborhood will hear me.' I got up and stood in front of Arun. 'I am serious. Get him out of here now!'

Arun and Peter knew I was serious. They had never seen me this angry before. It took some doing, but they finally convinced Varun to leave with them. I was alone again.

I still had Varun's phone. I went through his entire phone list and found two other US numbers...more evidence.

I don't know how much sleep I got that night, but I slept fitfully. I woke up as the morning sun was rising, made myself a cup of tea and opened my Bible without looking. When I glanced down at the page I had opened it to, I was shocked. It was Genesis 3:4 glaring up at me. I had underlined it months ago. I read it again with a totally different perspective. 'That's a lie!' the serpent hissed. 'You'll not die! God knows very well that the instant you eat it you will become like him, for your eyes will be opened—you will be able to distinguish good from evil!'

'Yes Lord,' I said sadly, 'My eyes have been opened.' There was a deep, dark, cloud that had settled into my very soul. All the emotions I had felt the night before, the betrayal, the anger, revenge and yes, even hatred, had all simmered together deep inside of me and became a heavy, sticky goo of overwhelming sadness.

I saw everything differently now, as if a film had been lifted from my eyes. What a fantasy world I had been living in. Varun didn't love me at all. Our marriage, the one I was willing to die for, was a fake. He was a fake. How easily he said 'I love you' to another woman.

Just as I was building myself up into another royal rage,

God stepped in. I knew He was trying to show me more, another side of the picture...I saw the Bible study we had last night. I saw all of the men again singing and reading the Bible. Not really wanting to see this right now, I resisted the memory. It was interfering with my righteous anger.

But then I saw the moment when Varun was praying for all of the men...and my heart quivered.

'Okay, Lord, I see this,' I said, 'But what about the rest of it? The e-mails and messages on his phone? What about Debbie?' I was starting to cry again. 'What am I supposed to do Lord?' I wiped my eyes and stared across the room.

There, lying across my chair was the blue shawl that Varun's family had given me. My eyes remained on the shawl as memories connected to it filled me with warmth. I remembered the peace that came over me when I prayed for blessings for the family. Was that only yesterday? How I wanted to feel that peace again.

I looked outside the barred window by the bed. Four feet away was a concrete fence. The morning sun was just beginning to touch the top of the fence, its rays lighting up the green moss. I studied the patterns the moss had made. The tiny plant seemed to stand up to catch this brief moment of warmth.

I knew that, no matter how much pain I was feeling, I had to forgive Varun. The Bible was very clear on this. Even the Lord's Prayer said, 'Forgive us our trespasses as we forgive those who trespass against us.' If I was able to forgive Varun's family, why was it so hard for me to forgive him? Because this offense hit at the very core of my being, our marriage.

By now all of the men knew that Varun and I were fighting. We were their spiritual leaders. They all looked to me to set an example. I had been preaching to them about anger and forgiveness over the past years, but how could I at this moment, be forgiving, when I was full of raw emotion? The answer was, I couldn't, not by my own strength, but with God, anything was possible. He knew my heart and my weaknesses. He knew I couldn't bear the pain much longer. Filled with resolve, I took a deep breath and swallowed hard. 'Okay, Lord, I need you to help me forgive Varun because I can't do it on my own.' As miraculous as it may sound, a few seconds later I looked back outside the window and watched as a white feather came into my view. It drifted slowly down, rocking back and forth in the air and caught itself on the rough concrete fence.

It was just a feather to anyone else, but between me and God it was a sign that He heard my prayer, that He was with me. I smiled and whispered a 'Thank you' up to heaven.

It was about half an hour later that I heard the motorcycle and voices outside. There was a knock on the gate. I took a deep breath and braced myself as I went to unlock the front gate. After opening it, however, I turned on my heel and went back into the house.

'Help me Father,' I prayed as Peter, Arun and Varun walked in.

Peter and Arun looked very serious and tired. Varun's eyes were red and he was drunk, swaying as he stood there.

'He's drunk at 10 o'clock in the morning,' I stated matter-of-factly.

'Drinking since seven,' Peter offered. 'He tell us he sorry.'

Arun pushed Varun towards me. Peter pulled me towards Varun. 'Forgive now,' Arun ordered.

That was my cue, my big opportunity to set a good example…and I blew it. It was my pride that stepped in. 'Who is Debbie?' I asked Varun.

'Sheeze nobody, Janisss,' he slurred, 'Has no meaning to me.'

Then he did something that broke my heart, he began to sob uncontrollably. 'I wanted to tell you waaaay back,' he cried, 'I'm glad you know now.' He collapsed in my arms, leaning heavily on me. 'I'm sorry honey.' I sat him on the bed before we both fell over.

I wanted to ask him so many questions, to really tell him everything I had felt last night. But he was so drunk, it made no sense. I thought I'd go into the kitchen to make some tea. Maybe I could sober him up, and then really rip into him. But as I started to move, Arun grabbed my arm. 'Forgive now,' he said firmly. I stood there looking at Varun. He had his head buried in his hands and was mumbling something about the devil.

Then Peter said something that was like a slap across my face. 'Janice, you old! Varun young!' Then he pleaded gently, 'You holy woman of God.' That last statement was my final cue, my last chance to set the example of forgiveness.

My shoulders drooped as I dumped my pride on the floor. Slowly I smiled and nodded at Peter and Arun, and then I went over and got down on my knees in front of Varun and wrapped my arms around him. I said plainly, 'Varun, I forgive you.' He lifted his head and I looked into the most tortured face I had ever seen. 'No,' he sobbed, 'You can't forgive me because I am the devil!' I smiled at him, 'Yes, you are a devil sometimes, but you are also the man I love,' I said, and repeated, 'I forgive you honey.' We both stood up and held each other closely, blended together in forgiveness.

Arun said, 'We go now.' And I heard them leave, still wrapped in Varun's arms. He began to give me wet kisses on the cheek, saying 'I'm so sorry,' over and over again. 'It's okay, honey,' I soothed, 'Now let's lay down on the bed.' He nodded and collapsed on the bed. Within minutes he was sound asleep.

~

Over the next few days Varun and I talked at great length about what had happened. First, he admitted that he had been taking the 'stomach medicine' since the visa was denied. He felt that it calmed his mind more than the prescription medicine for his ADD. He said that none of the guys approved of it, because they all had tried it once and it gave them hallucinations.

He confessed that the visa denial hit him very hard, because he didn't want me living in his world where he knew our marriage wouldn't be accepted.

'I wanted that visa to protect you, Janice,' he said, 'I am so proud of the way you adapted here and changed our lives, but I knew that sooner or later, the hard realities of my culture would hurt you.' He went on, 'Plus there was God with us, and I wanted to have faith that He could make a difference here, using us to change the terrible old customs. I thought that if I just had enough faith, everything would be okay.'

He told me that when I arrived, his dad was suspicious and began to ask lots of questions about our ministry and what we were doing. Each morning when he went for breakfast at his home, there were talks about planning his marriage. At the same time, I was pushing him to tell his family that we were married.

As the days went by and the pressures mounted, he went to the internet to escape. That is when he turned to a little pornography, which led to online sex, which recently led to online dating. He felt guilty about it, but at the same time he couldn't stop.

'I swear to you, honey, Debbie was the first one I started chatting with.' Then he grinned, 'You are a regular 007 when you are pissed! I don't know how you got into my mail and sent that message to Debbie.'

I smiled, 'Never underestimate the power of a woman scorned! What did she say?'

He looked disgusted. 'I had asked her to send me a picture of herself before all this happened,' he said, 'She is connected to Satan himself.'

'Why do you say that?' I asked, surprised.

He blushed as only an Indian can blush. 'She sent me a picture of her private parts and she was so fat!' We both burst out laughing.

Varun threw up his hands, 'I swear to you honey, I have learned my lesson. From now on it is just you, me and God.'

Later that day I heard Varun laughing like crazy. I was in the kitchen and he was on the computer in the bedroom. I went in to see what he was laughing about. 'My 007 wife!' he said, shaking his head, and started laughing again.

'How in the hell did you get into my profile on this dating site?' he asked. Before I could answer, he said, 'I was just going into it to cancel my membership and I read what you had written...good job, honey!'

'Thanks,' I said, 'I thought it was an accurate description at the time.' I smiled. I didn't tell him that I had no idea how I was able to get into his mail or the dating site. I figured it must have been a 'God thing.' It was best to keep him guessing.

~

Our lives, our marriage became stronger after that terrible trial. We talked and laughed more and loved more. Peter and Arun were so happy to see us together again, and took pride in the fact that they were a major factor in our reunion.

Though the death threats lingered like a shadow in the background of our lives, and sometimes hovered near the surface, it never again controlled us.

I know Varun missed his mom terribly and that the pain of the rejection of his family was a daily battle for him. But the drugs and the pornography were no longer a part of our lives.

It was one night, a few weeks later, just after our Bible study, that Varun received a phone call from the church secretary in Jhalda. He wanted to meet with us the next day. I was fighting a cold and knew I couldn't make the trip, so the guys all volunteered to go.

It had been a while since we had done anything on the church and I felt terribly guilty about it. Not only did we not have any money to add to the construction, but we had been dealing with our own personal issues, and had not contacted them.

Even the cost of renting the car and driver had to be considered before agreeing to meet with them. After much discussion, it was decided that renting the car was out of the question. Whoever wanted to go had to leave early the next morning on the bus. Five of them volunteered to go. Varun called the secretary back and told him to meet them at the bus stop in the afternoon.

I spent most of the day in bed, taking medicine and sleeping. Varun left his phone with me, so he called to check on my condition and to let me know that they had arrived.

I had woken up from my afternoon nap feeling very calm and peaceful. I wondered what happened in Jhalda. I also remembered the feeling I had when I was last there. How wonderful it was that one day, that church would bless others when it was finished.

I thought about all the events that had happened over the years and the relationships that had been built as the bricks had been placed one by one on the church. I remembered a scripture that said something like Christ was the cornerstone of the church and I smiled. Yes, He was...and I fell back to sleep.

I was woken up with the noise of the guys returning. They all gathered around the bed. Varun sat next to me. 'How are you feeling?' he asked.

'Better, I think,' I replied, trying to clear my head. 'What's going on?'

It was then that I noticed the solemn looks on the faces around me. 'We had a fight with the people,' Varun said, adding quickly, 'But we were very controlled, no violence.'

'What people?' I asked, 'The people at the church?'

'Yes,' Varun replied, 'We first had lunch with the secretary and then he took us to his house and the church board was there.' My brain was finally clicking into gear. 'So what did they say?' I asked.

'They wanted to know when they were going to get their money back for the deposit on the church door.'

'Really?' I asked, 'After all the money we have put in to build the church? I thought that this was their contribution.'

'Exactly,' Varun said, 'But then they started to complain about the time it was taking to finish the church.' At this point the rest of the guys began talking all at once. From what I could gather, we were fired by the church board and a verbal fight ensued. I sat there and listened quietly. 'They say bad things!' Peter said, indignant. Arun, who was our accountant said, 'You spend more than one lakh on church.' I was surprised at the figure, I hadn't realized it was that much. Rajat piped in, 'We will make a sign, "This church built by Janice Paul and The God Squad, Purulia."' Everyone nodded their heads. I just smiled.

I could see that all of them felt terrible and were afraid

to tell me exactly what had happened. I signaled for all of them to come close.

'I know you all are feeling bad about what happened today,' I began. 'But what you are forgetting is that from the very beginning we were building that church for God...not the people.' I waited while Varun translated. 'God used all of us to start that church. Don't you see? The church was what brought all of us together. Because of the church we began the Bible studies and we all became like a family. While we thought we were only building the church, God was building us up, testing us, and changing our lives.' Varun translated again. 'We don't need a sign made for the world to see. We are building treasures in heaven. God knows what we have done here, and one day the world will know too...I believe this. I am so proud of all of you. And I know God is also proud.'

Arun, not willing to let go, said. 'But church is not finished.'

'I know,' I said, 'But our part in it is finished. We planted the seed. Someone else will finish it and the harvest will begin.'

Rajat, who understood more English than the rest, said sadly, 'Sometimes seed falls on shallow ground.'

I smiled at him and said, 'Yes, that is why we must keep planting seeds.'

I knew what God was doing. Just as He had opened doors for me to come to India, He was closing doors now. It was as though my mission in India was over.

The church in Jhalda was no longer a part of us. The orphanage was gone.

In spite of the family threats we remained, trying to continue to do God's work. But I knew that Varun lived with a daily reminder and questions about his family. The only way for him to heal and move on was for us to leave the area. But Varun, still clinging to hope that his family would change their mind one day, didn't want to leave.

A phone call came that changed all of that.

It was Varun's mother. She said that she was sending a rickshaw to our house with all of his things. His dad wanted everything out of the house that belonged to him. She was told to tell him that he had lost all of his inheritance, all the land and the money. He was now declared dead.

'It is better for you, and for us, if you go away from Purulia, much better...safer,' she said. Then she added, 'You are not dead to me. You will always be my son. I love you and will be praying for you and Janice. You stay with Janice,' she said emphatically, 'She is good for you.' Then she hung up. It was an extremely emotional moment for both of us.

His mom knew that Varun would never leave until she told him to. The bond they had was very strong. She was giving her blessing and warning for us to leave.

When the rickshaw arrived, I was surprised at how few things there were, mostly clothes. I left Varun alone as he sorted through the things.

Another door had closed.

We knew we had to get completely out of India to survive.

If we were going to stay together, the US was out. There was Bangladesh, but there was trouble brewing there between the Bengalis and the Bangladeshis, so that wasn't an option either. Our finances wouldn't allow us to fly very far, so that pretty much eliminated the rest of the world. Our only option was Nepal.

Once we had decided on our destination, all we needed was a financial breakthrough, even for Nepal. And it came, from a most unexpected source—a refund check from the US government! The strange thing was that this check had been traveling around India for about six months and just happened to arrive at the Purulia post office when we needed it the most. More miraculous was that the address on the envelope was Varun's parents', but as the postman was new and didn't know where their house was, he asked someone in the village for directions. That person was a friend of ours who knew where we were staying, so he told the postman to return it to the post office and he would send us over to pick it up. The next day we went to the post office, not knowing what this letter could be. After showing my identification and paying the postage due, we went outside to open it up. When we saw that it was a check and what the amount was we both nearly fainted! Most people would consider it a small amount, but to us, it was just the amount we needed to pay for our flights to Kathmandu and a bit left over to survive on.

That letter had been to Mumbai, New Delhi, and Kolkata. The odds of it ending up in our hands, at just the right moment were incredible. But as someone once said to me, 'When it comes to God, nothing just happens to happen.' We booked our flights to Kathmandu.

Things were changing amongst the guys too. Bharat and Nitesh were studying for exams to enter the Indian Police Service. Peter had already married and had a little daughter, Arun decided that he would never marry, though I thought he would be a good catch for any woman. Rajat stopped chewing betel nuts and was starting to look at women more than politics. He and Jonas went into business together raising fish in the local ponds. Ajit didn't know what he was going to do, but whatever it was, I knew he would show up late, dressed like a star. My young men were growing up and getting serious about life.

We had told Hira and Minu that we were leaving a week before our departure. It was difficult, not only because they had become so close to us, but also knowing that they would be losing an income that they had depended on.

A few days later, when I went out in the rickshaw to do

my daily marketing, the children in the neighborhood came out to meet me. Over the time that I was there, I taught them the sign language for 'I love you.' All the children knew it and as I rode past them in the rickshaw, I heard echoes of 'I love you', as they all made the sign and waved at me.

We had one last party at the house. It was planned two days before our departure to Kathmandu, and it was all paid for and put together by our men.

Before the party, we had our last Bible study in which I prayed over each of them and anointed them with oil.

The guys all knew how I loved to hear them sing. Poor Rajat could not sing in tune, but what he lacked in talent, he made up for in enthusiasm and volume. He always made me smile, but made the guys angry because he would throw them off key. But that night their voices blended in perfect harmony as they sang a few of my favorite songs, almost making me cry.

It was a great party. We all shared memories of picnics, fishing trips, the trips where I gave my testimony in churches. We laughed at the memory of our last night in Kolkata at the old church, when they got caught smoking and I was able to calm the pastor down. The guys teased me about the many things I did the first year I came, including my attempts to wear a sari.

I tried to show them how to dance American style and we waltzed around the floor. There was a bittersweet feeling in the air. The winds of change had blown through our lives and I think we all knew that we couldn't return to this moment in time, so we cherished it all the more.

On the morning of our departure, three rickshaws were ordered to take our luggage and us to the railway station. We woke up at 4 a.m. so we could catch the 5:30 train to Kolkata. Sleepily, and in candlelight, I made our last tea.

The Secret Wife

We did our final packing and closed the suitcases just as the rickshaws arrived. As the luggage was being loaded, one by one the men showed up.

Dawn was just breaking as I gave them each a last hug and we said our goodbyes. Everyone was waiting for me outside as I took one last glance at our house.

When I walked outside towards the gate, the men were all whispering, then in unison they said, 'Jesu sohai'—God be with you. 'Jesu sohai' I called back to them as I climbed into my rickshaw, trying to keep myself from breaking down.

The sky was growing light as we left the house. It was as we were leaving the narrow alley where our house was, that I noticed that on both sides of the pathway stood all of our neighbors. I was both humbled and very surprised as I rode along hearing them call out one after another, as we passed, 'Goodbye, madam, namaskar, madam.' I couldn't keep my tears in check any longer as I returned their greetings. As we reached a turn in the path that lead toward the main road, I saw that many of the children had gathered there and with one voice they did the hand signs I had taught them and shouted, 'I love you.' I turned to see where Varun was. To my surprise, Varun and all the men were walking in twos behind me, their heads held high.

I was overwhelmed with emotion as I saw all our neighbours quietly walking behind the men.

When we reached the main road, I was waving and crying as I heard more 'goodbyes' and more 'I love you's' from the children. Varun shook hands with each of the guys, got up on his rickshaw and we sped away just as the morning sun began to send light upon the faces of our neighbors and my guys.

There are moments in our lives that remain frozen in our memories. For me, this was one that will always bring a lump in my throat.

Epilogue

We landed in Kathmandu as refugees escaping the death threats and the persecution we felt in India. It was five years after I had left my country to come to India.

Nepal was the only country that would accept our marriage, our age difference, our nationality difference. Though we still shocked people when they found that we were married, at least we didn't feel our lives threatened.

We tried eight times to get our file reopened and reconsidered in the US, but failed each time. My own country would not accept our marriage, Varun's country wouldn't either.

Varun and I continued with our mission in Nepal, working with a leprosy organization for several years. I gave my testimony in many churches throughout the Kathmandu Valley... But that is another story.

My testimony was first published in 'The Bible Society of India' magazine, which was distributed throughout the world in December 2006. I also gave my healing testimony before 4,000 people in Biratnagar, Nepal, in 2010.

The church in Jhalda was finished by the same church that tried to stop us from building it. I hear it is growing in attendance.

I never forgot the command from God to 'Go out and tell the world.'

I am now sixty-seven years old. I move a little slower, and some days I can hardly move at all, but each day I wake up knowing that, in spite of myself, I can go out and show the love of Christ. The fibromyalgia still lingers in my body with days of fatigue and occasional trembling in my hands.

I think God chose to keep it there as a reminder of where I used to be.

In 2013 we visited some remote villages in West Bengal, to speak to them of the healing power of Jesus and pray over the sick. It is still my heart's desire to reach Christians in the far corners of the world who struggle alone, and face daily persecution for their faith.

My old wheelchair sits in a corner of Varun's family home in Purulia, yellowed with time and collecting dust. Its design was not intended for the dusty roads of India and the battery charger was lost years ago. But every time I looked at it I was filled with praise and gratitude. I admit sometimes I used to go over, wipe it off and sit in it, close my eyes and remember all that took place during those days of pain and suffering, rejection and loneliness…and I wept…not because of all of that, but because I knew that without that, I would have never believed as I do today. I would have never dusted off my Bible and begun the journey of faith, redemption and tremendous grace given to me over the years. So yes, I wept, but with joy! And just as I did on that glorious day of my healing, I say over and over again, 'Thank you Jesus!'

God did answer my prayers and Varun's family finally accepted our marriage and I was welcomed into his family home. They are good people caught up in the pressures of their world, but chose to believe in us.

Varun's mother, Sabita, passed away in August of 2012. We returned to his village to attend her funeral, a twenty-four hour journey by road. There were changes back home too. Rod passed away in April of 2011, and my father in February 2013.

I flew back to the US after dad died, to be with the family and sell the mobile home that Rod and I had bought together.

It was the only home I had left in the US. Then I returned to Purulia, to resume my life with Varun, who had returned there while I was away, with our two dogs and all our belongings.

But in a bitter twist of irony, that same year, after nearly ten years of marriage, Varun and I went our separate ways. I learned that no matter how much I loved him, prayed for him, prayed with him, in the end, he had to make his own choices...and they were not mine.

Pranab was right, Varun was a very brave man to marry me and to continue to fight for our marriage. He tried, but in the end, the pressures, temptations, and differences of our world wore us both down.

I wish our story had a happier ending...that we could have overcome the barriers and the prejudices within both of our cultures. I wish we had been able to break away from our own emotional chains that bound us up back then. I wish we could have brought the love back, Christ back, into our relationship, but it was not to be.

But I don't regret any of it.

Because...A miracle happened and I was walking. I experienced love again.

For a while, Varun and I were warriors! For a while, we believed in our love and in our dreams to serve God with all of our hearts and minds. For a while, we overcame insurmountable odds, we sacrificed everything...for love... for God.

We dared to dream a very big dream because we knew that we had a very big God...for a while. We each did what we could according to our own measure of faith.

I met some wonderful and amazing people in Purulia, and in India. I fell in love with the community and culture. I learned that you can endure any kind of hardship and suffering, if you have love around you. I can only hope and pray that we planted mostly good seeds in India. I still feel so honored and privileged to have been able to visit the villages and pray over the people.

There were a lot of lessons that came out of those years together. Some will say that we failed in everything we did. Those that say such things, weren't there with us during the struggles and the triumphs. I can tell you that it was a battle well fought and not an easy one to walk away from.

In those years, I learned how to lean on God completely, for everything. My faith was toughened up and polished there, through daily lessons.

I have come to realize that there really is no such thing as a permanent failure.

We all must stop and 'lick our wounds' now and then. There is nothing wrong with that at all. We only fail when we linger in self-pity over the thing we lost, or carry bitterness and anger inside because we lost. Everyone loses now and then. You are not an exception to this law. Loss and failures are simply lessons we needed to learn to achieve our successes later.

I also learned the hardest lesson of my life, and it was a big one…to know when to leave, to let go. I had to respect myself, and trust God enough to walk away. I knew my time with Varun was over, and I had to let him go. For love must be poured in overflowing, in order to pour it out onto others. God is love, and without love, there is nothing.

∼

So once again, I packed up my suitcases, and flew to the one place where I knew I had friends waiting. Friends who would support me and help me recover from my broken heart. For me, Nepal truly was my Shangri-la, and Kathmandu had been our home for nearly five years. It was there I found solace.

In the heart of Kathmandu, is Thamel, the tourist area. It was the place where Varun and I had wandered on our first trip to Nepal, where he learned about sizzling chicken, and where the strikes had delayed our flight back to India.

But in the years that we lived in Nepal together, we never lived near Thamel.

Varun never liked it much, but I was always drawn to it, and would sneak away, now and then, to spend a few hours by myself, just to wander and look in the many shops along the narrow streets. There was a sort of energy, a rhythm there, that softened me, and made me smile, and a surreal quality about it, that made me think it surely must have been designed by some Disneyland architects.

It had a musky mix of old and new energy swirling around in the air, along with the tourists from all around the world, their foreign languages tickling my ears. It was intoxicating... back then.

Sita, beautiful, wonderful, Sita, who had taken care of Varun and I over the years, as our housekeeper and cook, met me at the airport. She was, and is, like a sister to me. I wept in her arms like a baby, as she listened to my story and comforted me. She and her husband helped me get settled into my room before leaving me alone for the night.

I spent the first few weeks in a 'trekking' hotel that a friend helped me find. My room wasn't fancy, but it had a hot shower, clean sheets, and a view of the busy street below. I had arrived with very little money. I was mourning for the loss of the life I had known, my purpose, the ministry, and, what broke my heart the most, the dogs, 'our kids', that I had to leave behind in India. I was in a state of shock.

Emotions bubbled up inside me and exploded as I screamed into the pillow on my bed, sometimes striking my fists at it in uncontained rage and anger. I wandered aimlessly through the streets, stopping occasionally to chat with a store owner, or sit alone in a garden and sip on Nepali tea. I slept fitfully and talked to God a lot, and wept until I fell asleep again. I filled my empty hours reading books, and staring down at the streets teeming with tourists and vendors. The clatter and clamor of noises below were somehow comforting in my sorrow.

I met with old friends and cried on their shoulders. I made new friends, and cried with them too. I am overcome with embarrassment, when I think of it now, but everyone was patient and kind. It seemed like the sadness would never leave me. I was consumed by loss, by failure.

Fortunately, everything in life is temporary, including sorrow. It's not that you 'get over it.' It's just that it mellows and blends into your life, slips into the background.

One day, a few weeks later, I caught myself humming as I walked down the street. There was a feeling of lightness and power within me. I felt like I had been in a cocoon for a very long time and was beginning to spread my wings and break it away. It was as though the scales had fallen from my eyes and I began to see things I hadn't seen before.

Like: For the first time, no one required anything from me. It was no longer up to me to make all the decisions. I was not stared at, or followed around, or guarded.

No one was taking pictures of me or asking me for money (except the local street vendors).

And, I was not in isolation, without other women friends—this was one of the best realizations. I was just like any other white tourist on the streets. And more importantly,

I blended in! People spoke in English to me. There were things familiar to my own country, especially the food. I even met other Americans who lived in the area. At first, I am sure I talked a mile a minute to them. How good it was to speak my own language so freely again.

I drank, the three-drink limit, nearly every night, and smoked a pack a day, with abandonment.

I knew that this was all part of the healing process for me. Because I also knew that sometimes, rest, taking care of one's inner self, is a very good weapon. I sensed that this was the place and time I needed to heal. I didn't feel God's disapproval at all. Instead I felt him comforting me, reassuring me that He loved me and understood exactly where my heart was.

So I went about my days smiling, and greeting people that were fast becoming a part of my new life. I was being renewed, slowly and gently. I was in the perfect place for renewal...and I knew to cherish every moment because, I knew now, everything is just for a season.

∼

It was nearly two years later, Christmas Eve, 2014 that I realized my rest time was over. I could feel it...that God was stirring things up around me.

It was 2 a.m., and the music coming from the three pubs across the street, made the windows rattle and the floors vibrate. I stood on the balcony watching the activity. I had stood there many times before, even praying over the city, but this time as I looked around, sadness enveloped me. I felt like a rudderless ship lost at sea. I was itching for a real purpose again.

I had some concerns, not the least of which was my Nepali visa. It was expiring soon. I often wished that Nepal would embrace me as enthusiastically as I embraced it. Sadly I didn't qualify for their retirement visa, so I had to move on. Secondly, there had been changes in my health. It was getting harder to climb the stairs to my room. Walking itself had become more painful, requiring me to take breaks often.

I began to worry about becoming a burden to those around me, and about the medical care available, if something serious were to happen. A feeling of urgency was rising up inside of me. What was this feeling? Why now?

Was it time to return to the US? Was I homesick, or too old to live overseas, as some had suggested? The thought saddened me.

One day I Skyped my son and daughter, and talked to them about returning to the States. I had been gone for a decade, so I didn't expect a lot of enthusiasm about me returning to their lives. But after our conversation, I had second thoughts about returning at all. Perhaps it was my own doubts nagging me? I shook them off and began calculating a budget for life in the US. It would take me four to six months to save enough. That seemed a very long time.

This sense of urgency kept nagging me, becoming a grain of sand irritating my spirit. What was I missing?

That was on 20 April 2015.

On 25 April, the earthquake hit Nepal.

My physical injuries were minor, but the toll it took on my emotions was immeasurable. I watched my whole world fall apart, literally. This was like the Titanic, without water. This was the moment in time when our courage and our character were measured for the entire world to see. Most of my friends were superheroes.

Everyone ran for open grounds, away from the swaying, crumbling, buildings. With each aftershock, we were all terrorized. And the aftershocks kept coming, night and day, relentlessly tearing into our sleep and our sanity. Most people stayed outside and dashed inside their buildings to retrieve their things, praying an aftershock wouldn't hit while they were inside. I did the same.

So many stories, memories, remain in my head from the earthquake and all it did to my beloved friends and the entire country of Nepal. I can't complain. I was one of the lucky ones. Over 9,000 people lost their lives. I flew back to America.

~

15 May 2017

Two years and six days have passed since I returned to my own country.

It was a very rocky re-entry and the struggles haven't stopped since I arrived. But neither have the miracles. (I believe that with each struggle, there is a miracle attached.)

I have tried very hard to settle in, to adapt, to change, to become a part of the community and to blend in with the church here and my own family. And while I have made some wonderful friends and have had memorable moments reuniting with my daughter and son and grandson, I must say that, in all honesty, I do not belong here.

I am like a fish out of water, gasping for air. I see no purpose in sitting around getting older in the hustle and bustle of this place, while the battlefield is out there, waiting, calling me to begin again.

I have read some biographies of missionaries, over the years. And I have met a few in my wanderings. The truth is, we are a stubborn lot! Tough and determined to carry on with the mission assigned us, without regard for our own safety or health, or the approval of many of those around us. So when we are told to take a 'sabbatical' or to retire from the field, it is more often with trepidation or strong objections. I think it is because we become so much a part of the culture and the lifestyle of the people amongst whom we live, that we adopt their country into our blood.

I believe that, many years ago, when God healed me, my DNA was changed completely. I was joined together with Christ on that day and sent out into the world to preach the good news. That has never changed.

Some have told me that there are many needs and causes right here, that I could take up. I have examined and pursued many of these possibilities but none tugged at my heart as much as the lepers, or the street children in India, or the widows in Nepal.

There are always battles in these lives we live. We must choose the ones most worthy to fight. Some battles are thrust upon us. In the two years I have been 'home', I have been fighting for my life, physically and spiritually. After the earthquakes and aftershocks, my blood pressure never dropped down to normal. My body was in a constant 'flight or fight' mode.

When I stayed at my daughter's house those first few weeks, I woke with nightmares and tears. I needed desperately to simply rest, but there was no time. I needed to find a place to live quickly and get a car. This required me to cash in on an investment I had for years, which brought even more anxiety.

I was told later that I was suffering from PTSD (post traumatic stress disorder). All I knew was that I was feeling overwhelmed and over stimulated by the new culture. Things I had done before without a problem were now terrifying. I was living in a mental state of fear as I navigated my way through the days ahead.

To be alone, I literally escaped to the local supermarket and drove their electric cart around for hours.

The store seemed huge to me. So many choices of everything! It made my mind dizzy as I traveled the food aisles. I was amazed that they had two full aisles for snacks and candy alone. When I had lived in the US earlier, I had been in supermarkets many times, but that was a lifetime ago.

It was in that store that I became reacquainted with America. Everything was there for me to learn, from current fashion and prices, to the latest gadgets. I observed the natives in their natural habitat, so to speak, and had conversations with employees and customers. In June 2015, I rented a one-bedroom apartment within walking distance from this store.

In the middle of July, my son, Kevin arrived. It was meant to be just a visit to spend time with me and his sister. But life threw us another challenge we weren't expecting at all.

On 9 August, I had my first heart attack. Three more followed. Within the next six months I had four angioplasties and two stents implanted in my heart.

The statin drugs, and four other medicines, commonly prescribed for heart patients, made me like a zombie, yet I was told I had to take them for at least one year, and maybe for the rest of my life. Those meds, triggered diabetes…and if that weren't enough, while struggling to keep my blood sugar under control, I had a few mini strokes. Kevin and I moved into a two-bedroom apartment, so that he could continue to live with me.

I was told to write my Will and prepare to die. Instead, I found a new cardiologist who helped me to get off the prescription drugs and begin a diet and exercise program, swimming laps at the local gym nearly every day. I stopped smoking on the day of my first heart attack. I still enjoy a cocktail now and then with friends, when my body allows it.

The important thing was that I had taken back control over my life's choices and stopped listening to the negative voices in my head.

I learned that when a doctor gives me a diagnosis, I simply turn it into a challenge to overcome. I believe it, but I refuse to accept it as a final word. I consider it, pray about it, and leave it in God's hands.

Luckily I had the support of my church and the foreknowledge of a healing God.

I know He heals me daily. It's in my DNA.

Though my body may be dying, my inner strength in the Lord is growing every day. I live in a perishable container, and death is sure to come one day. But I choose to fight for every breath, every minute that I can live.

I still live my life straddling the spiritual and physical worlds. I am only a human, with God-given gifts, like all of us, and weaknesses like anybody else.

If there were a message to this story, I would hope it would be that God uses us in spite of ourselves, our addictions and our weaknesses. That shows that He can use anyone, even you, just the way you are. You have been given gifts that are very unique, made just for you. Usually those gifts show up in the things you are passionate about. Follow your passion!

I am still passionate about everything life has to offer. I wake up each morning wondering what new adventure God will take me on next. Whatever it is, my luggage waits in the corner...I am still willing!

I will never forget a conversation I had, a few years back, with a British couple, over cocktails, in The New Orleans

Café in Thamel. It was a few months before the earthquake. We were talking about religions and our beliefs. I had shared the story of my healing, and the ministry in India. I said, in reflection, 'It seems like I live my life not fitting in the "Christian world" and not fitting in the world in general.' The man laughed and said simply, 'Neither did Jesus.'

Indeed...and Amen.

Printed by Libri Plureos GmbH in Hamburg, Germany